Sir Crawford McCullagh

Belfast's Dick Whittington

Susan B Cunningham

Published by Ballyhay Books,
an imprint of Laurel Cottage Ltd.,
Donaghadee, Northern Ireland.
Copyrights reserved.
© Susan Cunningham 2016.
Printed in the EU.
ISBN 978-1-910657-09-6

*This book is dedicated to
Sir Crawford's great great grandchildren
Michael and Shelley*

Introduction

I suppose most people, from time to time have looked at old photographs and wondered what the people in them were really like. In my family there was one face that seemed to dominate all the photographs. A tall, handsome and kindly looking man. My great grandfather, Sir Crawford McCullagh.

I first became aware of my great grandfather when I was shown a photograph of him standing on the steps of his home, Lismara, with General Dwight D Eisenhower and other members of my family, including my father Lionel Henderson. I was probably about fifteen years old at the time and remember thinking that he must have been someone of some importance. I was told that not only had he been the longest serving Lord Mayor of Belfast, but also he was the longest serving Lord Mayor in the United Kingdom. At that time there were still quite a lot of people who, if I mentioned his name, would say "Oh, I remember him. Wasn't he Lord Mayor?" That was usually followed by "I've seen his very large portrait in the City Hall." Or "Didn't he own Castle Buildings Department Store?" Or "Didn't he have something to do with the Zoo and the Floral Hall?"

In 1997 my family and I moved to Comber and by sheer coincidence, the previous owners of the house had in their possession a number of books that had been owned by Sir Crawford and his children, in fact most of the books were inscribed by my grandmother

Daisy. The books were bought at Rosses Auction Rooms in Belfast when the owners moved to the house in the 1960s. Needless to say they allowed me to keep them and they are one of the reasons why I decided to write this book. Then a few years later, in 2000, I was contacted by a woman living in Canada who informed me that she was coming to Belfast to donate to the Linenhall Library 5 volumes of press clippings relating to the years of Sir Crawford's Mayoralty. There were also numerous photographs, some private papers and most importantly an unpublished manuscript by an Ulster journalist called Alfred S Moore. The woman in question turned out to be Sheilagh Hearnden McCullagh, daughter of Sir Crawford's nephew Ernest McCullagh and so my cousin.

Sheilagh, by this time, was in her 70s and had already done an enormous amount of research into Sir Crawford's life and was very keen that it should be written down and published. She asked me if I would take it on and so I decided then that I would write it as a hobby. I went through her notes, read the unpublished manuscript, had visits to the Linenhall Library the Public Record Office of Northern Ireland (PRONI) and over the years found a number of people who were enormously helpful and genuinely interested in someone who has now been almost airbrushed from the history books.

It has taken me nearly 15 years to write his story. This book is not an academic or analytical study of his career in politics. Instead it is a profile of his life and family, the people he met throughout his distinguished vocation as First Citizen and the extraordinary times through which he lived. For those wanting a more detailed analysis of his debates on Municipal Politics and issues such as housing, transport and public health, these can be accessed online[1]. Access to the Belfast Corporation archive is held in PRONI under the reference LA/7. The Lord Mayor's correspondence consists of 219 files, 1931-71. Most of the material relates to the Lord Mayor's official duties, but there are some references to wider political and social interests.

---

1.   The Stormont Papers – 50 years of Parliamentary Debates Online.

While every effort has been made to ensure that the information is accurate, I apologise for any errors or omissions that have occurred in the writing of this book.

I would like to thank all those people who have given their time and patience in helping to finally bring this book to closure. First and foremost to Sheilagh Hearnden McCullagh for bringing the 5 volumes of press clippings to Belfast and providing me with the material to start writing in the first place. Jane Crosbie for her excellent editing skills. Richard Graham for his wealth of knowledge and meticulous research. James Lynne for his patience in providing me with continuous requests for information. I would also like to thank the staff of both the Public Record Office of Northern Ireland and the Linenhall Library for their patience, courtesy and helpful advice. Henry Rowley provided the inspiration for the title of this book and the following have all played their part in bringing this work to print: Alf McCreary; Orv Lyttle; Miss Cecil Garrett; Jim McDermott; Tom Brown; Moyne McConnell; John Harcourt; John Bradbury; Nurse Mary Hagan; Martin Crozier; Angus McConnell; Donald Cheyne; Robin Masefield; Professor Richard Clarke; David Cooke; Keith Haines; Seamus Henderson; Cllr. Jeffrey Dudgeon; Robert Corbett; Ian Montgomery; Matthew Gamble; Nigel Macauley; Stanley Hearnden; Winsome Linton; Susie Carnson and last but certainly not least my husband Alan who encouraged me from the start and told me not to give up.

It is with regret that I must record that Sheilagh is not with us today to see the book she inspired in print as she passed away in 2014.

Contents

CONTENTS

Chapter One
1868 - 1882

Humble Beginnings

"I cannot tell how the truth may be,
I say the tale as 'twas taught to me'.

McCauley on Ancestry
from Margaret Henderson.

Crawford McCullagh arrived into Grand Central Station in Belfast early on the morning of 24 April, 1882 from a farm in Aghalee, Co. Antrim. He had visited Belfast only once before and one can only assume that the experience was an impressionable one as, aged fourteen, he decided to leave his family and set out on a journey that was to radically alter the course of his life.

Brimming with self-confidence and enthusiasm, the young adventurer stepped off the train that spring morning bringing with him drive, ambition and attitude. He knew these headstrong and determined character traits were needed for the role he would ultimately fulfil. He had little by way of formal education and was disobeying his father's wishes. However, within his lifetime he became a millionaire, a leading public figure, and the longest serving Lord Mayor in the British Isles.

Crawford McCullagh was born on 14 December 1868 at Annaghdroghal on the shores of Lough Neagh. In astrological terms, those born under the sign of 'The Archer' often have the ability to look ahead and make shrewd judgements as to the outcome of future events. Crawford was guided not only by his impulses but also an intangible force that determined his character and his destiny.

He was one of six children born to Robert McClave McCullough and Mary Jane Hawthorne, daughter of Francis Hawthorn of Meenan near Poyntzpass. Robert was brought up on a farm at Dinnahora in the Parish of Mullabrack, County Armagh, with three brothers and three sisters. His elder brother was the Reverend Joseph Crawford McCullough, (see Appendix 1) Minister of the First Presbyterian Church in Bangor, County Down 1857-1878, while his other brothers, Samuel and Ebenezer were merchant buyers in the drapery business in Lurgan.

According to Crawford, his father Robert McCullagh was a stocky, thickset man with a homely whiskered face. He remembered him being reserved amongst strangers but with his own family and friends he was genial and possessed a keen sense of humour. He could also be firm with the boys when they needed disciplined, but he was respected and obeyed by all the family. His mother Mary Jane McCullagh was a tall handsome woman, capable and strong, whose life revolved around her family. In later life, Crawford would take on his father's determination and strength of character as well as his mother's warm and generous personality.

Crawford's paternal grandmother Nancy Crawford was the daughter of the Reverend Joseph Crawford of Cremorne, Co. Armagh. The children were brought up understanding that she was descended from Scottish nobility. In his memoirs Crawford recalled sitting at his grandmother's feet with his brother while she fired their imagination with heroic tales of her alleged ancestor Sir Reginald de Crawford who lived in the 13th Century in Monoch in Scotland and was Sheriff of Ayr in 1297.

There is evidence to suggest that John Crawford (1660-1736) a descendent of Sir Reginald de Crawford came to Ireland from Scotland and settled in Co. Monaghan where he purchased considerable property near Newbliss, including Aghadrumkeen and Drumbain. His estate was at Kilcrow, which he named Monoch after the family seat at Ayr. The armorial bearings on his tomb in Kilcrow Churchyard are the same as those of the Crawfords buried in Kilbirnie Parish Church in Ayrshire, Scotland. Although John Crawford lost most of his estate due to bad luck and gambling, there still remains today a small parcel of land that is farmed by a Crawford, the eighth generation of the family to work the ancestral lands.

In later life Crawford McCullagh was heard to remark "Ancestors, after all, are like potatoes the best part of them is underground! It's not what a man's grandfather was that counts today, or even what his father was, the only thing that matters is what a man has made of his own life"[1].

Shortly before Robert McCullagh married Mary Jane Hawthorne, his father and uncle died leaving him a substantial inheritance. With this money he leased 78 acres of agricultural land at Annaghroghal on the shores of Lough Neagh. The property was owned by Colonel Waring, a descendant of Colonel William Waring after whom nearby Waringstown is named.

The two-storey farmhouse was situated at the end of a mile long rutted lane with a garden at the front of the house touching the shoreline. When Robert McCullagh moved into the property it was badly in need of restoration but it had the potential of becoming a very comfortable home in which to bring up his growing family. The holding had two covered barns, a pig pen, stables for the horses and a courtyard at the back of the house with a well and water pump. Robert spent considerable time, effort and money improving the property. He brought with him livestock, ploughed the land, planted crops and trees and made the farm very profitable. They settled into the property in 1858 and in 1859 their first child Annie was born, followed by Jemima in 1863, Jenny in 1864, and then a son, Samuel in 1866. Crawford was born in 1868, and baptised in the name of his

---

1. Crawford McCullagh, *An Account Of My Early Life*

uncle the Reverend Joseph Crawford McCullagh [see appendix 1]. Selina, the youngest of Crawford's siblings, was born in 1876.

It is significant at this point to note that Robert McCullagh and his brother Joseph were already planning Crawford's future. Robert McCullagh tried to influence the lives of everyone about him. He was governed by the highest principles and possessed a most assertive personality. Often these traits would have great influence on the fortunes of the family although not always in the way he had planned. The McCullagh family were typical farming tenants, renting their land on long leases, sub-letting a small acreage to cotters and engaging in commercial crop cultivation and cattle rearing. For centuries the backbone of rural Ulster society, they enjoyed social respectability and a privileged standing in the rural community around Lisburn and Moira. A census taken in 1802 characterises this social stratum as 'respectable, sharp and clever'. A modern historian describes them as 'obstinate, hardy, self-reliant and direct'.[2]

At the time when Robert McCullagh leased Annadroghal, Tenants' Rights were a controversial issue in Ulster and rifts often developed between landlords and their tenants. In 1870 the lease at Annaghdroghal expired. The landlord, Colonel Henry Waring, was prepared to renew the lease subject to an increase in the annual rental and Robert McCullagh was adamantly against this option, as he had greatly improved the property and considered the increase grossly unfair. He maintained that it was an agricultural holding, whilst Colonel Waring held that it came under the legal classification of an estate or residential tenure. Convinced that he was being unfairly treated, he took the matter to court but subsequently lost. A lesser man would have stood down, but not Robert McClave McCullagh. He took the case to the High Court, unfortunately the court again ruled in favour of Colonel Waring. Robert had no choice: he would either have to pay the increased rent or leave the premises. To a man of his character there was only one thing to do. Robert stubbornly

2.   Nick Baron, *The King of Keralia*.

refused to pay the increase in rent and was given ten days to leave the property. Driven by resentment he razed all the crops and piled them on the side of the road where they lay to rot or were taken away by passing travellers.

Had this been a few years later, Gladstone's revolutionary Land Act (1881) would have secured the property for the act guaranteed the 'three F's" – *Fair Rent,* if it could be amicably agreed, would be set by land courts to last fifteen years; *Free Sale* enforced compensation for improvements to property; and *Fixity Of Tenure* gave protection against eviction provided the rent was paid.[3] Subsequently the property lay vacant and derelict until 1963, when it was once again restored to a family home and farm.

In 1871, with limited resources, and depleted finances, Robert moved his family to the Parish of Aghalee, in the Barony of Massereene, County Antrim. The village of Aghalee lies on the main road between Lurgan and Antrim town, one mile from Moira and a few miles from Lough Neagh. The parish enjoyed the name Soldierstown from 1641 when there was a barrack quartering two troops of horse and foot. The parish countryside was very fertile with no bog or wasteland. Limestone was plentiful and huge quantities were shipped through Lough Neagh to Belfast via the nearby Lagan canal. Many of the local farming community at that time were employed weaving linen and cotton at home used for manufacturing in Belfast twenty odd miles away.[4] The parish was prosperous and it was a good place for the McCullagh family to grow up.

The property of 90 acres was leased from the Marquis of Hertford at 25 shillings an acre and consisted of farmland and paddocks divided into well arranged fields enclosed by hawthorne hedges and iron gates. The plain stone 18th century farmhouse was set back from the main road up a long lane and had good views of the surrounding countryside. It was a comfortable roomy house with adequate

---

3. Alfred S. Moore, *A Merchant Prince*

4. Samuel Lewis, *The topographical dictionary of Ireland*

accommodation for the family. There was a yard and stables for the animals, and the grounds at the front and side of the house were laid out with fruit trees. Crawford was three years old when they moved to Fortland and his memoirs reveal a happy childhood, playing with his brother and four sisters.

In an account of his early life he recalls one Sunday afternoon when he and his brother went out to find the horses while his sisters slipped quietly upstairs and changing out of their best clothes. The girls then sneaked out the back door and scampered down the garden barefoot dressed in little more than petticoats and bloomers. One of their favourite haunts in the summer was a stream that ran at the bottom of one of the paddocks. Here they would play with an old whisky barrel taking it in turns to float down the stream in the bobbing vessel until it eventually filled up with water. Then forced to swim to the grassy bank, they took off their drenched bloomers and draped them over the hawthorne hedges to dry in the summer sun.

In 1875 at the age of seven, Crawford joined his brother and sisters at Upper Ballinderry National School, three miles from Fortland, where he acquired a sound grounding in the "three R's" – reading, 'riting, and 'rithmetic" from John English Bolton. Robert McCullagh wanted Samuel to become a doctor and for Crawford to become a Presbyterian Minister and follow in the footsteps of his uncle, the Rev. Joseph McCullough. For once their father was not to have his wishes fulfilled.

Life on a farm in the 1870s was not an easy one and when not attending school the boys were expected to help out on the farm. A normal day meant rising in the darkness at 6.00am when water and corn had to be brought to the horses before breakfast. At 8.00am all hands were assembled in the fields and work went on without interval until midday. The caw of the crows, the champing of the bits, the jangle of the harrow chains, and the call to the horses at the changeover of the furrows was a familiar routine to all the McCullagh family. Normally the farmyard bell sounded at 6.00pm indicating the transfer of work from the field to the farmyard. The teams were unyoked and when they were stabled, they had to be brushed down, fed and bedded before supper. The boys, filthy and exhausted, were expected to wash, tidy up, and join the rest of the family for their evening meal. Crawford recalled that every evening the family would gather in the parlour while their father read a substantial passage from the bible. Religion was a part of the spiritual air breathed in Ulster Presbyterian households. It was an orderly system of faith for country folk at that time. When Samuel and Crawford's education at Ballinderry National School came to an end, Sam's fees were paid for him to continue his education at Lurgan College so that he could continue his father's wishes of becoming a doctor. Within a short while it soon became clear that Sam was not suited to the medical profession and instead of matriculating at Lurgan College, he was apprenticed as a trainee accountant with the firm of William Boyd and Sons, drapers in Londonderry.

Crawford meanwhile, was sent to stay with his uncle the Rev. Joseph McCullagh in Bangor, Co. Down. This seemed only to strengthen his resolve that a life in the confines of a parochial Presbyterian ministry was not for him and this was strengthened when his aunt took him on a shopping and sightseeing trip to Belfast. This was Crawford's first trip to the city and the afternoon's experience had an indelible effect on the impressionable thirteen year old. What he saw during his tour of the city and the fine drapery stores in Donegall Place may well have established an ambition to own a business of that nature. At any rate, he left his uncle's Manse and returned to Fortland, where he decided he did not want the ecclesiastical career his father had mapped out for him. When his father told him he was to enrol at Lurgan College for his secondary education for matriculation, he flatly refused. As far as Robert McCullagh was concerned, there was only one alternative: if Crawford would not have the pulpit, then he could have the plough! So for one spring, he put in the long hours and strenuous work of the farm labourer. It was hard work for a boy of fourteen, but he had grown into a big, strong, sturdy lad with a robust constitution which later stood him in good stead. His father thought this farm work would bring Crawford to his senses and make him change his mind.

About this time, Crawford received a letter from his brother Samuel, who had left the firm of William Boyd in Londonderry, and was now working as an apprentice in Belfast with Brands and Co., Ladies Outfitters in Donegall Place. Attached to the letter was an advertisement cut out from the Belfast News Letter.

WANTED
Well educated boy as apprentice to the drapery trade.
Apply, Messrs. Robertson, Ledlie and Ferguson Co., Ltd.,
Bank Buildings, Castle Place, Belfast.

The next day Crawford told his father that the work he was doing on the farm could be better and more cheaply done by a hired farm hand getting paid 8/6p (roughly 45p) a week. He furthermore told his father he was going to Belfast to find a job to his liking and he would not have one chosen for him. Robert, who had such high expectations for his younger son, was angry and bitterly disappointed. As Crawford was set on going to Belfast the next day his father refused to let him go until he had done his day's work.

Crawford recalls in his memoirs getting up at 4.00am in order to complete the day's work in time to catch the afternoon train from Moira to Belfast. His father refused to give him the train fare but he had saved a shilling and two pence for a return ticket. When he arrived in Belfast, he went straight to the Bank Buildings. The manager, impressed with his manner gave him the job. "You can start here on Monday morning", was all he said, adding "Your wages will be free board and lodging during your five years apprenticeship".

When he returned home his mother pleaded with him to refuse the job and comply with his father's wishes and go to Lurgan College. He said nothing she could say would change his mind and told her he was going to Belfast to make his own way in life.

On Monday morning 24 April, 1882, he rose early and had breakfast with his mother and sisters. The trap was brought to the door, but there was no sign of his father. Crawford recalls in his memoirs how his mother left him to the end of the lane and before saying goodbye turned to him and with tears in her eyes said "Crawford, I want to give you some advice, have nothing to do with bad company, always tell the truth, and do what your superiors tell you. When you meet with a difficult problem, as you will, and you do not know which way to turn, ask yourself the question, 'What would my mother like me to do?' If you follow this advice, I have no fear that you will come out alright". Crawford never forgot her advice, and in the coming years he relied implicitly on her wisdom and her unfailing vision.

Chapter Two
1882-1895.

The Young Apprentice

> *Do you remember how, before dawn*
> *we were awakened by peeling notes,*
> *By sudden outcry as of Titan voices*
> *shrill, prolonged, shrieking together?*
>
> Alice Milligan.

The Bank Buildings

The five years of Crawford's apprenticeship in The Bank Buildings was to be his introduction to commercial life. The original building in Castle Place was erected by Waddell Cunningham in 1785 and later opened in June 1787 as The Belfast Bank. The bank was known as 'The Bank of the Four Johns', as the four founders were all called John – Ewing, Holmes, Brown and Hamilton.[1] In 1800 the Bank ceased trading and the building became the home of the Bishop of Down and Connor. In 1805 it was converted into a shop. Around this time the area in front of the building was used to execute criminals, however this gruesome practice came to end in 1816. In 1853 the store was established as a wholesale drapery firm by Messrs. Robertson, Ledlie, Ferguson and Co., and in 1900 the premises were rebuilt with a front exterior of red Dumfries sandstone and large plate glass windows.

---

1.   Raymond O'Regan, *Hidden Belfast*, p.106

Crawford remembered his first night in the Bank Buildings boarding house where he was to sleep with twenty-two other apprentices. He related in his memoirs:-

> 'The room consisted of two rows of single beds that ran up the centre and behind these taking up wall and window space were small cubicles to house our belongings. A couple of gas jets spluttered a cold blue flame at either end of the room. On my first night I retired to bed and was lying there, when I was suddenly caught by the heels and pulled out onto the floor. I got up, very cross, and struck out at the ringleader landing a blow on his face. His nose started to bleed and he cried out that I had tried to kill him! Some of the other boys attended to him and I got back into bed. Then they started to annoy me again. I said, "Look here, the first boy that comes near me, the same thing will happen to him", and I got no further trouble'.

The next morning when Crawford walked through the side door of the Bank Buildings the manager showed him round the various floors of the department store where he would be employed for the next five years. He was to arrive every morning at 8.00am sharp, when all the apprentices would be given breakfast. The floors were then to be brushed, counters polished, and gas lamps cleaned in preparation for the store opening at 9.00am. They were given a substantial dinner at 3.25pm with a break of one hour and then it was back to work until 6.00pm when tea was taken in the canteen. The apprentices were then free for the evening, and if they wished to go back to their lodgings, the Bank Buildings boarding house provided an excellent library where journals and newspapers were available.

The business itself gives us an insight into commercial life in Belfast. The ground floor had an area of half an acre, and the total floorage space of the building extended to fully three acres. The ground floor and first floor areas housed the principle showrooms. Damask tablecloths and napkins, sheets, pillow-cases, towels, fine cambric hand-embroidered handkerchiefs, silks, satins and ribbons, feathers and bows for the adornment of ladies hats were just some of the high-class goods on display to tempt the numerous customers who frequented the store. The top floor was used for manufacturing purposes where weaving, embroidering, stitching and hemming combined to produce the highest standard in design texture and finish. Altogether, there were two hundred and fifty people employed by The Bank Buildings.

Crawford's willingness to accept all jobs at the Bank Buildings singled him out from the other apprentices, many whose ambitions stretched no further than working behind a counter for the rest of their lives. The floor manager appointed to induct the apprentices was ruthlessly efficient but protective of his young charges making sure they were well instructed in all departments. The linen-draper, he told them, was a tradesman of considerable stock and a very useful member of society. His skill should consist of a perfect knowledge of linen manufacturing, the difference between linens and the properties of other fabrics from different countries. The Bank Buildings was one of the largest department stores in Ireland and an apprentice was moved from department to department so that after five years he was trained in every branch of the trade. Crawford entered into his apprenticeship enthusiastically but to be 'in trade' from a family with gentlemanly aspirations was considered somewhat degrading. One could be a gentlemen farmer or go into one of the professions without losing face, but to be a 'counter hopper' was not considered suitable for a gentleman.

In an account of his early life Crawford reveals an interesting incident during his apprenticeship:-

Following my mother's advice I always did what I was asked to do. Consequently, I found it was not long before I got more to do than I should have, because if there was any difficult or important work to do, I was always delegated to do it. One afternoon I was sent on an errand to Great Victoria Street station to deliver some heavy parcels to a customer. I ran along the platform with the boxes and the first person I bumped into was my Uncle Samuel who was wearing his customary silk topper, frock coat, coloured vest and gold cable watch chain. He was well over six feet with a long red beard and was of a very prepossessing appearance. He caught me roughly by the arm and asked me where I was going. I told him that I had left home and was working as an apprentice in the Bank Buildings and he seemed very annoyed. He said, "You will have to leave and come home with me, get on this train at once". I told him that I would do no such thing and wrenching myself free from his grasp I ran down the steps of the G.N.R. as fast as my feet would carry me.'

Samuel McCullagh was so worked up about the incident that instead of heading home to Lurgan as usual, he took the train to Moira and went to see his brother. When he confronted Robert McCullagh with the evidence of his son's impropriety Crawford's father could only reply, "I can do nothing, the boy has a will of his own". Crawford had chosen his career in defiance of his father, he worked hard and was determined to further himself. During the five years training he acquired an uncanny knowledge of the public's wants which was to become a major asset in his future career.

All this time he remained close to his brother Samuel who with some help from his mother had paid for Crawford's apprenticeship. With no additional financial help from his father, he fell back on his own resources selling newspapers to augment his income outside the Great Northern Railway station and at Gibson's Corner in Castle Place.

Belfast had grown from virtual obscurity at the beginning of the nineteenth century. Between 1835 and 1850 the population of the town had doubled to almost 90,000; between 1850 and 1901 it increased about fourfold to almost 350,000 people.[2] In his memoirs Crawford recalls the tremendous noise and hazardous conditions of a city centre undergoing a major transformation, where horse drawn trams, hackney cabs and jaunting cars with iron shod wheels rattled around the White Linen Hall. Georgian architecture of symmetry and restraint was being replaced with high Victorian individualism. The city's boundaries were extending as never before. Narrow cobble stone streets were giving way to wide boulevards such as Royal Avenue and Ormeau Avenue and he remembered the unrelenting tapping and hammering of the stonemason's chisel and the endless procession of carts and wagons carrying hundred of red bricks and sandstone blocks to the building sites. As many as 1000 horses were kept in stables and byres throughout the city for the purpose of pull-

2.   J.C. Becket et al, Brenda Collins, *The Edwardian City*, p.166

ing horse drawn trams and he remembered watching ragged urchins in dirty caps and short trousers wheeling wooden hand carts then stopping to shovel up manure from under the horses hooves. He also recollected the cold winter evenings when the linen mills and factories around the city were closing up for the night and observing undernourished barefoot children, and sad looking women, shawls wrapped tightly around thin shoulders and pinched faces as they trudged home after a twelve hour shift.

However, like cities in the north and middle of England, Belfast offered the unskilled worker the opportunity to climb up the social and occupational ladder. An apprenticeship with a number of industries in Belfast could be had for a small indenture and provided the possibility of gaining knowledge, experience and education along the way.

Harland and Wolff were building the biggest ships in the world. The *Teutonic* and *Majestic* were launched in 1889 and the *Oceanic* in 1899. It also encouraged the growth of other shipbuilding firms in Belfast and provided work for a fast growing populace. Men and women from all over Ireland flocked to work in the expanding textile factories, engineering, and rope works. The York Street Flax Spinning and Weaving Company, the largest of its kind in the world employed 4,000 workers. By 1894 there were nine hundred thousand spindles in use in Ulster's Linen industry. Thomas Gallagher employed 600 people in his tobacco firm growing his own leaf on extensive estates in North Carolina and importing raw tobacco to the value of £480,000 in 1889.[3] Belfast was also becoming a world centre for the production of aerated waters. Ross's, Evans and Cantrell and Cochrane who produced Aromatic Ginger Ale, Fruit Flavoured Lemonade, Sparkling Montserrat, Club Soda, as well as Kali Water.[4] Marcus Ward on Dublin Road claimed to have pioneered the mass produc-

3. Jonathon Bardon, *A History of Ulster,* p.391

4. Ibid

tion of Christmas cards and was awarded the Legion of Honour in 1878 by the President of France.

Although Belfast was pre-eminently an industrial city it was still a place of export for agricultural produce. May's Market was open daily to sell corn, grass seed and flaxseed, with cattle and horse fairs being regularly held there. The butter market operated six days a week in Great Patrick Street, where heavily salted butter could be bought in firkins, crocks, lumps and prints. Friday saw great herds of cattle being urged on by drovers, down the city thoroughfares for sale in Oxford Street; and in nearby St. Georges Market, meat, poultry, eggs and fish were sold by traders from innumerable stalls. The Turnley Street Hay and Straw Market was open every day to supply the needs of the city's six hundred jaunting cars, in addition to horse-drawn trams omnibuses, traders' carts and private carriages.[5]

Crawford remembered how Great Victoria Street was at this time a rather grand residential and mercantile thoroughfare popular with doctors, dentists and professionals alike. William Boyd, Director of the Blackstaff Mill lived at No. 43. His neighbour Sir William Whitla, physician, philanthropist and benefactor to Queens University lived at No. 41 and John Brady, a surgeon lived at No.11. In 1890, No.71 was a hospital for Nervous Diseases. There was also an Ophthalmic Hospital, and in 1901 No.69 was the Belfast Hygienic Institute. Great Victoria Street also boasted no less than five hotels. The Adelphi, The Dublin and Armagh Hotel, The Ulster Railway Hotel (now the Crown Bar), William Robinsons Hotel and the Crown and Anchor Temperance Hotel.[6]

The commercial areas of Bedford Street and Linenhall Street surrounding the White Linen Hall were known as 'Linenopolis' in deference to the importance of the linen trade in Belfast. These wide streets were lined with three and four storey warehouses occupied not only by linen and muslin manufacturers but cabinet makers, car-

5. Jonathon Bardon, *A History of Ulster,* p.389

6. Alfred S Moore, *A Merchant Prince*

riage assemblers, furniture handlers and funeral furnishers. Although Belfast was experiencing industrial and demographic growth, the long hours and meagre wages were detrimental to the health and output capacity of the workers. The conditions in which these people worked were amongst the most unhealthy imaginable. For almost all types of linen spinning and weaving the atmosphere needed to be very hot and humid. In the wet spinning rooms, where the majority of children worked, the floors were always wet and the workers went barefoot. The spinners were liable to get a condition known as onychia, a very painful inflammation of the big toe nail which was caused by walking barefoot on floors covered with hot contaminated water. Clothes became saturated with spray from the spindles and it was commonplace for children working in these conditions to develop lung diseases when they were very young.[7] For women workers in the linen mills life was particularly hard. Rising at 5am they had to go to work in all weathers, sometimes travelling barefoot. Their clothes were cheap, crudely made and consisted of a striped petticoat made from 'Newtownards Strip', a cotton blouse was added and a thin 'drugget' shawl thrown over the shoulders providing scant protection from the harsh weather.[8] The women characterised by these garments became known as 'shawlies'.

A Board of Trade enquiry listed average earnings of linen operatives working full time in September 1906: men £1 2s 4d., boys 7s 8d., women 10s 9d., and girls 6s 7d. Adelaide Anderson, one of the first female factory inspectors, added that the wages 'of an immense number of women … did not rise above 7 or 8 shillings out of which came deductions for disciplinary fines, charges for damage or purchase of damaged articles, so that for many young women 5 or 6 shillings was nearer the mark.'[9]

---

7.   W.A. Maguire, *Belfast*, p.79

8.   Alfred S Moore, *A Merchant Prince*. (Further research has not uncovered any more information regarding 'Newtownards strip'. I can only assume it is made up of remnants of material.)

9.   Jonathon Bardon, *A History of Ulster*, p.333

Crawford sympathised with these workers and was later regarded as an employer who took the welfare of his employees seriously, paying fair wages and rewarding loyalty. His memoirs reveal how at the time he would make a little extra money by selling editions of the Belfast Telegraph outside the Great Northern Railway station, where across the street at the Ulster Railway Hotel thick set, stalwart men in greasy aprons off-loaded barrels from horse-drawn wagons onto the pavement, the air filled with the stench from Heddle and Reeds Glue Factory, a smell he said that lingered in the nostrils and made the eyes water. Every day refuse carts filled with the city's excrement and manure were left at the Great Northern Railway Station to be collected by train, taken to the country and then used as valuable fertiliser. The state of major streets in Belfast at this time have been described as 'being very imperfectly cleansed' and even when swept 'the offensive accumulation is sufficient to remain in festering heaps for whole days'.

Belfast at this time was well known for its range of entertainments, and theatres such as The Alhambra, the Theatre Royal and the Ulster Hall were very popular venues. The Theatre was also successful in winning a new working class audience. Writing in 1891, the actor Whitford Kane recorded the Theatre Royal's Gallery included 'shipyard workers in their dungarees, men from the linen and rope factories, shawled mill girls, clerks young and old, and stage-struck apothecary apprentices like myself'.[10] With its proximity to the Bank Buildings boarding house, it is very probable that Crawford would have visited Fred Ginnett's Circus on the corner of Glengall Street, the tents displaying massive posters showing clowns, trapeze artists, performing ponies and elephants with elaborate head pieces. With the price of admission only 1d it was easily affordable. This site would later be home to the Grand Opera House built in 1898. It opened with the Pantomime Blue Beard, Frank Matcham's lavish

---

10. John Grey, Belfast: *The Making of the City*, p.109

interior, the Belfast News-Letter observed, created 'a most brilliant and charming Eastern Effect'.

Rising incomes and particularly the emergence of a skilled working class, a very marked feature of Belfast society, created new possibilities and entertainment became a flourishing industry. Crawford recalled his first evening at the Bank Buildings boarding house reading the Belfast News Letter for the first time and being enthralled by the numerous entertainments that were advertised – Robinson Crusoe was being performed as the Easter Pantomime at the Theatre Royal and Hengler's Grand Cirque at The Ulster Hall proclaimed a laughable sketch entitled 'Papa and his son Johnny in search of Equestrian exercise!'

Seen through the eyes of a young Crawford McCullagh, Belfast would have seemed an imposing city, his walk to the Bank Buildings each morning took him down Great Victoria Street, past Fisherwick Presbyterian Church[11] and the bronze statue of the Reverend Henry Cooke, 'The Black Man' overshadowing the railing of the Belfast Academical Institution. Wellington Place and the White Linen Hall built in 1787 enclosed behind its landscaped gardens and elegant railings. Thomas Carnduff in his Life and Writings remembers the old White Linen Hall in the glory of a summer's day, with its cool and shady grounds festooned with stately foliage, jealously watching the inevitable destruction of what was at one time the aristocratic residential quarter of the city. This was indeed the hub of Belfast with its hotels and restaurants such as The Castle, The Imperial and The Royal Hotel and then Donegal Place, a shopping thoroughfare known as the 'Flags' with its elegant shops and plate glass windows displaying expensive silverware, elegant clothes and luxury merchandise.

---

11. In 1897 the Fisherwick Place congregation agreed to sell their building to the Presbyterian Church in Ireland to provide a site for their headquarters to move to their present site on Malone Road, Belfast.

At weekends the apprentice boys played football at Chapel Fields, which stretched from Joy Street to Linenhall Street bordering on Ormeau Avenue. In the holidays this large wasteland was a bustling playground with roundabouts, circuses, wild beast shows and boxing booths.[12] If they couldn't find space to play football at Chapel Fields there was always 'the Plains'. These comprised acres of flat grassy meadows which were situated between Botanic Avenue and Rugby Avenue. It was one of the largest open spaces in Belfast. At weekends thousands would gather to cheer on their favourite clubs from Sandy Row or Donegall Pass.

Holidays were few and far between but on days off Crawford recalled exploring the city with his friend Tom Brand, a fellow apprentice from the Bank Buildings whose family later built Brands and Co., Ladies Outfitters. They would walk through the leafy grounds of the old White Linen Hall, fish for sticklebacks along the banks of the Lagan, visit Carter's Waxworks in Castle Place or venture up the newly flagged and paved Royal Avenue. This broad, handsome and modern thoroughfare replaced the old, stinking and insanitary Hercules Street and Garfield Street. Up until 1882, Hercules Street had been narrow and full of alleys, entries and rank slums. It was a foul smelling and stinking butchers' quarter where slaughtering was carried out on the premises, and traders dealt with the various products of the carcases of cows and pigs. It also functioned as a daily street market thronged with farmers and fish-mongers, egg-wives and knife-grinders. Among the shops that survived was the only menagerie in Belfast, a strange and exotic establishment owned and run by Messrs. Bostock and Wombwell. Crawford recalls in his memoirs how he and Tom were regular visitors fascinated by the shrieking of monkeys and colourful chattering parrots. The dark interior, made more sinister by the presence of pythons and reptiles kept them spellbound and fired his imagination with images of dark jungles and lost

---

12. Thomas Carnduff, *Life and Writings*, p.15

continents. These premises were demolished in 1884 to make way for the Grand Central Hotel.

In 1881 John Robb, entrepreneur and owner of Robb's Department Store in Castle Place formed the Belfast Estate Company which developed a section of Royal Avenue from what had previously been Hercules Street. In 1883 he presented plans before the Town Council for a large central railway terminus based on the Grand Central version of New York City. By 1892, Robb had become totally disillusioned with the delays caused by the City Council and dropped his plans for the railway terminus, opting instead to build a magnificent new hotel which would dominate Royal Avenue. In the same year he formed the Belfast Central Hotel Company Ltd. The Grand Central Hotel opened it's doors on Thursday 1 June 1893, reputedly the finest in Ireland and the largest ever built in Belfast. Passing through the revolving doors the patrons of the day could enjoy a table d'hote Luncheon in one of the magnificent dining rooms for the princely sum of two shillings comprising of 'Soup, Fish, Joint, Poultry and Cheese'. The evening dinner menu was available at four shillings and eight pence.[13]

In his memoirs Crawford recalls going one Sunday, with his brother Sam, to the Custom House Steps. This was a famous meeting place for lay-preachers, religious and political agitators. It was an ideal venue, for the space in front of the steps allowed room for thousands of people and it was not uncommon for riots to erupt as the aggressive public speakers whipped the crowd into a frenzy. Apart from public speakers there were other attractions. In amongst the throng were stalls selling 'yellow man', 'bulls eyes' and 'half-penny chews'. There were oystermen and pie-men, ballad singers and musicians, and quack doctors displaying dark brown bottles containing magic elixirs that cured everything from headaches to constipation. Toothless old women in black shawls sold mussels and whelks, and old men with rotten teeth shouted 'knives, scissors and razors to grind'. He vividly

---

13. Alfred S Moore, *A Merchant Prince*

recalls walking around the dockside admiring the tall masts and spars of square-rigged sailing vessels and cross channel steamers moored at Donegall Quay. On the other side of the river at Queens Quay coal-boats and river barges bobbed gently on the evening tide, and as they stood on Queens Bridge they could see two or three massive ships under repairs at the Abercorn Basin on Queen's Island. On their way back to the boarding house the boys would have stopped at the White Linen Hall to mingle with the city's town folk, and listen to the military band that played in the grounds every Sunday evening.

Belfast Riots Of 1886

In the spring of 1886, the Liberal Prime Minister William Ewart Gladstone introduced the first Home Rule Bill for Ireland which resulted in a series of severe disturbances which continued throughout the summer of that year.

On 3rd June a skirmish between a Protestant and a Roman Catholic navvie in the Alexander Graving Dock led to a vicious fist fight. Anger over the issue of Home Rule evoked strong feelings of sectarian animosity. The following day rioting broke out in the shipyard between Protestants and Catholics resulting in one man drowning and hundreds being hurt. Civil disorder erupted on the streets of Belfast with numerous fights taking place between various mobs. Pavers, cobbles and stones were hurled at the military and disorder and killing continued throughout the summer.

Between May and September 1886 at least thirty-two people were killed (including women and children) and 371 policemen injured.[14] Shops and public houses were vandalised and burnt, and dozens of families, both Catholic and Protestant were intimidated out of their homes. By the end of July the worst of the rioting seemed to be under control, although spasmodic disturbances continued in and around the Bowers Hill district at the bottom of the Shankill Road.

---

14. Alfred S Moore, *A Merchant Prince*

The General Election in July 1886 provided reassurance for those Protestants who opposed Home Rule. With the defeat of the Home Rule Bill the danger of rule by a Dublin Parliament had passed and the defection of so many Liberals made it impossible for Gladstone to carry on.

Crawford was now becoming a valuable young man in the eyes of his employers. In 1887 the company engaged him as an assistant manager. The salary offered, twenty-five pounds a year with board and lodging, was good for the time, and he stayed on at the Bank Buildings for a further two years, increasing his knowledge and understanding of the drapery business. This was only five years since he first came to Belfast and it gave him the confidence and experience he needed in order to further his ambition of owning a shop of his own.

Belfast at this time was experiencing many momentous occasions and it was Crawford's good fortune that he was there to witness them. One such event occurred on the morning of Saturday 13 October 1888 when Crawford came out of the boarding house to see the Great Northern Railway terminus being lavishly decorated with flags and banners. When he reached the Bank Buildings there was great excitement as the 6th Marquis of Londonderry the then Lord Lieutenant of Ireland, and the Lord Mayor Sir James Hazlett were soon to pass down Donegall Place in the state carriage. They were to attend a banquet in the Town Hall where Queen Victoria would confer on Belfast the title of City. When the dignitaries passed through the town at just after noon that day, business came to a standstill as everyone came out onto the streets to cheer and clap. Every available space around Castle Junction was occupied as people craned their necks to get a better view of the procession. The whole city was pulsating with energy and optimism, for at last Belfast was being acknowledged as one of the leading industrial cities in Europe.

At about this time his brother Samuel went to work for William Boyd & Sons in Londonderry. Crawford stayed on in the boarding house for another year and then moved to Sunnyside Street, Lisburn Road, where he shared a house with Joshua and Robert Beckett, boyhood friends from Aghalee. When he finally left the Bank Buildings, it was to transfer his services at a higher salary to John Hanna's drapery shop at 38 High Street situated at the corner of Sugarhouse Entry.

High Street in 1889 was a thriving, commercial thoroughfare with furniture shops, insurance offices and medical halls. There were drapers shops and haberdashers, glove shops, hat and coat emporiums and no house was complete without a photographic print from the studio of William Abernethy who provided all purpose love letters to accompany his photographs. John Arnott and Co., at the corner of Bridge Street and High Street displayed the latest styles from London and a Quaker tea merchant called Forster Green had his warehouse at No.15 which characteristically featured a giant golden tea canister on the front of his store. This was the site of the Old Market House where the United Irishman Henry Joy McCracken was hanged in 1798.

Crawford had only been employed by John Hanna for a few months when he heard of a vacancy next door at the drapery shop of John Porter at 34 and 36 High Street. He immediately applied for the job and was accepted, beginning first as a buyer in their dress department. His business acumen was immediately obvious. One evening John Porter called Crawford into his office and told him that he was to be promoted to General Manager upon Porter's retirement. John Porter attributed the success of his business to Crawford's efforts and he immediately raised his salary to fifty pounds a year.

Another important event marked that year. Crawford met and fell in love with a young girl called Mary McCully.

Shortly after taking up employment with John Porter, Crawford moved out of the house on the Lisburn Road and took up residence with Mr. and Mrs. McCully, who ran a boarding house in Salisbury Terrace on the Antrim Road. The McCully's had an only daughter called Mary, known affectionately by her family as Minnie. She was seventeen, exceptionally pretty and great fun. Crawford reveals in his memoirs how he fell for her the moment they first met. They had the same sense of adventure, were both bright and ambitious and it wasn't long before a close bond developed. When Crawford came home in the evenings they would go for long walks. Alexandra Park with its well tended paths and rose gardens was a favourite venue but sometimes they would walk down the leafy boulevard of Fortwilliam Park to admire the large mansions owned by linen merchants and ship builders. Other times they went as far as Whiteabbey and imagined living in one of the grand houses built on the shores of Belfast Lough with their well manicured lawns hidden behind high hedges and ornate wrought iron railings. Within a short time they decided they wanted to spend the rest of their lives together.

With this promotion Crawford felt in a much stronger economic position. His future was now more secure than ever and he was confident that the right time had come to settle down and raise a family. Crawford and Minnie were married on 7 April 1890 and moved into a house in Stranmillis. The rent on the terrace house was four shillings and sixpence a week, a significant amount of money at that time. It had a parlour on the ground floor with a scullery at the back, a privy and ash pit in the backyard and two bedrooms on the first floor. The parlour with its bay window and deep cornices was the 'good' room and essentially used on Sundays or for visitors. Minnie had to walk no further than the Stranmillis Road to buy her groceries. Parlour shops sold fresh eggs, butter and vegetables and the nearby Lisburn Road was becoming increasingly commercialised as shops were selling everything from household goods to fresh meat and poultry.

The old estates of Belleview and Sandymount had not yet surrendered to the developers and the area surrounding Stranmillis with its old Jacobean style mansion and estate of woodland, lake and meadows still provided a quiet oasis close to the River Lagan.

When the couple moved into their new home, Crawford was earning fifty pounds a year, and with the amount he had saved from his days in the Bank Buildings he and Minnie were able to live very comfortably.

The newly developed area between Friars Bush and Mount Pleasant where they now lived was walled in by red brick terrace houses with bay windows, diminutive gardens and well trimmed privet hedges that still stand and are so characteristic of Victorian Belfast.

Meanwhile his brother Samuel had become engaged to Catherine Boyd, the daughter of William Boyd. They married in Londonderry in 1891. When Sam returned to Belfast he secured for himself a position in Brand's Fashion House in Donegal Place, and the couple took up residence at No. 4 Stranmillis Gardens. They were a well-matched pair in looks and temperament. He was tall and handsome, with an engaging personality, and she was his equal in looks and charm. The two brothers and their wives would spend many happy times together and in fine weather they would go sailing on the river Lagan. For a shilling they could rent a boat from Tom Boyce who ran a ferry service from River Terrrace across the Lagan to the pier on the Ormeau Bank. From Boyce's boathouse they could row up as far as Stranmillis lock and sit in the river garden of Molly Ward's Tavern, the girls would have curds-and-cream while Crawford and Sam would get a big plate of Carrick oysters for only 4 pence a dozen. On other occasions they would stroll through Botanic Gardens and admire the exotic blooms in the magnificent iron and glass hot house. All through the year there was entertainment in the form of band concerts and military tournaments, firework displays, fancy dress parades and gymnastic performances.

Their happiness seemed complete when Minnie became pregnant but her confinement was dogged with sickness and ill health and, after a long and difficult pregnancy, Minnie finally gave birth to a son in January 1891. Tragically he died a few days later. To add to their sorrow, they were told by the doctor to not risk having another child. A year later Sam's wife Catherine announced her own pregnancy and on 25 September 1892 she gave birth to a boy. They christened him Ernest Crawford McCullagh and Samuel asked Crawford and Minnie to be god-parents.

Shortly after the birth of Ernest, Minnie's health deteriorated rapidly and it soon became apparent that she was suffering from tuberculosis. In those days this respiratory disease was called phthisis, or the more sinister 'White Plague'. There was no cure other that complete rest, plenty of fresh air, and sunlight. A strict adherence to hygiene was also highly recommended. Infectious diseases such as smallpox, scarlet fever, measles, whooping cough, typhus, diphtheria and typhoid fever were termed zygotic diseases and were responsible for nearly 1,000 or 15% of all deaths in Belfast every year in the 1880s. However, tuberculosis accounted for another 15% of the deaths, so that, in total, specific infectious diseases were responsible for nearly one third of all deaths in Belfast at this time.[15]

A new hospital for the treatment of tuberculosis had opened in Fisherwick Place in 1890, but with only a small number of beds it was almost impossible to gain admission. Minnie recovered somewhat and in 1892 she became pregnant again. Almost immediately her fragile health began to deteriorate. Ernest McCullagh, Crawford's nephew, in his biography *A Merchant Prince* writes a poignant account of her life at this time:-

> 'the last few months of her life, Minnie spent in bed with the shadow of death hanging over her, and my mother (Catherine McCullagh) was with her on her last night, when she kept saying, "I don't want to die". She was twenty-one at this time and her short life was over before it had begun'.

Crawford, Sam and Catherine were with Minnie when she passed away on 26 October 1893. She had given birth to a daughter but sadly she died within twenty-four hours of her mother. Crawford found great comfort and support in the relationship he had with Sam and Catherine but this however was to be short lived as tragedy struck again when in February 1894, Samuel suddenly took ill and died of acute appendicitis. Immediately after Sam's funeral, Catherine and Ernest were taken back to Londonderry by her father William Boyd.

---

15. Dr. Roger Blaney, *Belfast: 100 years of Public Health*, p.34

Crawford was devastated. A loner by nature he had for a long time withdrawn into himself treating his friends with indifference and avoiding his family who tried to comfort him. However, such things as these are character forming. In Crawford's case, they simply added to the traits which made him such a success in life. One of his outstanding characteristics was self-reliance. He learnt it the hard way. Deprived of those in whom he found love and understanding he learned to depend upon himself.

Chapter Three
1895-1900

A Fresh Start

There is a force that drives us on and yet
We are that force and sometimes have controlled it.

Paul Engle.

The sudden death of a loved one can affect those bereaved in many ways. When Crawford lost his family and his brother his first thoughts were to start a new life away from the things that reminded him of the past. Major decisions made in the spur of the moment can often lead in the wrong direction but sometimes fate comes along and the right choice becomes obvious. Crawford was now twenty-five years old and general manager of a successful draper's shop but he thought the place out of date and old fashioned and John Porter's policy of 'what was good enough for my grand-father is good enough for me' was holding him back from his goal. He was clearly at a cross-roads in his life and it was at this time that he decided to try his luck in South Africa. It was six years prior to the Boer War, (1899-1902), and South Africa provided opportunities with many Ulstermen, such as the Cuthbert brothers from Coleraine, having already gone there and been very successful.

In 1889, permission had been granted to Richard Charles O'Neill, whose grand-father came from Ligoniel, to call a settlement 'Belfast'.[1]

1. Alfred S Moore, *A Merchant Prince*

29

Crawford was seriously thinking about emigration in September 1894 when strolling down High Street one evening he bumped into someone who was to radically influence and develop his career.

William Gibson

William Gibson of Phoenix Lodge, Dunmurry was the son of a County Down farmer. Born in Drombroneth, Dromore he started life as an apprentice to his brother-in-law, James Crozier, who had a jewellery shop in North Street, Belfast. At the age of 27 William set up his own jewellery business, first in North Street and then in 1870 at Castle Junction later known as 'Gibson's Corner'. He advertised his shop as a 'watchmaker, jeweller, silversmith, optician and manufacturer of bog oak jewellery'2 . His range widened to include silver and gold objects of a very high standard. In 1880 he moved his business to London and opened the Manufacturing Goldsmiths' and Silversmiths' Company at 112 Regent Street. Gibsons's company was recognised as one of the leading jewellery houses in the United Kingdom. He attended exhibitions all over the world receiving Gold Medals at the Health, Indian and Colonial Exhibition and at the Paris Exhibitions. At the Paris Exhibition he had the distinction of receiving the Legion of Honour.[3] Gibson's Corner in those days was a fashionable meeting point for ritualised strolling and shopping and provided a convenient place in the centre of the city for young people to meet, flirt and gossip.

William Gibson had known Crawford since his days in the Bank Buildings, in fact their first encounter was when Crawford was selling the Belfast Telegraph newspaper at Gibson's Corner to earn pocket money. To illustrate the depth of Gibson's philanthropy and to maybe explain the extraordinary relationship that existed between Crawford and William Gibson it is necessary to relate a story told in the Belfast Telegraph at October 22, 1914.

2.   Ulster Architectural Heritage Society, *Central Belfast, An Historical Gazeteer*, p.105

3.   *Belfast Evening Telegraph* 27 June 1914

In November 1908 Dame Nellie Melba visited Belfast, and on the night she was to sing in the Ulster Hall the weather was very stormy and wet. A Belfast newsboy called Charles Pollock was selling copies of the Belfast Telegraph outside the Metropole Hotel where Miss Melba was staying. When she appeared at the hotel door to walk to her carriage, Pollock, promptly made a safe pathway for her by spreading his newspapers on the pavement. Madame Melba grateful for his act of chivalry gave the delighted newsboy a £5 note. Mr. Gibson on learning of the event offered to pay £25 towards the boys education.

In those days £25 was an enormous amount of money, a year's wages in some cases. So it is easy to see the influence that William Gibson had on Crawford especially at a time when he was unsure of what he was going to do with the rest of his life.

Crawford in his memoirs recalls how one evening when walking down High Street he had bumped into William and told him he was going to resign from Porter's shop and emigrate to South Africa. Reaching the corner of High Street and Bridge Street, William suddenly stopped at a vacant shop displaying a 'To Let' sign and told Crawford that if he were to take the lease and open up his own business he was bound to succeed. Crawford laughed and protested that he had scant capital, just enough to buy his fare to South Africa. Gibson told him not to make any decisions but to think long and hard about what was best for his future as he might make a move in the wrong direction and regret it for the rest of his life. They shook hands and went their separate ways. However, on Monday morning of the following week William Gibson walked into John Porter's shop and gave Crawford a receipt for £125, explaining that he had bought the lease and fittings of the vacant shop and that he would trust him to pay it back at a later date.[4]

Crawford McCullagh's First Business Venture

Crawford's personality and character must have impressed Gibson from their first meeting to have placed such an element of trust in his young protégé. When interviewed later on in his career Crawford

---

4.   Crawford McCullagh, *An Account Of My Early Life*

said "There is no such thing as luck. There is only opportunity and you have to recognise it when it comes along and grasp its particular message and train your hand to make capital out of it". Few men will easily relinquish their hold on what is tangible and secure. Crawford had a good position as manager of John Porter's, and he knew the future was uncertain but he knew that if he was to succeed it would require hard work an element of luck and his total commitment to the new shop.

In 1894 he opened his first shop at 28 High Street which proudly displayed the name as:-

C. McCULLAGH MILLINERY, DRESS, MANTLE
& LADIES' GENERAL OUTFITTING

The premises were flanked on one side by the haberdashery establishment of James Wylie and on the other side by the tailoring shop of John G. McGee, whose speciality became famous world wide. McGee began his business in 1840 as a 'practical hatter' providing 'Best London Hats'. He then extended to tailoring and produced the 'Ulster' which is described in the Oxford Dictionary as 'a long loose overcoat, usually worn with a belt, made from frieze or tweed, in Ulster, Ireland'. It was later made famous in the cinema by the actor Basil Rathbone in his portrayal of the sleuth Sherlock Holmes.

To purchase stock, Crawford went to London to open an account with a wholesaler. At this time any potential new customer was expected to pay half the total amount of their initial order prior to delivery. Crawford did not have the required amount for his purchases, but as luck would have it when he entered the London warehouse he spotted one of the account executives that he had met on a previous buying trip for John Porter. He immediately told him his predicament. The account executive took him into the office and introduced him to the head of accounts saying 'This is my friend from Belfast, Crawford McCullagh. He has just opened his first shop in a prime position, I know his reputation and guarantee this man will make a great success of his enterprise. I recommend we give him all the credit he needs,'

Emboldened by these remarks and realising he could purchase more than he intended, Crawford proceeded to go on a spending spree buying up much of the stock in the warehouse! When he eventually got back to the accounts manager to pay him half the cost the man surprised Crawford by not taking the money and told him that the guarantee of their mutual friend was so satisfactory that he could pay on the customary terms of an old and approved customer. Crawford seems to have realised the value of personal trust through this encounter and for the rest of his life he was to be a generous patron to any young person trying to make his way in life.

Belfast's attainment of city status meant a good deal of social mobility. In the middle of the 19th century Belfast was little more than a provincial town and although High Street was a thriving shopping area most shop owners lived above their stores and a considerable section of the population lived in the adjoining streets and entries. College Square remained residential throughout the nineteenth century, and until after the First World War. Occupied originally by prosperous merchants, industrialists and academics, it became favoured by surgeons and medical specialists. Donegall Place, laid out as part of Lord Donegall's improvements and built during the 1780s and 90s, became the most desirable residential thoroughfare in Belfast. The Royal Hotel at one time the town house of Lord Donegall had many famous visitors including the Royal Duke of Connaught, Daniel O'Connell, and Lord John Russell. William Thackeray thought it 'as comfortable and well-ordered an establishment as the most fastidious cockney can desire, and with an advantage .... that dinners which cost seven shillings at London taverns are served here for half-a-crown'.[5] In 1891 it was reported that 'It still preserves its ancient reputation as a high-class establishment, catering for the nobility and gentry who patronise it, and distinguished from other hotels which

---

5.   Ulster Architectural Heritage Society, *Central Belfast, An Historical Gazeteer*, p.105

seek their customers among the commercial classes. In fact no commercial accommodation is afforded here'. By 1898 the hotel had closed, perhaps because of this failure to move with the times, and Donegall Place became a thoroughfare for business and shopping.

Towards the end of the 19th Century a social elite emerged in Belfast and in accordance with its enhanced economic significance developed a taste for suburban living. Although many professional families continued to live in Belfast's city centre others moved to the leafy suburbs of Malone, Dunmuray, Holywood and Belmont. This drift out of Belfast led to the building of many impressive new homes.

Sir William Ewart Bt., Linen Merchant and Lord Mayor of Belfast (1859-1861) built Glenmachan House at Strandtown in 1862. William Dunville of Dunvilles Irish Distillery built a vast red brick mansion called 'Redburn' at Holywood on the shores of Belfast Lough (now demolished) and William J Pirrie, Chairman of Harland and Wolff lived at 'Ormiston' in a rather grand house in the Scottish Baronial style in the area known as Belmont.

One particular house where Crawford visited many times belonged to Joseph McConnell. One of his closest friends and colleagues, he was the son of Sir Robert McConnell, Estate Agent. Their family home 'The Moat', at Strandtown had been built in 1863 by Thomas Valentine a prominent linen manufacturer. The house was built in the Italianate style of brick, while the estate comprised thirty acres with six cottages, a walled garden, glass houses, garage and stabling accommodation, along with gardens and lawns.[6]

This area of Belfast was also home to Crawford's previous employer William Robertson part-owner of The Bank Buildings, who lived in a Victorian mansion called Netherleigh. The original land attached to the estate measured nearly 7 acres and was part of the old Belmont Estate with its extensive parklands, beech trees, rookery and lake. On

6.   Kathleen Rankin, *The Linen Houses of County Antrim and North County Down*, p.59

this estate stood the old Belmont House which was demolished in 1890 to make way for Campbell College.

There were other beneficiaries from the city's growth. The middle classes of Belfast society; such as accountants, bank managers and solicitors were also able to rent or buy comfortable suburban houses further away from the business section of the city centre in areas such as Ormeau, Knockbreda, Rosetta and Sydenham. While upper and middle class residents of Belfast sought to improve their surroundings, the working classes continued to live in streets of red-brick 'parlour' and 'kitchen' houses in the city. These streets stretched in monotonous rows with each house exactly the same as its neighbour.

Although the development of the linen and shipbuilding trades, the tobacco industry and the rope works etc., brought relative prosperity to every class, the wages of working people remained very low by modern standards. The average wage of an experienced tradesman was roughly 35 shillings a week. Nevertheless, the ingrained work ethic and thrifty nature of these people made a little go a long way, with a reasonable standard of living being enjoyed by most of the population and while pleasures and luxuries were few, there were music halls, theatres and circuses to be enjoyed. However a long walk in the evenings to the river Lagan, or on a Sunday to Cave Hill were the commonest pleasures for the great majority.

As Belfast had became more prosperous the distinct elite had seen their economic well being (and those of their employees) linked to the Union with Britain. This tendency had always been there but, as in 1886 it was to be threatened once again.

In his memoirs Crawford tells of the anguish felt once more by the people of Belfast when in 1893 the Liberals regained power and Gladstone introduced the Second Home Rule Bill. Once again the Unionist made plans for a convention. Twelve thousand delegates had been elected by Unionist associations across the province and they were to meet in a specially constructed convention hall at Stranmillis. It was estimated that three hundred thousand supporters filled the Botanic Gardens during the convention. Crawford relates in his memoirs listening to the Duke of Abercorn and the Liberal Unionist Thomas Sinclair and being amazed that the meeting remained a peaceful one with hostile references to Catholics being carefully avoided. This of course was to impress public opinion in Britain. In an account of his early life Crawford describes attending a rally and the atmosphere he experienced in the Ulster Hall:-

> a huge audience had gathered to listen to Lord Randolph Churchill. I had arrived a little late and was aware of the restless crowd pushing forward to get as near to the platform as they could without causing injury. I was standing at the back of the hall and could feel the excitement and tension of the evening as this charismatic speaker urged an enthralled loyalist audience to prepare themselves in the event of Home Rule. His speech was greeted with a great roar of applause, and the excitement and patriotic mood of the crowd continued into the night as the bands and processions made their way home.

There was a further demonstration on 4 April 1893 when one hundred thousand loyalists marched past Belfast's White Linen Hall. Although there were bands and banners and a copy of the Home Rule was publicly burnt there was no return to the violence witnessed in 1886.

Eventually the Bill was steered through the Commons with a majority of 30 votes, only to be defeated in the Conservative (controlled House of Lords) on the pro-Unionist majority. Gladstone wanted to call a general election but his cabinet refused to support him and dispirited by his second failure to get Home Rule for Ireland he retired in March 1894.

Although Crawford was to enter Belfast Corporation in 1905 his interests up till then were predominantly focused on his highly successful shop in High Street. A keen observer of the latest pioneering trends in fashion he was aware of the new revolution in the way women dressed. Magazines such as the *Delineator, Femina* and *Vogue* were popular in London, Paris and New York but he now saw that they were also being read by fashion conscious women in Belfast.

During most of the nineteenth century, shopkeepers conducted their business on conservative and traditional lines. Cloths and fabrics were standard in weave and colour and women were strictly limited in their choice of colours. Ready to wear garments were scarcely known in the trade and material was bought by the yard and made up at home from paper patterns that appeared in *Ladies Home Journal* or *McCalls Sewing Patterns*. Largely due to the influence of the popular press this was starting to change.

Queen Victoria's reign was coming to an end. It was the dawn of a brand new century and trends and fashions were rapidly changing. In Belfast the economy was prospering and the industrial society had produced a new middle class. This new moneyed class was now joining the consumer ranks and wanted only the best goods. Appreciation of art and beauty was becoming fashionable and the manufacturer and retailer, to be successful, had to offer goods of the highest quality and design. Progressive mass production too, must claim credit for widening the scope for the employment of creative artists and skilled crafts-people.

Creativity was central to Crawford's vision and whilst buying in London he was always conscious of fashion trends to interest the Belfast public. He used this judgement of customers' tastes coupled with his ability to identify trends to provide a varied range of products for his new shop.

From an early age Crawford showed a flair for publicity and style. In *An Account of My Early Life* he writes of his customer relations:

> When I opened my first shop, the first customer on purchasing an item was invited to inspect the range of costume cloths and choose a dress length of her preference. The second customer was similarly rewarded, in fact I ended up giving six customers a similar gift. This gesture of good will and appreciation proved an exceedingly effective opening advertisement. I made such a success of my High Street shop that I was able to move to larger premises.

The drapery trade in Belfast at that time was extremely competitive. His friend Tom Brand opened his first shop at 47 Royal Avenue in 1897 and established himself in business as a costumier and furrier.

In the same year Crawford moved from 28 High Street into larger premises owned by Mrs Hanson at 15-17 High Street. He placed an advertisement in the *News Letter* for an experienced draper's assistant and interviewed at least a dozen applicants. In the end a recommendation came from an old friend called Ginnie Faulkner. Ginnie's brother owned the vast Faulat shirt business in Belfast. Ginnie was acquainted with a young woman who worked in the Ladies department of Robinson and Cleaver's Linen Warehouse recently moved from Castle Place to Donegall Place in 1890. Maggie Brodie was 25 years old, single and an attractive brunette. She was hard working and ambitious and Crawford was looking for someone who could work well behind the counter as a sales assistant but would eventually take on the role of manageress. Maggie lived with her parents and siblings at 19 Greencastle Street in the townland of Ballygolan part of which lies within the Greencastle district of north Belfast. Her late father William had been a draper and her mother Ellen owned a grocers shop. Her sister Ellen worked in the grocers shop and her brother Hugh Kinsman Brodie appears to have started his career as a writing clerk. His death certificate in 1944 reveals that when he retired he had been a company secretary.

Maggie left home at sixteen to serve her apprenticeship with her Uncle Hugh Brodie, owner of a cotton manufacturing company in Bolton-le-Moors outside Manchester. She served her apprenticeship in the factory as well as learning all stages of cotton production, from the cultivation and preparation of raw materials to the making up and decoration of the finished fabric. She also had further skills in hand embroidery, drawn thread work and crochet. Crawford agreed to take on Maggie Brodie at a salary of £12 per annum. From the start she displayed a remarkable degree of resourcefulness and imagination in the decoration and lay out of the shop both inside and out. She soon became indispensable to Crawford often staying behind in the evenings to help him with his accounting books. It soon became the custom for them to leave together after work and walk to Castle Junction where she boarded the Whitewell Tram for Ballygoland.

Within a year their relationship had blossomed and they soon began to spend more time in each others' company. Evenings were spent at the theatre and it would appear from his memoirs that he was able to purchase tickets for the opening night of the pantomime Bluebeard at the Grand Opera House on 23 December 1895 in Great Victoria Street. It's likely that they also witnessed the celebrated trapeze artist and high wire walker Charles Blondin giving his last spectacular performance at the age of seventy-two. Balancing 100 foot above the ground on a manilla rope he performed variations on his celebrated act which included making a crossing blindfold, wearing a sack; pushing a wheelbarrow and then finishing by carrying a man on his back. Maggie was fun to be with and in her company Crawford appeared happy and relaxed. At weekends they would take the boat from Queen's Quay to Bangor and go for long walks along the promenade to Ballyholme.

It was now evident that their relationship had altered from being a professional one to being something entirely different and that a special bond had developed making their friendship more intimate and loving. Crawford realised how important Maggie was to him and she in turn made no secret of that fact that whatever he undertook in life she would be right there beside him. Although Crawford could not replace his first wife Minnie, he realised he had found someone with whom he could share the rest of his life. They held a party in the shop to announce their engagement.

Crawford McCullagh and Maggie Brodie were married in Fortwilliam Presbyterian Church on the Antrim Road, Belfast on 26 July 1897. They started their life together in Stranmillis but shortly afterwards it was decided that they would move to a healthier environment. Crawford had been suffering from recurring chest problems, probably brought on by smoking, however, fearing tuberculosis they looked at renting property in Helen's Bay, a small seaside village not far from Bangor in County Down. Helen's Bay at this time was a quiet little hamlet with only a handful of villas and summer houses either rented or owned by families who came to get away from the smog laden atmosphere of Belfast. With its clean air, picturesque walks and stunning coastline it was the perfect place to bring up a family.

This small rural village was clearly attracting significant number of visitors from Belfast lured by accounts such as this one from the Belfast and County Down Railway Guide 1898:

> The water is delightfully pure. The beautiful sylvan and coast scenery, the bathing facilities, the shortness of the railway journey (about 20 minutes) and the convenient refreshing-rooms near the station, combine to make Helen's Bay one of the favourites of the Belfast seeker of a day's enjoyment.

The sandy beach at Helen's Bay was a favourite with families during the summer months and the picturesque village of Crawfordsburn[7] with its famous Cingalee Tea Gardens was a pleasant walk on a Sunday afternoon.

In 1896 The 1st Marquis of Dufferin and Ava agreed to rent farmland for the construction of a golf course. Originally he had somewhat grander ideas for this scenic spot and had plans drawn up for a stylish seaside resort not unlike a mini Brighton or Eastbourne with long terraces of tall elegant villas facing onto a promenade and an elaborate pier extending out to sea for pleasure steamers. Lord Dufferin did commence the project with the building of a battery wall and promenade at the head of the beach,[8] but the elaborate plans remained just that. However, he did build a rather ornate 'gothic baronial style' railway station in the square of Helen's Bay in the hope of creating employment. He named the village after his mother, Helen Selina, Lady Gifford. Helen's Bay Golf Club was opened on 16 May 1896 on land leased from him.

In 1900, Crawford acquired the lease of number 5-7 High Street, then comprising the shops of Joseph Forde, bootmaker, and Edward and William Gribben, watchmakers and jewellers, with the Shelbourne

---

7. Further research has uncovered evidence to suggest that one Andrew Crawford, who gave his name to the village of Crawfordsburn in 1606 came from Kilbirnie in North Ayrshire. Whether he is related to John Crawford, ancestor of Crawford McCullagh, who settled in Monaghan is open to speculation.

8. Bayburn Historical Society, 'Twixt Bay & Burn', p.27

Dining rooms on the upper floor of Forde's. These buildings west of Crown Entry were demolished and superseded by an up-to-date establishment with Crawford introducing several novel features, principal among them being the use of brass in the shop front and a marble pavement at the entrance. The new building was especially designed by architects Aicken and Bangor and built by Mr. William Kerr. Crawford thought he now had a shop that would support him for the rest of his working life. However within five years the business had become so successful that he was faced with the knowledge that another major change had to be made in order to maintain his commercial success.

Chapter Four
1900-1908

A Sure Foundation

As we pay others, we are paid;
Life gives us back just what we give,
And so we do not live to trade,
But trade that we may truly live.

Anonymous.

Helen's Bay

When Crawford and Maggie came to Helen's Bay in 1898 there were relatively few residents living in the village. The 1901 census tells us that the McCullaghs occupied number 9 Ballygrot, Bangor, Co. Down where there were 330 inhabitants in 74 houses.

The advent of the railway line played a crucial part in the development of this part of the coast. In 1860 the population of Bangor was just 2,500 and the development of Helen's Bay had not begun in earnest. However, the extension from Holywood through Helen's Bay but bypassing Crawfordsburn was opened on 18 May 1865, it was greatly helped by the long standing offer from the Railway to all new residents of a free season ticket for two years.[1]

---

1. Bayburn Historical Society, *'Twixt Bay and Burn'*, p.31

When the McCullaghs moved into their new surroundings in 1898 the areas of Crawfordsburn, Ballyrobert and Helen's Bay had a number of farms and farmsteads. There was a market garden in Kathleen Avenue where the locals gathered on a Saturday morning to buy fresh vegetables, and milk, butter, buttermilk and cheese was sold from carts in the square. On Craigdarragh Road, before the arrival of mains water, a water supply was piped from Clandeboye. This often allowed small worms, frogs or even fish to arrive at unexpected destinations!

The McCullaghs soon settled into their new life in Helen's Bay seeing however little of their immediate neighbours in the first couple of months due to the demands of the business. Their move into the company of some of Ulster's 'elite' families was unnerving for Maggie as her upbringing had not prepared her for the social changes that would naturally occur due to the success of the business and the increase in their finances. One of the first things that made a huge difference to the McCullaghs' life in this small close-knit community was their commitment to the Presbyterian Church in Church Road. As long ago as 1882 there had been talk of building a church in Helen's Bay. Ballygilbert was then the nearest available and it was a long walk for many. A large tent was acquired in 1883 and services were held there during the summer months. In 1892 the Presbytery of Ards was asked to make provision for services to be conducted in the Temperance Hall, at the Station Hotel in the village. In 1895 Lord Dufferin came to the rescue and presented rent free a suitable site for the church.[2] Building started in 1895 and was carried out by the contractor William Kerr whom Crawford had employed when he undertook the renovations at 5-7 High Street, Belfast.

In a small community like Helen's Bay, worship was of paramount importance to the residents. After church, contacts were established, calling cards distributed, and it was in this community of respectable middle class families that Maggie formed lasting friendships. The

2.   Bayburn Historical Society, *'Twixt Bay and Burn'*, p.73

committee of Helen's Bay Presbyterian Church in 1900 consisted of a small group of prominent industrialists, merchants and professionals who had given their time, effort and money in order to establish a congregation.

One of the most influential members of the committee was Thomas Workman who lived at Craigdarragh House, Craigdarragh Road. He was Receiver General for Scotland, a Magistrate of the County of Down and one of the founders and vice-chairman of Workman Clark and Company, Ship-builders. He was also a linen merchant and carried on the family business of T.&G.A. Workman, started by his grandfather. He was a keen member of the Bangor Corinthian Sailing Club and one of the founders of the 'canoe club,' now the R.N.I.Y.C. at Cultra.

Another resident of Helen's Bay was James Mackie, D.L., head of the firm of James Mackie and Sons Ltd., who until 1897 ran the Albert Foundry. When Mackies became a limited company in 1902, he took over the Clonard Foundry one of the largest engineering works in the city. James, his wife Elizabeth and their six children lived in a house called Hazelbank at Whitehouse on the shores of Belfast Lough, but during the summer they rented a house called Fairholme in Helen's Bay.

George Herbert Brown was also a prominent member of Helen's Bay Presbyterian Church. He built 'Tordeevra' in Kathleen Avenue, now known as 'Bennet House' and both he and his wife Kathleen were the first captains of Helen's Bay Golf Club. In 1904 he was High Sheriff for County Down, Justice of the Peace and Member of the Down County Council. He was also Chairman of John Shaw Brown and Sons, Ltd., a prominent Belfast linen house. As a keen yachtsman, he won many prizes with his yacht 'Halcyone'.

One of the driving forces in the building of the new Presbyterian Church was W. S. Mollan. He lived at 'Thornleigh' and held Sunday school lessons in his house after church service. He was an Elder and Clerk of Session for fifty years at Fisherwick Church, Belfast as well as Hon. Secretary of the Y.M.C.A. Another church member, Hugh Ross, was a director of the Midland Railway Company. He was a summer resident who for some time lived in 'Rust Hall'.

John Smith built 'Dalry' on the Craigdarragh Road and dedicated much of his time to the Presbyterian Church. He was an impressive figure who walked through Helen's Bay every day wearing a caped 'Ulster', a cloth cap and silver topped walking stick.

Another resident in this small community was James Taylor. An Elder of Helen's Bay Church he was the organist for many years and a very gifted individual regarding music and appreciation of art. With his particular interest in stained glass windows in cathedrals he gave wonderful lantern shows on cathedrals and churches he had visited on his many holidays abroad. He was one of the founders and a partner in the firm of Taylor, Calvert and Co., Stockbrokers. He was also Chairman of John Milligan and Co., Ltd., steamship owners and coal importers. His daughter Stella was a great friend of the McCullagh children, especially Helen, and they remained close friends for many years.[3]

It was into this company that Crawford and Maggie found themselves when they started married life in Helen's Bay and very soon Crawford was encouraged to join the Presbyterian Church Committee. Recognising his business skills he was elected Honorary Treasurer in 1900. He was to hold this position until he resigned on 24 March 1908. *A History of Helen's Bay Presbyterian Church* by Margaret Garner records that on that date at a social meeting of the congregation in William's Hall he was presented with an 'Illuminated Address'. A few years later on 29 January 1911, Crawford and Robert Workman were elected Elders.

The contacts Crawford made and the friendships forged in Helen's Bay were significant stepping stones in his first encounter with politics and it was the influence of James Mackie, George Herbert Brown

---

3.   Margaret A.K. Garner, *A History of Helen's Bay Presbyterian Church 1896-1958*, pp.11-13

and Thomas Workman that encouraged him to enter city council a few years later.

By 1900 the McCullaghs were now more financially secure than they had ever been. Maggie, with the support of her new friends, was feeling more comfortable in her surroundings and with this in mind Crawford and Maggie decided it was time to start a family. Their first daughter was born on 4 November 1900 and christened Helen Brodie McCullagh. Helen was six months old when Maggie went back to work. Although this would have been unusual in those days for women in her position to continue working after the birth of a child, Maggie was determined to support Crawford in his work. She was fully supportive of her ambitious husband as well as finding the drapery business both stimulating and challenging. She therefore hired a cook and a nanny to look after Helen and manage household affairs.

In October 1901 not long after the birth of Helen, Crawford received a letter from his mother telling him that his father was gravely ill and did not have long to live. Arriving at Fortland to see his father for the last time it must have been a poignant moment when Crawford apologised to him for his stubbornness all those years ago. Robert McClave McCullagh died on 4 November 1901. After her husband's death Mary Jane moved in with her daughter's family at Cornakinnegar, Armagh, not far from their original farm at Annaghroghal.

Business success was by no means the only aim in Crawford's life. An entrepreneur ahead of his time, he was constantly looking for new areas of development and innovative ideas in fashion. One such example of his insight occurred the following summer at the Northern Counties Hotel in Portrush when the McCullagh family were on holiday. Crawford recounts in his memoirs how he designed an item of clothing for women which became known as the 'Guards Coat' and was one of his best selling garments:

'I was sitting in the foyer of the hotel when a woman walked in wearing a stunning navy blue coat lined in red satin. Shortly afterwards I spotted an illustrated weekly magazine called The Sketch in the reading room of the hotel and found on the front page a picture of a member of the Guards Band wearing a beautiful blue coat cut in military style fashion. The association of ideas, and the trend of taking the English masculine and making it feminine, intrigued me. So much so that, the next day I informed Maggie of my plan and went straight back to Belfast. With the magazine tucked carefully under my arm I took the train to Belfast and immediately went to see my friend and business acquaintance, Mr. Thompson, who had a manufacturing clothing company in Donegall Place. I asked him if he could produce a coat similar to the Guards Coat as shown in The Sketch, but with feminine lines. I was assured that this was indeed possible and the manufacturing of the garment was started almost immediately. Needless to say when the first batch of coats were ready for inspection, I was delighted and the demand so great that they literally flew out of the shop.'[4]

At this stage Crawford decided to start manufacturing coats under the name 'The Belfast Coat and Costume Company'. His first venture produced a garment called 'the Slieve Donard Coat', a version of the 'Raglan' a man's coat with wide sleeves popular in the 1890's. Crawford again using his imagination to turn the masculine into the feminine had the coat tailored to suit the female market. Crawford was just one of a group of men of similar age and ambition who had been apprentices together in the drapery trade. They were now successful businessmen in a city that already had five department stores.

His friend Thomas Brand was obviously successful because by 1902 he had relocated to larger premises at 21 Donegall Place which had become vacant the year before. He was now trading as Brand and Company 'Ladies Tailors, Costumiers, Milliners and Furriers'. Another good friend, Samuel Donald Cheyne had a successful drapery and shirt manufacturing company at 16/22 Donegall Place. His wife Anastasia had a strong influence in the company and invented The Cheyne Patent Skirt Gauge Co., which was awarded a Royal Warrant in 1914 by King George V. Stores such as Sawyers in

---

4. Crawford McCullagh, *An Account of my early Life.*

High Street, catering for the high end of the fish and butchery trade, Liptons grocery store, the Belfast Co-operative store and numerous furniture shops in the city were testament to the vitality of commerce in Belfast.

In 1902 Maggie discovered she was pregnant again and much to everyone's delight she gave birth to a second daughter, Margaret Eileen, born on 21 February 1903. Christened Margaret she was always affectionately known as Daisy.[5] Maggie was now content to stay at home and look after her two children. However, her social life in Helen's Bay was fairly limited. She had a small circle of friends like herself who were involved in Church activities. Certainly some of them played tennis and golf but there is no evidence to suggest that Maggie had any hobbies, other than reading. It would appear that her sole aim in life was to support her husband. In his memoirs Ernest McCullagh, Crawford's nephew states that Maggie was devoted to her husband "although I have no doubt she loved her children it would appear that within a short space of time much of the parenting of Helen and Daisy was left to housekeepers and nannies". At this stage in his career, Crawford was taking on a much bigger enterprise than ever before and for the time being preferred his wife to stay at home and spend time with his two daughters.

From his first days as an apprentice with the Bank Buildings, William Gibson had taken a paternal interest in Crawford McCullagh. Over the years he was to be mentor and business advisor to the young entrepreneur and so when Crawford made important decisions in his life he turned to William for guidance. Crawford wanted to build a large department store in the middle of Belfast and his plan was to design a modern innovative building using the best of materials and installing the latest technology that the modern era had to offer.

In January 1904 on the recommendation of Gibson, Crawford made plans to visit America and Canada. His intention was to spend three days in New York and a further three days in Toronto. William was

---

5.   Daisy McCullagh would become the author's grandmother.

a friend and business associate of Timothy Eaton who was President of T. Eaton and Company, the largest department store in Canada, and he had arranged for Crawford to visit his family for a couple of days. In New York Crawford stayed three days at the Waldorf Astoria Hotel visiting all the important department stores in the city, Macy's, Bloomingdales and Lord and Taylors, located in an area of New York called 'Ladies Mile'. He took his time talking to the managers, the assistants and floorwalkers, walking up and down the aisles taking notes, and examining the merchandise and type of products on display. When he was satisfied he had done a thorough examination of each store he travelled by train to Toronto to stay with the Eatons.

Timothy Eaton was born in Clogher, two miles north of Ballymena, County Antrim in 1834. His father John died in 1846, followed two years later by his mother Margaret Craig Eton.[6] In 1854 at the age of 20 he left Ireland for Canada with his brother James and in 1856 they started the J. and T. Eaton General Store in a log building on the banks of Fish Creek, St. Mary's. By 1868 Timothy had married Margaret Wilson Beattie, but the brothers quarrelled and the partnership dissolved. James remained in Fish Creek, however, Timothy and Margaret moved to Toronto where in 1869 they opened their first 'cash only' dry goods store at 178 Yonge Street. The business prospered to such a degree that sales at Eaton's rose from $24,000 in 1870 to $155,000 in 1880 when the number of employees totalled fifty, mostly female.[7] In 1883, Eaton's moved to 190-196 Yonge Street, where Timothy purchased a row of shops that gave him a fifty-two-foot frontage. There were twenty-five thousand square feet of selling space, tall plate glass show windows, and an interior atrium that allowed natural light to fall throughout the store's three floors. In 1884 Eaton's published their first mail order catalogue called *The Wishing Book*. By 1896 the catalogue ran to four hundred pages and

---

6. Rod McQueen, *The Rise and Fall of Canada's Royal Family*, p.7

7. Rod McQueen, *The Rise and Fall of Canada's Royal Family*, p.10

was published twice a year. In large type on the catalogue's cover Eaton's declared itself:

CANADA'S GREATEST STORE

In 1897 the Eaton family moved to a large, newly built Victorian house at 182 Lowther Avenue, a dwelling almost as grand as Government House. There were conservatories filled with palm trees, reception rooms hung with point de venise lace curtains, as well as French gilt chairs and ornament-filled glass display cabinets.

There is no doubt that when Crawford McCullagh visited the Eatons in 1904 their influence must have been overwhelming. Timothy Eaton was a man from the same Ulster farming stock, a man who had worked his apprenticeship in a store selling grain and hardware where he worked from before sunrise until after sundown, often sleeping under the counter because there was too little time to walk home and back. Like Crawford, he had wanted to do something different with his life and had left his homeland to go to Canada to make his fortune.

By 1904 Timothy Eaton was sixty-eight years of age and in poor health. An accident on his farm in 1899 had left him with a broken hip and injured shoulder. He now had to be driven to the store then pushed to his office in a wheelchair. On days when he did not leave home, a store employee would arrive at 7a.m. to read him the papers, make telephone calls and do other errands. By the time he arrived to stay with the Eatons, Timothy's son Jack had successfully taken over the running of the business.

According to Crawford's memoirs the Eatons were wonderful company and eager to hear about the rapid development of Belfast and Crawford's plans to open a department store. They arranged daily visits to the Toronto shop where the manager Mr. Allen was able to show Crawford the latest innovative technology. Telephones had been installed in 1884 as well as a system of overhead pneumatic tubes that carried cash from the counters to a central office where correct change was given and returned via the same device. Eatons first passenger lift, Fenson's Patent Hydraulic Elevator was installed in 1886. Crawford studied each floor, travelling in the elevator, completely mastering the layout of the building. He particularly studied the clever use of lighting in the various departments. On the ground floor they sold perfumes, leather goods and jewellery; on the first floor, scarves, hats, gloves, stationery; on the second floor were men's clothes and on the third floor women's whilst the fourth floor sold household goods and kitchen accessories. Crawford studied the position of the counters and the glass cabinets that displayed beautiful cashmere scarves and kid leather gloves. By the end of the third day he was in no doubt as to how he was going to have his own department store constructed and developed. Plans had already been drawn up to build his new store in Castle Place. With the help of his friend and mentor, William Gibson, these plans were about to become a reality.

The Redevelopment of Old Belfast

The style of architecture within Belfast city centre at this time was evolving at an amazing rate and many old buildings from the previous century were being demolished to make way for more modern premises. Crawford's present site in High Street was only a short distance from a block of old-style shops owned by William Gibson and situated on the south side of Castle Place, between Gibson's Corner and Cornmarket. In 1903 Gibson relinquished his holdings and leased the property to Crawford for re-development. It was Crawford's desire to build a magnificent building which would become a landmark of contemporary design and sound workmanship.

This area of Belfast known as Castle Place had been home to successive fortifications since the time of John de Courcy, an Anglo-Norman who came to Ireland in the twelfth century. However it was Sir Arthur Chichester (1563-1625), an English adventurer, soldier and Governor of Carrickfergus whose name is one of the most notable in the city's illustrious history and who is generally thought of as the founder of modern Belfast. It was his son Arthur, who was made

Earl of Donegall for his services to Charles I, who enlarged the old Belfast Castle originally built by his father and constructed a most elegant palace complete with turrets and gables, a large courtyard and a garden planted with orchards, cherry gardens, bowling green and ornamental ponds. The castle continued to be lived in by successive generations of the Chichester family until 24 April 1708 when it was destroyed by an accidental fire tragically killing three sisters of Arthur, the 4th Earl of Donegall. The castle itself was never rebuilt and in the 1780s a large section of the castle gardens was developed by the 5th Earl of Donegall, by building rather fine terrace houses in what is now known as Donegall Place. A Georgian house was built on the site of the castle about 1787 for Lord Donegall's agent. This was demolished about 1896 to make way for the shops which Crawford eventually knocked down in order to erect the new Castle Buildings.[8]

These antiquated buildings included the shops of Tom McClellan, cutler; the Cahoon Brothers, who were watchmakers and silversmiths, Burrows and Company whose window displayed a fine variety of lace and fancy goods and was also famous for Belfast's own Madame Tussaud's. There was also a freak theatre owned by a Mr. James Carter. The shops had a combined frontage of over two hundred feet, and were demolished in this first phase of the erection of 'Castle Buildings'. Architects Blackwood and Jury drew up elaborate plans for an extremely ornate edifice. The *Irish Builder and Engineer* magazine referred to it as 'a nouveau siècle spirit'. It formed a new and striking feature in the architecture of Belfast. No expense was spared in the construction by McLaughlin and Harvey of this very modern building, which was completed in just over six months.

The building had an elaborate façade of plate glass windows and Carraraware ceramic cladding. Castle Buildings was erected in two phases, the first being the three big arched bays to the west, crowned by a voluted Dutch gable bearing the date '1905'. The other two

8.   Alfred S Moore, *A Merchant Prince*

arched bays to the east, one of them rising to a prominent drum-like attic storey were added in 1907. The two lower storeys of the building were devoted to shop space and showrooms, and apart from the granite pilasters these two storeys consisted almost entirely of glazing. At ground level there was originally a plinth of polished brass, with mullions also of brass and ornamental caps and bases of copper. The entrance doors were of polished mahogany mounted with repoussé copper panels. The grand ornamental stairway of carved balusters were decorated with copper panels at the base and surmounted by wrought copper electric standard lamps. The ceilings were panelled with friezes of Anaglypta in bold relief; the floors were of black and white marble. Having been influenced by his trip to Canada and the department store of T. Eaton and Company in Toronto, Crawford installed a pneumatic tube cash-delivery system, the first of its kind to be installed in Ireland. The innovatory features of the interior of Castle Buildings have long gone but the building still stands in Castle Place, a monument to his good taste and vision.[9]

Crawford had now moved from the relatively busy shopping and commercial thoroughfare of High Street into the bustling hub of Victorian Belfast. This upper part of High Street opening out into Castle Place and extending to the junction of Castle Street, Royal Avenue, Bank Street and Donegal Place, was probably the busiest street in Belfast. This bustling mini metropolis also known as Castle Junction, was the turning point for all trams entering and leaving the city where a fare of two pennies was the maximum regardless of distance. Castle Place in 1905 was now home to other modern and prestigious buildings. Here could be found the Ulster Club, the Provincial Bank, The Ulster Medical Hall and The Bank Buildings, where Crawford did his apprenticeship. Also in Castle Place on the site of the old castle gatehouse, was Leahy Kelly and Leahy's tobacco warehouse, described in *Industries of the North* as 'the largest and

---

9.   The estimated loan from the Ulster Bank in 1903 for building the property was £5,000. The current shops at this time occupying Castle Buildings are Mothercare and The Early Learning Centre.

handsomest establishment of its kind in the world ... of an exceedingly rich, artistic and costly character'. Across the road at No. 1-15 Castle Place was Crawford's competitor John Robb and Company, established in 1861 and one of the largest retailing shops in the area.

Although Robb's was a well established and dependable family store it was nonetheless 'old fashioned' compared to the new emporium of C. McCullagh & Co., Silk Mercers and Milliners. When Crawford himself opened the doors to his palatial emporium on Friday 6 May 1905 his customers found themselves in a most modern and fashionable 'Art Nouveau' establishment. No expense was spared in purchasing the latest styles from the continental and London markets. Crawford had travelled to London, Paris and Toronto for inspiration, and for the opening day he had arranged one of the most dramatic and attractive displays ever seen in Belfast. Whilst the ground floor displayed novelties, ladies and gentlemen's accessories, children's clothing and general drapery, the second floor showroom was magnificently equipped with 'art deco' mirrors affording light to fall at strategic levels to show off to their finest advantage the latest styles in dainty gowns, Paris millinery, ostrich stoles, silks and furs. His aim was not only to maintain a shop of distinction as a centre for ladies' requirements of all kinds, but to ensure that he would be regarded as a leader of Belfast's fashion.

The rise in the McCullaghs fortune, mirrored the development of Belfast city centre. In 1896 the old White Linen Hall was demolished to make way for the new City Hall. Funded in part from the profits of the municipal gas industry, the City Hall took eight years to build and eventually cost over £360,000 to complete. In today's terms, using the index of average earnings, that is equivalent to £128 million. Moreover, in the spring of 1907 the architect, Alfred Brumwell Thomas (1868-1948), issued a writ for almost £14,000 for the balance of his fees. The builders H. & J. Martin also threatened to sue the Corporation for an outstanding balance of £67,000 but before litigation (and after a private conversation with the Lord Mayor) the company agreed to settle for £33,000).[10] Constructed from Portland stone, the interior was lavishly and expensively decorated with fine Italian marble and the dramatic façade was topped by a dome 173 feet high. Opposite the City Hall on the corner of Donegall Place stood one of the most impressive and fashionable department stores in Belfast. Robinson and Cleaver's Linen Warehouse was a six storey building built with white Scrabo sandstone complete with balustraded parapet featuring fifty sculpted heads of the firms' patrons. They supplied Queen Victoria with linens for the Royal Households, and in 1902 were awarded a Royal Warrant.

Donegall Square was undergoing extensive redevelopment with the newly erected Scottish Provident Institution, the Northern Bank, the Ocean Buildings and the Scottish Temperance Buildings. The interminable noise and pollution that was caused by this enormous project of rebuilding and redevelopment did little to dim the pride and confidence that the citizens felt for Belfast. For historian Cornelius O'Leary, the ambition of Belfast City Hall articulated a desire to compete and outdo the great English cities, rivalling 'any British civic temple' in scale and magnificence. The city was now thriving and famous for its shipyards, rope-works, foundries and linen mills. These were a true reflection of Belfast's industrial and commercial wealth and helped businessmen like Crawford have confidence in the city's future. It was this that influenced Crawford's decision to enter Belfast City Council. He had moreover, at the age of thirty-six, a further incentive to civic interest in Belfast. In 1906, only twenty-four years after he had entered the city as a mere boy, he was ranked as the largest individual ratepayer. The rateable value then of 12-18 Castle Place, was £1,400. With the rates fixed at 7s 1d in the pound, his personal contribution to municipal rates was almost £500 annually from that property alone.[11]

10. Gillian McIntosh, *Belfast City Hall, One Hundred Years*, p.17

11. Alfred S Moore, *A Merchant Prince*

When Crawford was elected to Belfast City Council in 1905, the city's municipal government was run from Belfast's modest Town Hall in Victoria Street. His business acumen and enterprise had earned him a considerable reputation among the successful business-men of Edwardian Belfast so that when Cromac Ward councillor-ship became vacant he was urged by his Unionist associates to put his name forward. He was so substantially supported that no other candidate stood against him and he was therefore duly elected city councillor.

One of the organisations that Crawford joined when he began his career in Belfast Corporation was the Belfast Citizen's Association formed in 1905 and who had as their objective, 'Promotion of effi-ciency, economy and reform in municipal administration'. A specific aim in relation to reform was to:-

> 'Inquire into such abuses as may exist to the detriment and of loss of the citi-zens, to further every prudent scheme for the betterment of the city, including the removal of slum areas, the better housing of the poor, and the extension of the City on a systematic street plan with adequate open spaces, as opposed to jerry-buildings in contravention of the bye-laws, and by an enlightened and humane policy to secure the best results as to health and comfort for every citizen.

The Association which had its offices at 9 Ocean Buildings, was managed by a Central Committee of 50 individuals together with a President, 25 vice-presidents, Honorary Secretaries and Honorary Treasurer.[12]

With the same firm resolution and energy that he had exercised in his business career, he entered into this new adventure with typi-cal drive and enthusiasm. His readiness to take action at any crisis never left him and in 1906 he was unanimously appointed a mem-ber of three of the most important committees entrusted with mu-nicipal administration, Improvement, Finance and Law. He was still only thirty eight years old, and at half an inch over six feet tall and weighing fifteen stone, he presented a striking figure. He had never

---

12. Dr. Roger Blaney, *Belfast: 100 years of Public Health*, p.63

spoken publicly in his life and although devoid of the experience of practiced orators, he impressed his audience with his vigour and directness. Avoiding irrelevant and petty side issues he hammered home his points with force and sincerity. The absence of practised flourishes were more than compensated for by his ability to appear both natural and unaffected. He recounts in his memoirs his first day at a city council meeting when he was to address the committee. The Lord Mayor, Sir Daniel Dixon took him to one side and gave him some advice:

> "Don't be like some members, trying to talk on every occasion. When you have something to say I will give you an opportunity to speak, but always remember that your real strength will lie in what you don't say. My advice to you is, never speak unless you are aware of all your facts and their implications. Therefore when you have anything important to say it will be listened to and in time you will become a power in the Corporation."[13]

Crawford accepted the Lord Mayor's recommendations and that advice was an unchangeable principle throughout his career.

During its history, Belfast's municipal council held meetings in various venues. The first council meeting held was in the Old Market House, which stood until 1810 at the corner of Corn Market and High Street, its upper storey serving as the combined Town Hall and Courthouse. In 1820, when the Commercial Buildings, (now the 'Northern Whig' building) was erected, some rooms were rented there, and then during the subsequent thirteen years the Police Chambers served as the third Town Hall.

Belfast's municipal control, prior to the 1841 Municipal Reform Act, was concerned only with civil disturbances and cleaning and lighting the streets. With regard to cleanliness, frequent complaint was made regarding butchers in Hercules Street and other parts of the city where they allowed the blood and offal of their slaughter houses to run into channels and ditches. Although Belfast had built its first public abattoir in 1869, butchers still continued to throw their rub-

---

13. Crawford McCullagh, *An Account of my early Life*

bish into the streets until the city council enacted that all offal and garbage must daily, under a twenty shilling fine, be taken out into the tide at least twenty yards beyond the 'full sea marks.'[14]

In 1831-32, the progress of the town was outpacing both its Town Hall and its local Government. The council could now afford to have a specialised Municipal Building instead of renting rooms. Plans were drawn up for a new Town Hall to be erected on the then vacant site at the corner of Fountain Street and College Street. These plans never came to fruition and instead a site was selected in Poultry Square, now Victoria Square. This was not a new building but an old bacon curing store to be refurbished at a cost of over sixteen hundred pounds. Not much bigger than a large house it had to accommodate not only the Council Chamber, but the offices of the Mayor, Borough Accountant, Sub-Treasurer, Town Surveyor, Rates Collectors, and Inspector of Provisions, Weights and Measures. Henderson's 1852 Street Directory specified it in candid terms:

> It is a mean and inconvenient structure. But it is in contemplation to erect a new Town Hall in a commanding site, and on a scale of great magnificence. If constructed according to the model of the Corporation Architect, Mr. A. T. Jackson, already completed, it will be by far the most noblest building.[15]

When in 1888, Belfast was raised by Royal Charter of Queen Victoria to the rank of City, this became Belfast's first City Hall. However, within a very short time it was felt that this red brick gothic edifice was not sufficiently grand enough for a city that had just been raised by Royal Charter and so in 1890 the site of the White Linen Hall was purchased in order to build the current City Hall. In 1892 a charter was granted by her Majesty Queen Victoria, conferring upon the Mayor of Belfast, the title of Lord Mayor, and upon the Corporation the name and description of 'The Lord Mayor, Alderman, and citizens of the City of Belfast'. Under the act passed in 1896 for the extension of the boundaries of Belfast, the increased city, which was

14. Alfred S Moore, *A Merchant Prince*

15. Alfred S Moore, *A Merchant Prince*

originally divided into five wards for the purpose of municipal representation, was in 1897 divided in fifteen wards, and the number of members of the corporation was increased from 40 to 60.[16]

As a Unionist and prominent businessman in Belfast Crawford decided to become a member of the Ulster Unionist Council which had formed in 1905 to bring together Unionist MPs and influential businessmen opposed to Home Rule. Comprising two hundred delegates, drawn from all nine Ulster counties the objective of Ulster Unionism was to preserve the union between Britain and Ireland. Its leaders therefore consistently aimed to create a strong, united, disciplined movement in the province whose purpose was to convince the British government that Ireland should not be granted self-government. However, in 1906 the Liberal landslide in Westminster ensured that the Irish Parliamentary Party (Irish Nationalists) did not hold sufficient power or influence so the Home Rule issue was put on hold for the time being.

16. Alfred S Moore, *A Merchant Prince*

Chapter Five
1908-1912

Civic Duty

The years lessons are written on the walls -
No Surrender – Ulster says No.
I see in the sky a Presbyterian Rainbow,
Orange and unforgiving, woven of fire.

Iain Crichton Smith.

Royal Commission on Sewage Disposal

In 1908 Crawford was appointed Chairman of the Improvement Committee. There were still many deprived areas of Belfast where living conditions were so appalling that many infectious diseases flourished as a result of bad sanitation and chronic overcrowding.[1] Dr. L. W. Darra Mair writing in 1908 had the following to say about typhoid in Belfast,

> It thus appears that the mortality from this disease in Belfast has been not only great, but excessively great, and that over a series of years, no other town of the United Kingdom equals or even approaches it in this respect". Typhoid fever is almost always acquired by ingestion of solid or liquid water contaminated with excreta from a patient with typhoid or from a carrier.[2]

---

1. Infectious diseases such as smallpox, scarlet fever, measles, whooping cough, typhus, diphtheria and typhoid fever were termed zymotic diseases and were responsible for nearly 1,000 deaths in Belfast every year in the 1880's.

2. Dr. Roger Blaney, *Belfast: 100 years of Public Health*, p.27

Overall housing conditions in a city are closely associated with public health. Healthy houses have satisfactory water supplies, they have adequate toilet facilities, have adequate provision of heating and lighting. The fabric of the house should be in good repair and there should be no dampness.

When some or all of these elements are missing there is a greater likelihood for the inhabitants to develop tuberculosis, respiratory diseases including pneumonia, many forms of infectious disease, high infant mortality, accidents and psychiatric or social symptoms such as delinquency or depression.

The aim of the Improvement Committee was to demolish those houses that were unfit for human habitation thus reducing the risk of death and disease. Crawford's obligation to slum clearance and the re-housing of tenants in these areas was critically important to him. While he was Chairman of the Improvement Committee, the Corporation introduced an Improvement Order in which seven hundred slum dwellings in the Millfield Area were demolished and were replaced with new houses. These dwellings were not only over-crowded with people but in many cases contained livestock as well. The most serious problem at that time concerned the removal of waste matter. Thousands of working class houses had their privy and ash-pit combined in a small back yard, with no access to the yard except through the house. This involved all the accumulated filth and refuse being carried through the living area to the street where it was then collected by the Corporation Scavengers. In these appalling conditions, tuberculosis, pneumonia and typhoid flourished with very high mother and infant mortality. The Corporation houses that replaced these slums now had access at the back of the house, a yard at least ten feet square and a separate privy (dry closet). Streets shutters were erected on downstairs windows in order to ensure heat and privacy, and foot scrapers were inserted in the wall at the side of the front door to enable residents to clean their boots of street dirt before entering the house.[3] At the same time, the Corporation provided every house with free gas fittings in the form of one light bracket, one gas ring and a meter. Other issues that the Improvement Committee

3.   Dr. Roger Blaney, *Belfast: 100 years of Public Health*, p.17

was concerned with were the construction of street lights, the need to replace cobble stones with paving, the widening of existing streets and the need to construct new ones where demand for housing was greatest. Although the Corporation made housing inspections and reports were carried out to determine which areas were most in need of demolition and repair, it did not make special provision for their replacement. The building of new homes was still left mainly to private enterprises such as Sir Robert John McConnell. The typical new dwellings for working men in this Edwardian period were either kitchen and parlour houses, with the area that people chose to live in being dependent on their earnings and their religion. McConnell was responsible for building a large number of houses behind Queens University. These streets were given the names Damascus, Cairo, Jerusalem and Palestine, hence the area became known as the Holy Land.

In modern Belfast the disposal of body waste is so efficient that it is rarely given a second thought but the water closet, which had been invented by Joseph Bramah in 1778, was initially very slow to catch on. A century after its invention Belfast had only a very few houses equipped with the device, and these usually the houses of the wealthy. The methods of sewage disposal were considerably varied. Effluent which reached the sewerage system was discharged into the River Lagan, which then was in a very foul condition as were the Blackstaff, the Forth River and the Connswater. Some houses had built private sewer pipes and some of these flowed into cess pools or into blind drains, creating a nuisance when they began to over-flow. The Bog Meadows were frequently flooded with sewage and the Blackstaff was a chronic nuisance.[4]

In 1900 a new sewerage system built under the Belfast Main Drainage Act of 1887 had been put into operation. The intention of the de-signers of this new system was that the sewage should be released beyond the West Bank into Belfast Lough through a wooden 'shoot'.

4.   Dr. Roger Blaney, *Belfast: 100 years of Public Health*, p.21

This proved to be defective and liable to breakdowns which led to serious contamination of the nearby shorelines giving rise to offensive smells at low tide. It also gravely prejudiced the wholesomeness of the shellfish which were still gathered from the banks. In 1902 the system proved particularly inadequate when heavy rain and high tides flooded Donegall Place with a mixture of rain, sea water and sewage. In Glengall Place and Grosvenor Road, ground floor premises had to be vacated and workers ferried out of the area in shallow boats.

In 1906 the Improvement Committee of Belfast Corporation had undertaken to purify the city's outflow of sewage to the satisfaction of the Local Government Board at Dublin Castle. However, an official complaint was lodged by Captain Harrison, a landlord from Tillysburn, near Holywood, concerning the offensive smells emanating from the foreshore during the summer months. He alleged that the sewage was the cause of the smells and took action to restrain the Corporation from depositing crude sewage into the Lough. As a result of these complaints, the Citizen's Association succeeded in getting the Local Government Board at Dublin Castle to appoint a Vice-Regal Commission to enquire into the proper method of sewage purification. When the experts arrived they asked for facilities to investigate the problem and were taken to the Outfall Works, where seventy-two acres had been acquired to install purification sprinklers. The Health Commissioners discovered that the problem was an innocuous weed called *Ulva Lattissimma*, or *Ulva Lat* as it became known. The weed grew most profusely on the County Down side of Belfast Lough particularly around the Holywood, Tillysburn area and it gave off a foul odour, particularly when the sun shone. In order to observe the growth of the Ulva Lat, the Commissioners separated the weed into containers, putting some in with crude sewage, some into the water from the Lough, and some into the purified sewage. In gathering the weed from the foreshore it was discovered that it did not grow well in the crude sewage, but grew most profusely in the purified sewage. The commissioners discovered that by placing a mussel into the container the Ulva Lat attached itself to the mussel and the weed grew very quickly. It was then discovered that the weed had no roots and could not attach itself to the rocks or to the seashore, but it had anchored itself to the mussels which covered the foreshore at Holywood.

After consultation with the County Borough Surveyor, and the Health Commissioners, Crawford and members of the Improvement Committee met at Tillysburn foreshore at ebb tide to see the Ulva Lat in its natural habitation. The mussels were then forcibly removed from their substratum of black slimy mud. Consequently on a return visit to the site a few days later they discovered that not only was the white sand clean, but the removal of the mussel had eliminated the Ulva Latissimma! During the investigations into the matter, Crawford travelled to London to interview the greatest expert on the subject at that time, Professor Dibdin. He was shown many experiments in dealing with the problem in the Thames, and the Professor took him to see a system that had been adopted known as the 'Dibdin Beds'. These were composed of large tanks with a series of slate beds, the sewage was allowed to percolate through the slates to the outlet. After examining it he could clearly see the sewage going into the tanks and eventually the effluent coming out. Professor Dibdin took a large mug and filled it with the effluent and invited Crawford to drink it. When he smilingly declined, the Professor, without a qualm raised the mug to his lips and drained the lot!

In 1911 a Royal Commission on Sewage Disposal recommended that the wooden 'shoot' which had taken from 1883-1893 to complete, should be replaced by a culvert capable of delivering the effluent from the tanks during the first three and a half hours of ebb tide. In 1913 the construction of the concrete culvert was commenced. The construction of a pumping station along with other culverts also helped to prevent the flooding to which Belfast had always been susceptible.

Although Crawford was first and foremost a businessman, his interests were varied and widespread. His business relationship and friendship with the McConnell family was forged when Crawford bought into the housing market in Belfast and from as early as 1900 with help from the McConnells he acquired a considerable property portfolio from which he attained rent. One venture that he very wisely did not invest in at the time, as he was in the process of building his department store in Castle Place, was R. J. McConnell's Garden Colony.

Cliftonville Circus Garden Colony

The development of middle-class suburbs was greatly assisted by the extension and electrification of the tramways. McConnell was a member of the Corporation's Tramways and Electricity Committee and it was no doubt due to him that the longest one-penny stage in Belfast in 1908 stopped at the entrance to Cliftonville Circus. In 1905 an attempt was made to found a Garden Colony in Belfast by Robert McConnell, Lord Mayor in 1900, Estate Agent and Land Developer, with his head office at 37 Royal Avenue, Belfast. It was claimed by Jonathon Bardon in his book *A History of Ulster* that McConnell's firm was probably the largest of its kind in Ireland. It was responsible for the erection of large numbers of houses throughout the city for every class of person. By far the biggest builders, contractors and brick makers in Belfast, and almost certainly Ireland, were H. and J. Martin, from their 'Ulster' building yard on the Ormeau Road they controlled 300 acres of building land and brickfields dotted all over the city.[5] Herbert Martin married Margaret (Meg), the twin daughter of R. J. McConnell. Their son Ian, born in 1902 would eventually take over the business from his father. McConnell was noted for being a garden city enthusiast and was influenced by Victorian social visionary Ebenezer Howard, whose book *Garden Cities of Tomorrow* achieved international acclaim and was the inspiration for new towns in many countries, not least in the U.K.

Horrified by the squalor of Victorian city slums, Howard envisaged a utopia where people would live in cities in perfect harmony with

5.   Jonathon Bardon, *Belfast: An Illustrated History,* p.140

nature. McConnell's plans were ambitious. He realised that cities were ideal for social opportunity, amusement and higher wages. But he also could see no reason why those advantages shouldn't be combined with the joys of the country; the beauty of nature, fresh air and an abundance of water, woods and meadows. His plan was to construct new housing at Cliftonville similar to that of Welwyn and Letchworth in Hertfordshire.

In 1906, the Company promoted a competition to be judged by the editor of the Building News, Maurice Bingham Adams, in which the entrants were to build 'convenient and homely artistic homes' on 33 plots on the site rather than simply entering designs. The site at Cliftonville Circus in North Belfast was within a penny tram fare of the city centre, in open country looking up towards Cave Hill, Belfast Castle and downwards towards the Lough. The landscape proposed by W. J. Walshe of Bangor, Co. Down provided for three open gardens; tree-lined roadways; a central pleasure garden with a tea house, flag staff and bandstand with no two houses in the colony to be exactly the same. The streets were to be called Aster, Begonia, Daffodil, Hollyhock and Fern Gardens; and Sir Robert undertook to plant 100,000 shrubs, flowers and fruit trees. The houses were to be sold at cost price – the cheapest costing £240 – and the advertisement promised:

> 'You will see some of the prettiest villas that have been erected since Noah left the Ark …The beautiful panorama unfolded cannot be duplicated … tennis lawn for the girls, cricket pitch for the boys, playgrounds for the children'.

While, unfortunately, the venture did not survive in its entirety, it is an indication of the ambition of some of Belfast's entrepreneurs that a number of survivors of the original scheme may still be seen in the leafy streets between Westland Row and Knutsford Drive.[6]

On 16 February 1911 Joseph McConnell, R. J. McConnell's eldest son, presented a paper to the Auctioneers' Institute of the United Kingdom, in London, on 'Garden Suburbs', in which he discussed

---

6.   C.E.B Brett, *Buildings of Belfast 1700-1914*, p.61

legal, financial, landscaping and practical aspects. He argued strongly for home ownership and that garden suburbs would provide "the greatest benefit to the greatest number".

Joseph McConnell or Jo-Jo as he was known to his family and friends was the eldest son of Sir Robert McConnell and probably one of Crawford's closest friends. They both enjoyed fine dining and would meet regularly in the Carlton Restaurant in Donegall Place and when in London would very often dine together at the Carlton Club in Mayfair, an indulgence which contributed to both men being over-weight. Crawford described him as mild mannered, courteous, generous and very much liked and admired by both family and friends. Jo-Jo had a 'head for figures', was hard working and credited by the family for getting the estate agency business and developmental activities back into credit after near bankruptcy.

When Crawford entered Belfast City Council in 1905 becoming Councillor for Cromac Ward, his colleague Tom McConnell, was elected to Windsor Ward. The two men worked together both in business and in Belfast Corporation and during Crawford's mayoralty no reception or dinner would have been complete without at least one member of the McConnell family being present. Whilst Crawford and Tom McConnell's relationship centred around work within City Hall and the Housing Committee, the bond that linked Crawford with Jo-Jo was their love of cinema, their penchant for fine dining and shared property enterprises. Their joint investments in Belfast city centre included College Square East, Wellington Place, Howard Street and the Classic Cinema in Fountain Street. Crawford utilised the services of the McConnells over many years, building up an impressive personal portfolio consisting of properties in Glengormley, Cherryvalley, Orangefield, Lisburn Road, University Street and the Belmont, Castlereagh and the Willowfield areas. He also owned commercial property in Belfast which included Bedford Street and Clarence Street. His main business, Castle Buildings, was based in property he owned in Castle Place, Castle Lane and Castle Arcade.

In 1927 R.J. McConnell died and Jo-Jo inherited the title. In 1929 he was asked to represent Co. Antrim in the House of Commons at Westminster by George Reid, Chairman of the Antrim Unionist Association and as its longest-serving member was 'Father of the House' when he died. Jo-Jo's election to Parliament further reduced his activities in Northern Ireland where he was a prolific horseman, riding to hounds each winter. It is probably the case that the physical inactivity of parliamentary life, living in London and eating too well hastened the decline of his health and led to his death. He eventually died of stomach cancer in 1942.

The Launching Of The Titanic

By 1911, Harland and Wolff had earned its reputation, not only for building the biggest ships in the world but also for their very high standard of work. The Chairman, William James Pirrie served on Belfast Corporation and was Lord Mayor in 1896-1897. A small man with a dynamic and controlling personality, yet full of energy, he was the driving force behind Harland and Wolff and instrumental in securing orders for ships from companies around the world. Modern steel-making revolutionised shipbuilding, and Pirrie was at the forefront of development in marine engineering and naval architecture. Their most valued customer was The White Star Line who had always had their ships built by Harland and Wolff in Belfast. In 1899 the company launched *The Oceanic*, the biggest and longest ship in the world. The *Freeman's Journal* described the occasion as 'the greatest event of its kind the world has ever witnessed, and in a certain sense, perhaps the most epoch-making incident of the century'[7]

The construction of their most famous ship *Titanic* and her sister ship *Olympic* took over two years. The massive gantry that dominated the city's skyline with its mobile cranes built to lift the hydraulic riveting machines (there was a total of three million rivets fitted on the whole ship) towered 100ft over Belfast. A contemporary account

---

7.   Jonathon Bardon, *A History of Ulster*, p.394

tells of "pavements of oak and great cradles of timber and iron and sliding ways of pitch pine, with 20 tons of tallow spread on them and hydraulic rams and triggers built and fixed against the bulk of the *Titanic* so that when the moment came the waters she was to conquer should thrust her finally from the earth". The cacophonous clamour and racket of hammers, chains and bolts being fitted to the ship would have reverberated around the city from early morning until the shrill whistle at 6pm called an abrupt end to the day's work, rendering the vast shipyard eerily quiet.

As High Sheriff of Belfast, [see appendix 2] Crawford McCullagh and his wife Margaret received an invitation to the launch of the White Star Royal Mail Triple-Screw Steamer *Titanic* at Belfast on Wednesday 31 May 1911 at 12.15pm. When they arrived the great shipyard of Harland and Wolff was buzzing with activity as the dignitaries and press took their seats in the three stands erected specially in the yard close to the Titanic to watch the launch. Among the guests was investor, J. Pierpont Morgan, effectively the owner of the Titanic. He had acquired White Star Line in 1902, and had travelled from the United States for the occasion. For the public, Belfast Harbour Commissioners had fenced off a section of Albert Quay with a good view of the proceedings, charging a few pence for entry, with all proceedings going to the city's hospitals.

At 11am, special trams ran down Corporation Street towards the waterfront. There was an expectant audience of 150,000 – a third of Belfast's population gathered for the occasion. As the launch time approached, the stands were filled to capacity and the banks of the River Lagan lined with spectators. At noon, the chairman, Lord Pirrie, led his invited guests to an observation platform, giving a splendid view of slip No 3, where the hull of the *Titanic* shone with a fresh coat of black paint. Along the top of the gantry, flew three flags – the Stars and Stripes, the Union Jack and, in the middle, the big red company pennant with its five pointed white star. Below them flew a row of signal flags spelling out 'Good Luck'. To facilitate the ship's passage into the water, the slipway had been covered in twenty-two tons of soap, grease and train oil, spread an inch thick.

With everyone comfortably installed, Lord Pirrie, sporting a yachting cap for the occasion, inspected the launching gear. At 12.05pm, a red signal flag was hoisted on the sternpost of the Titanic to warn tugboats and other small craft to keep clear. At 12.10pm, a red rocket was fired – the five-minute signal, and at 12.14pm, a second rocket was fired and there was a hush of anticipation as Lord Pirrie conveyed his instructions to the launch foreman.

As the last of the timber supports were knocked away, the ship stood motionless for a time before a mighty cheer erupted, followed by a cry of 'There she goes!' The soap and tallow did their job and the ill-fated Titanic slid slowly into the water at 12.15pm. As the McCullaghs left the quayside for the celebratory lunch, little did they know that the maiden voyage of this supposedly 'unsinkable ship' would end in tragedy.

The *Titanic* sank on 15 April 1912 with the loss of approximately 1,500 lives. The US Senate (involved due to the number of US citizens on board the ship) estimated that 1,517 people had died. The British Board of Trade, who had the responsibility for the inquiry, estimated that 1,503 lives were lost. Both of these figures were revised to 1,500 and 1,490 respectively. There have been so many other official and unofficial revisions that the exact number of souls lost will probably never be known.

An ironic twist of fate in this story of the *Titanic* sinking was that its sister ship the *Olympic* was making a return voyage from New York to Liverpool and passed the scene where the *Titanic* had sunk. It sent the following grim message:

Carpathian reached Titanic position at daybreak. Found boats and wreckage only. Titanic sank about 2.20 a.m., in 41.16N; 50.14W. all her boats accounted for, containing about 675 souls saved, crew and passengers included. Nearly all saved women and children. Leyland liner California remained and searching exact location of disaster. Loss likely 1800 souls.8

The tragedy of the 'unsinkable ship' dealt a terrible blow for Belfast and the many individuals who were connected to the poor souls who perished on that fateful night. In villages and towns all over Ireland people spoke in shocked tones, women dressed in black and most men wore black arm-bands. In Belfast department stores draped big swathes of black crepe in their windows. Memorial services were held in churches and schools were closed in mourning. The McCullaghs attended a memorial service in the Presbyterian Church in Helen's Bay and Crawford wrote a moving account in his memoirs of men and women shedding tears and not feeling ashamed to be seen crying in public.

Crawford McCullagh and Thomas Andrews had crossed paths on many occasions and when Thomas went down with the *Titanic* on her maiden voyage those that knew this quietly-spoken and well-liked Ulsterman were deeply saddened. Andrews was born in 'Ardara', Comber, Co. Down. He was the son of the Rt. Hon. John Andrews, chairman of the board of the family's linen mill. He attended the Royal Belfast Academical Institution until 1889, when at the age of sixteen, he began a premium apprenticeship at Harland and Wolff where his uncle Lord Pirrie was part-owner. His apprenticeship began with three months in the joiners' shop, followed by a month in the cabinetmakers' and then a further two months working on the ships. The last years of his five-year apprenticeship were spent in the drawing office. In 1901, after working his way up through the many departments of the company he became manager of the Institute of Naval Architects. In 1907, Thomas was appointed managing director and head of the draughting department at Harland and Wolff. On 24 June 1908 he married Miss Helen Reilly Barbour, daughter of John D. Barbour of Conway, Dunmurry. They made their home in

8.   Raymond O'Reagan, *Hidden Belfast*, p.238

Windsor Avenue, South Belfast and on 27 November 1910 they had a daughter, Elizabeth Law Barbour Andrews.

In 1909, Thomas began to oversee plans for the super liner RMS *Titanic* for the White Star Line. He familiarised himself with every detail of the *Titanic* and was in continuous attendance on the ship from her keel days until 11.40 pm on 14 April when the ship collided with an iceberg on its starboard side. His body was never recovered from the Atlantic. In his home town of Comber, Co. Down the life of Thomas Andrews is commemorated by a Memorial Hall built by public subscription and opened in 1915. He is remembered in the family grave as

> *'pure, just, generous, affectionate and heroic.*
> *He gave his life that others might be saved'.*

Home Rule

The dark eleventh hour
Draws on and sees us sold
To every evil power
We fought against of old.
Rebellion, rapine, hate,
Oppression, wrong and greed
Are loosed to rule our fate,
By England's act and deed.

Ulster 1912 - Rudyard Kipling

A Family Affair

Since the death of his brother Samuel, Crawford had kept in touch with his sister-in-law Catherine. On 12 February 1903, Catherine (Kate) married James Donaghy of the firm Moffat and Donaghy, drapers from Limavady, County Antrim. Although ten years older than Kate. James was charming, charismatic and a successful businessman with considerable assets and a thriving family concern in Limavady. In 1905 Crawford wrote to Kate suggesting that her son Ernest, who was now fourteen, should come to Belfast and serve his apprenticeship in his new Department Store. Ernest had visited his aunt and uncle in Helen's Bay on many occasions and felt very much part of the family.

The following year Ernest arrived in Belfast and started his apprenticeship in much the same way as Crawford had started his own career. Ernest quickly settled into his new life with his aunt and uncle and his young cousins, Helen and Daisy. He was a charming boy, with good manners and an enthusiastic attitude towards reading and study. Every morning at 8.15am, Crawford and his nephew would walk to the square in Helen's Bay and board the train for Belfast. The journey passed quickly as the carriage trundled through the Co. Down countryside, stopping at Holywood to pick up passengers. They were very much at ease in each others company and Crawford enjoyed discussing the day-to-day running of Castle Buildings and his responsibilities which also included representing the residents of Cromac Ward, assisting them in getting jobs and better housing. His role involved providing services for old age pensioners and the handicapped. In his commitment to the civic community he was giving his time and money to serve and work for the city as a whole, and in so doing bring him into personal contact with his constituents.

In 1907, Maggie gave birth to a boy whom they christened Joseph Crawford after his uncle the Rev. Joseph Crawford. The family always called him 'Boysie' and referred to him by that name for the rest of his life. As it happened, Ernest McCullagh celebrated his fifteenth birthday on the same day as his cousin Boysie was born and it was at this time that he told his aunt and uncle that he wished to become a Presbyterian Minister. Ernest had already discussed it with his mother and step-father who apparently did not oppose the idea and it would appear that he had been influenced by the Reverend John Edmund Hamilton who had replaced the Rev. Archer in Helen's Bay Presbyterian Church. John Hamilton was a kindly scholarly man with a great love of history and travel. He had a youthful and energetic approach to his sermons that appealed to the young people of the congregation, and his popularity increased when he started a Boy Scout movement and initiated a summer camp in Helen's Bay. He took a special interest in Ernest who attended bible classes held by one of Mr. Hamilton's sisters and he was sympathetic to the spiritual and emotional calling that had taken hold of young Ernest who now had his mind firmly set on entering the ministry.

In the limited account of Sir Crawford's life story that was written by Ernest in later years it was apparent that his Uncle wasn't entirely happy with Ernest's sudden inclination towards the church, in all probability because Crawford wanted his nephew to follow him into the drapery business. At any rate, at that time Crawford was spending more and more time involved in matters at City Council and less time at Castle Buildings in Donegall Place.

In 1911, Crawford had been elected High Sheriff of Belfast and to accommodate his extended family moved into a larger house in Helen's Bay called Rust Hall. It was and still is a beautiful white stucco detached villa set in spacious grounds with mature trees and manicured lawns. When Crawford bought the house it had thirteen rooms. As was usual in those days there would have been a collection of sculleries, pantries and store rooms, the second floor had four spacious bedrooms and on the third floor bedrooms for any live-in staff. The census reveals they had a 29 year old cook called Ellen Jane Armstrong and a 20 year old nanny called Lizzie Patterson. The house was located in Dufferin Avenue, later renamed Bridge Road and just a short stroll away from the railway station, St. John's Presbyterian Church, the square which was effectively the centre of Helen's Bay, Thompson's Hotel, the Post Office and a few shops. Every morning Maggie would accompany her husband to the station where they would catch the 8.15 am train into Belfast. From Queen's Quay it was then only a ten minute walk to High Street.

Although relations between Crawford and his father had been strained for many years, the bond that existed with his mother and sisters remained very strong. When his father died without leaving a will he supported his mother financially until her death in 1914 and when his sisters visited Belfast he let them purchase outfits without any cost to themselves. Although Crawford was known for his business acumen, he made an investment for his sister Jennie that failed and at the age of 40 she found herself virtually penniless.

In June 1885, at the age of twenty-one Eliza Jane or Jennie, as she was known, married a farmer called James Lyttle. He owned a substantial farm and cotter's house called 'Little Acres' in Clare, County Down. At fifty-four years old and a widower, he was considerably older than Jennie, he was also a close friend of her father, Robert McCullagh. In 1887 Jennie had the first of her children James Alexander who died in infancy, she then had her second son James Andrew in 1889. Her third son Johnny was born in 1892 but tragically died when he was only 4 years old. She went on to have two more sons Howard Francis born in 1894 then Albert Samuel in 1896. She also had two daughters, Florence Jemima known as Florrie Pat who was born in November 1890 then Rachel Violet in 1895. In October 1901 Jennie's husband died. Shortly afterwards Jennie sold the farm in County Down and moved to No. 5 Antrim Road in Belfast with her children. In 1904 at the age of 40 she married 36 year old Thomas Brown, the only son of James Brown a successful grocer specializing in imported foods. They moved to 334 Woodstock Road in East Belfast. However their marriage was short-lived as Thomas tragically died of bronchitis two months before their son Tommy was born. Thomas left Jennie £913 in his will, a considerable amount of money in those days. Having little knowledge of how to handle her inheritance, she approached her brother for advice on what she should do with her savings. Crawford invested her money in a trading company which provided her with a steady income. At the same time Albert, Howard and Florrie Pat went to work for their uncle Crawford in his Castle Buildings department store while James Andrew was apprenticed to a Lisburn grocer called John Gibson. Unfortunately in 1910 the trading company that held Jenny's investment went into liquidation and she suddenly found herself financially insecure with her only income now coming from her children's wages. For a man like Crawford losing his shares would have been viewed as a financial setback whereas for Jennie losing her precious savings was a nightmare. After lengthy discussions with her brother it was decided that the family would make a new life for themselves in Canada.

On Friday 12 May 1911 Crawford paid $50 for Florrie Pat and James Andrew to sail second-class to Toronto via Liverpool. Before the ship left he took them into Castle Buildings and gave them outfits for their new life. Although they had employment references from Crawford, on arriving in Toronto James and Florence actually knew no one other than their milkman's brother. They were given directions to his house on Wellesley Street and the family put them up for the night. The next day, they approached Mr. Allen, a Director of T. Eatons department store in Toronto with a letter of recommendation from Crawford who was an old friend of Mr. Allen's and they were given jobs straightaway.

The following year on 12 May 1912 Crawford bought passages for Jennie and the rest of her children on the Canadian Pacific travelling 'Saloon Class'. Before their departure to Canada, Crawford brought them into the shop in Castle Place and asked them to choose outfits suitable for their new life in Toronto, he also gave Jennie enough money to put a down payment on a house which she subsequently managed as a successful bed and breakfast. Jennie's eldest boy James Andrew worked at Eaton's Store and started university courses by correspondence and in 1920 was ordained in Hanbury, Ontario as a Presbyterian Minister. In 1926 he married Marguerite Brown, grand-daughter of Sir George William Ross, former Prime Minister of Ontario Province and Senator in the Canadian Parliament, and daughter of Cameron Brown, former editor of the Toronto Globe Newspaper. Florrie Pat who had received extensive training at Crawford's Castle Street Department Store eventually qualified as a buyer for Eaton's. When Pat married she and her husband set up their own business as buyers for North American firms, retaining Department stores including Bergdorf Goodman, Neeman Marcus and Sachs Fifth Avenue. Albert Samuel was a talented pianist but had a nervous disposition and always lived with his mother. Howard Francis married and had two sons, Crawford and Ronald. They settled in Clarksburg, Ontario. Rachel Violet married Robert Donald who worked in advertising and lived in Toronto raising three daughters, Jackie, Betty and Patsy. Thomas Brown, only son of James and Jennie Brown, changed his name to Lyttle, and married Margaret Mitchell.   Throughout his life, Crawford made numerous trips to Canada and the United States and always kept in touch with his sister, her children and his nephew Ernest.

Resistance To Home Rule

As High Sheriff of Belfast and Commissioner of the Peace Crawford was required to monitor and keep an eye on any disturbances in the city. Although the actual maintenance of law and order was in the hands of the Chief of Constabulary, the post of High Sheriff was not without its responsibilities, minor incidents of unrest had already occurred in the city and the tension in the Corporation was palpable. The Unionists under Edward Carson were stepping up their campaign to resist Home Rule and further demonstrations were planned. A series of minor disturbances highlighted the degree of unrest in Ulster.

As a member of the Ulster Unionist Council, he was aware of a special committee that had been set up in 1910 to implement the buying of weapons and the creation of an army in the event of Home Rule. Crawford felt a sense of unease about the measures being taken but he and Margaret believed it to be in the best interests of his fellow countrymen. The men instrumental for eventually bringing the weapons into Ulster were Major Fred Crawford, Secretary of the Ulster Reform Club, Captain James Craig and Captain Wilfred Spender.

When Crawford McCullagh was elected as Councillor for Cromac Ward in 1906, Captain James Craig entered Parliament as a Unionist representing East Down and when the leader of the Orange Order, Colonel Sanderson, died in the same year, James Craig took over the position and became spokesman for the Orange Order. When it became clear that the Prime Minister Herbert Asquith was going to go ahead with a Home Rule Bill, Craig approached Edward Carson and suggested he come to Ulster and prepare the ground for resistance.

Carson, although a liberal in terms of domestic policy, was a Unionist zealot. Robert Kee in his book *The Green Flag*, quotes Carson's two statements of principle - "It is only for Ireland that I am in politics" and "It is only for the sake of the Union that I am in politics". He assumed that Home Rule must be resisted and could only be defeated by what amounted to rebellion.

Although Edward Carson assumed the mantle of Unionist leader, his partner Captain James Craig had the organisational skills with which to mastermind the loyalist resistance. Delegates from the Unionist associations and the Orange Institution met to implement a 'Commission of Five' which was appointed to frame a constitution for a provisional government of Ulster, 'having due regard to the interests of loyalists in other parts of Ireland'. This commission, which was to work in consultation with Carson, consisted of Captain Craig, Colonel Sharman Crawford, Colonel R. H. Wallace, Thomas Sinclair and Edward Sclater.[1]

On 3 October, the Home Secretary Winston Churchill held a meeting in Dundee and told the assembled company that the government would introduce a Home Rule Bill in the next session. Churchill was convinced that Edward Carson was bluffing and that the outcome would result in no more than a few prolonged riots. Churchill was invited to speak at a Home Rule Meeting by the Ulster Liberal Association in the Ulster Hall but when he arrived at Larne on a cold winter morning in February 1912 he was confronted by a hostile crowd chanting the national anthem.

When Gladstone had introduced his first Home Rule Bill in 1886, Winston Churchill's father Lord Randolph came to Belfast and spoke at length to a cheering crowd in the Ulster Hall. In his speech he urged them "to wait and watch, organise and prepare, so that the ca-

---

1.   A.T.Q. Stewart, *Ulster Crisis*, p.48

tastrophe of Home Rule might not come upon them 'as a thief in the night' or find them unready." His son was now to stand in the Ulster Hall, but his sentiments were in stark contrast to those of his father in 1886. Churchill did not appreciate the resentment and aggression that was felt by his presence. The idea of standing in the Ulster Hall to make a speech supporting Home Rule was the ultimate insult.

The Chairman Lord Pirrie, insisted on extra troops and police being brought in in the event of a riot. In the end, the Ulster Liberal Association decided to change the venue and Churchill agreed to speak at the nationalist Celtic Park football ground in a marquee which had to be brought in specially for the occasion from Scotland.

Regardless of the presence of so many troops in and around the city, the streets of Belfast were heaving with people cheering, singing and waving loyalist flags. The only real disturbance was when Churchill and his wife Clementine left the hotel where they had been having lunch. A group of shipyard men closed in upon the car with the intention of turning it over, but they desisted with cries of 'mind the wumman' when they saw that Mrs Churchill was by her husband's side.[2] The crowd then followed the car to the Celtic Park football ground where a slight drizzle in the morning had now turned to heavy rain, flooding the ground and making the tent damp and uncomfortable. When the meeting was over Churchill and his wife were taken back to the station, and made it to Larne without any more trouble.

Parliament opened less than a week later and the Government issued a statement announcing that Home Rule would not be introduced in that session. In Belfast, the Unionists, believing that the Home Rule Bill would be introduced before Easter, organised a huge demonstration at which Bonar Law, the new Conservative leader promised to speak. The rally was held on Easter Tuesday at the Agricultural Society's show grounds at Balmoral, a prosperous Belfast suburb. It was a massive demonstration with one hundred thousand men and women assembled under the largest Union Flag ever made. No

---

2.   Budge and O'Leary, *Belfast: Approach to crisis; a study of Belfast Politics 1613-1970*, p.53

less than seventy trains had been needed to bring in loyalist supporters from the surrounding provinces. The proceedings opened with prayers by the Primate of all Ireland and the Moderator of the Presbyterian Church. Inspired by the sight of so many supporters, Bonar Law stood up and informed the expectant crowd that their cause was not Ulster's alone, but that of the Empire.

On 11 April 1912, the Home Rule Bill was introduced in the House of Commons. A few months later in June an amendment to the Bill was put forward by a Liberal member for St. Austell Cornwall, which planned to exclude the four counties of Antrim, Armagh, Down and Londonderry. The proposal resulted in a meeting of the Unionist members and peers at Londonderry House, Park Lane, London, home of the Marquis of Londonderry to decide what action should be taken. Carson was presented with a dilemma : if they supported it, they would seem to be abandoning the loyalists in other parts of Ireland; on the other hand, if they opposed it, they might well be accused later of turning down the offer of the peaceful exclusion of 'those districts which they could control'. Carson persuaded the conference to support the amendment, and in doing so, he opened the way for the recognition in the autumn of the following year that only six counties with a significantly large Protestant population could make an effective resistance. After three days the amendment was defeated by sixty-nine votes.

Feelings of anxiety and uncertainty were mounting. Unionists under Edward Carson were stepping up their campaign to resist and further demonstrations were planned, however a series of minor disturbances highlighted the degree of unrest in Ulster.

On Saturday 29 June, a Sunday school outing from Whitehouse to Castledawson in County Londonderry was attacked by members of an Ancient Order of Hibernians procession. In the scuffle that followed a number of children were hurt and so terrified by the attack that some were later found hiding in bushes about a mile away from the assault. The following Tuesday there was a clash between

Protestant shipwrights and Catholic workmen in the Belfast ship-yards. These disturbances escalated in and around the 12 July with a number of assaults being reported both inside and outside the ship-yards and on 14 September at a football match between Celtic and Linfield fierce rioting broke out in the stands and the fighting was so severe that a number of spectators were admitted to the Royal Victoria Hospital.

When Crawford attended a meeting the following day with Captain Craig and the Unionist Council, it was agreed that the only person who could bring confidence to the Ulster people and avoid mayhem was Edward Carson. The danger of outright sectarian warfare seemed imminent. Crawford voiced the opinion that only by holding a series of massive displays of loyalist solidarity could British sympathy be won and violence be avoided.

The next step for Craig and Carson was to find some way for the people of Ulster to resist Home Rule.

The Signing Of The Ulster Covenant

On 18 September 1912, Edward Carson arrived back in Ulster from London. The next day he travelled to Craig's home at Strandtown, Belfast and made public the terms of Ulster's Solemn League and Covenant. Thereafter there were meetings in different towns all over the province with the single resolution carried through at each gathering ; 'We will not have Home Rule'. The crusade had its finale in the Ulster Hall in Belfast. A faded yellow silk banner, which according to legend had been carried before William III at the Battle of the Boyne, was handed to Edward Carson by Colonel Wallace. He was also given a silver pen by his friend, and co-conspirator James Craig, with which to sign the Covenant.

On Saturday 28 September 1912, Belfast city was quiet. The ship-yards, the rope works, the linen factories, the foundries were all silent. People from all over Ulster attended services in various churches. The Protestant population of Ulster stood quietly in mounting queues outside Orange Halls, patiently waiting their turn to sign the historic Covenant. In Belfast the sun shone as Edward Carson, James Craig and the rest of the Unionist leaders walked down Bedford Street from the Ulster Hall to the City Hall where they were met by the Lord Mayor McMordie, the High Sheriff Crawford McCullagh and the Councillors and Alderman of the Corporation. As they stood around the circular table draped with the Union Jack another flag was borne into the chamber. This was supposed to have been carried by the Inniskillen regiment at the Battle of the Boyne. The flag was woven of silk with a crimson five-pointed star in the top left hand corner. Surrounded by these patriotic symbols of allegiance to the Crown Edward Carson was the first person to sign Ulster's Solemn League and Covenant. The area around the City Hall and the streets of Belfast was filled with cheering crowds waving flags and banners while waiting their turn to sign the Covenant. When the signing finally ended at 11pm, Crawford recounted in his memoirs the relief when being told by the police that during the event there had been no disturbances and the signing had been completed peacefully. Women were not permitted to sign the covenant by the Ulster Unionist Council and had to negotiate to be allowed to draw up a separate Women's Declaration. The wording on that Declaration was drafted by Thomas Sinclair and approved by the Ulster Women's Unionist Council's advisory committee. Women were told to make separate arrangements to set up signing the Declaration and signatures were collected in various town halls, courthouses, schools and church halls. Some signed in their own homes and in Ballymena there were house to house collections. The signatories to these documents provide one of the best examples not only of the popularity and determination of unionism, but also the comparative strength of women's unionism: a total of 228,999 women signed the Declaration in Ulster compared to 218,206 male signatories to the Covenant.[3] In Dublin, the Declaration was signed by two thousand men, in

---

3. Dr. Diane Urquhart, *In defence of Ulster and the Empire: The Ulster Women's Unionist Council, 1886-1940*

Edinburgh it was signed on the 'Covenanters' Stone'. Signatures were collected in London, Glasgow, Manchester, Liverpool, Bristol and York. When the signatures were checked and counted in the Old Town Hall in Victoria Street, Belfast, they totalled 471,414.[4]

On New Year's Day 1913 Edward Carson moved an amendment to the Home Rule Bill which would have allowed Ulster to remain outside the new jurisdiction. His recommendation of partition was rejected by the Prime Minister Herbert Asquith, arguing that John Redmond and the Irish Nationialists wouldn't accept it at any price. In early January, the Ulster Unionist Council held their annual meeting and decided that volunteers from the Orange Order and Unionist Clubs could be formed into a military organisation calling itself the Ulster Volunteer Force. Radical steps such as this were put forward partly because the protest demonstrations against Irish self-government appeared to be having no impact. In fact, their activities had been dismissed as 'bluff and blackmail' by the Government and Irish Nationalist MPs. By the end of February, 12,000 men were drilling with dummy rifles at 100 centres scattered throughout all nine northern counties, having been given legal sanction by sympathetic magistrates. By the summer of 1913 the Ulster Volunteer Force had recruited Sir George Richardson, a former Indian Army General to be their Commander. His headquarters were in the old Belfast Town Hall and he was joined by Captain Craig who was appointed Political Staff Officer and Major Frederick Crawford, Director of Ordinance of the HQ Staff of the UVF.

In September the Ulster Unionist Council came to a crucial decision. A 'Provisional Government' would have to be formed that would take absolute control of the province in the event of Home Rule. By the end of the year, the UVF had over 90,000 part-time volunteers, its own communication system, an elaborate immobilisation plan, motor-car and motor-cycle system and a nursing corps. Although Major Crawford had set up a secret arms network and had ordered

4.   ATQ Stewart, *Ulster Crisis*

several thousand rifles, six machine guns and a large quantity of ammunition, there were few weapons yet available. In December the British Government completely banned the importation of arms and ammunition into Ireland.

Immediately the UVF held a meeting in London with Edward Carson and other political leaders to discuss ways of illegally importing arms into Ulster. Two days later another meeting was held, this time at the home of Captain James Craig. Sir George Clarke, the chairman of the arms committee of the Ulster Unionist Council was asked if he would be prepared to bring in 20,000 rifles and 2 million rounds of ammunition quickly if there was an emergency. Major Fred Crawford was the only man who could carry through such an operation. He was born in Belfast in 1861 the son of Alexander Crawford, a manufacturing chemist. By 1894 he had joined the Artillery Militia and later served in the Boer War where he was mentioned in Lord Roberts's last dispatch. By 1906 he was secretary of the Reform Club and in 1911 was a member of the Ulster Unionist Council and actively involved in raising the Belfast Volunteers. He became Director of the Ordinance of the Headquarters Staff of the UVF and led the men of West Belfast into the Balmoral grounds at Easter 1912; he was commander of the Praetorian Guard in bowler hats who escorted Carson on Covenant Day, and he signed the Covenant in his own blood.

McCullagh recalls in his memoirs a comment made by a member of the Reform Club in 1914:-

'There are numbers of Irishmen who have done great deeds but none will stand out more prominently in history than the man who made it possible for Ulster to resist, and that man was Fred Crawford'

At this time an incident occurred involving The Ulster Provisional Government and it's attitude to women's suffrage. In September 1913, Edward Carson promised that in Ulster women would be admitted to the vote, and that there would be a woman on each of the committees of the central authority. In March 1914, he was confronted with a suffragette deputation reminding him of his promise. He had to inform them that some Ulster members were divided on the matter, and that he could not allow division in the ranks as long as the Home Rule question was before them. Betrayed by their leader, the women formally declared war on the Ulster movement. A wave of vandalism swept the province. Crawford recalls in his memoirs how he was showered with glass when the suffragettes smashed windows in the Old Town Hall, and a few days later as Carson was waiting for his train he was attacked by two suffragettes who loudly accused him of 'betraying the women of Ulster'.[5] A few days later General Sir Hugh McCalmont's home in Whiteabbey was set on fire. Orlands House, once the palace of the Bishop of Down and Connor, was also burned down by female activists; in Belfast they set fire to the Tea House at Bellevue, Annadale Hall at Ormeau and the pavilion of the Cavehill Bowling and Tennis Club.[6]

At the beginning of 1914, new negotiations were being held with John Redmond and Carson in regard to the possibility of partition. In these discussions Lloyd George proposed an amendment to the Home Rule Bill whereby each of the Ulster counties would remain outside Home Rule for six years, at the end of which time they would be included unless Parliament should have decided otherwise in the meantime. At the beginning of March the Prime Minister Asquith introduced the amendment on the second reading of the Home Rule Bill, however, Carson rejected the proposal outright declaring that Ulster wanted the matter dealt with immediately. 'We do not want sentence of death with a stay of execution for six years'[7] Carson's reaction to the proposal was met by the Cabinet with considerable anger and alarm. Churchill described the Ulster Provisional Government as a 'self-elected body, composed of persons who, to put it plainly, are engaged in a treasonable conspiracy'[8]

5.   ATQ Stewart, *The Ulster Crisis*, p.222

6.   Jonathon Bardon, *A History of Ulster*, p.447

7.   ATQ Stewart, *The Ulster Crisis*, p.141.

8.   ATQ Stewart, *The Ulster Crisis*, p.142

By the end of March, the War Office was putting into operation a military manoeuvre to overwhelm the Ulster Volunteers. The scheme involved the occupation of Ulster by 15,000 armed men and the blockade of its coast by battle squadron and destroyer flotilla. As it happened, the plan was aborted, largely through the refusal of the Army officers on the Curragh at Kildare to undertake any military operations against Ulster.[9]

While these events were occurring in Ireland, Fred Crawford was arranging his gun-running scheme in Germany. The plot to bring guns into Ulster was fraught with difficulties and took several months to conclude. There were disagreements as to where the arms should be landed and Fred Crawford was anxious in case the plot should be discovered and be made to look a failure. However, on the night of 24th-25th April the S.S. Clydevalley landed her shipment of rifles at Larne, Donaghadee and Bangor where they were unloaded and secretly distributed throughout the province.[10]

While the British Cabinet were making preparations to appoint a Military Governor to take over the running of the Belfast Police Force, there was little evidence of civil unrest that lovely spring morning in early April 1914 when Crawford McCullagh was elected by the City Corporation as the new Lord Mayor of Belfast. Although Ulster was in the middle of a crisis, and the threat of civil war seemed very real, the people of Belfast still carried on with their lives as normal. Crawford's department store Castle Buildings was trading as usual as were all the other major stores in Belfast. Banks, hotels and commercial businesses throughout the city were supplying their customary service as they had always done. Belfast City Hall carried out its functions and councillors also performed their many and diverse duties as usual.

---

9.   ATQ Stewart, *The 'Curragh Incident'*, p.145

10. A detailed account of the infamous 'gun-running coup' is to be found in *Fred Crawford – Carson's Gun Runner* by Keith Haines

Councillor McCullagh Elected Lord Mayor

On 1 April 1914, the General Purpose Committee of Council (the Belfast City Council in Committee) nominated Councillor McCullagh J.P., as Lord Mayor and Chief Magistrate of the Corporation of the City and County Borough of Belfast in succession to the late Councillor McMordie. In moving his election, Councillor James Johnston predicted his nominee would make an excellent Lord Mayor. Alderman King-Kerr, seconding the motion, confirmed that everyone to whom he had spoken expressed the opinion that the right decision had been taken. Although only 46 years of age, Councillor McCullagh was not new to municipal affairs.

His youth, his intelligence, integrity and dignity were noted. His acquaintance with law and order and his diligence were without question. Considered obliging, civil and polite, and coupled with his grit and knowledge of the Corporation, he had the prerequisites required to meet the onerous demands of the Lord Mayor's position. Having built up, for himself, a major business, he would bring to the position experience of success in corporate affairs. This alluded to the one requirement, never mentioned, that of having the financial resources necessary to meet the social demands of the position. All corporate entertainment was at the personal expense of the Lord Mayor.

In response, the Lord Mayor expressed the feelings of the assembly in paying respects to the family of the late Lord Mayor, Councillor McMordie who had died suddenly of a heart attack, that necessitated his appointment. He recognised the great honour conferred upon him and his wife Margaret (no longer Maggie!) and vowed to uphold the honour and dignity of the City.

The position of Lord Mayor of Belfast was an onerous one, even at the best of times. Not only was he following in the footsteps of a highly esteemed predecessor, who had been elected for five consecutive years, 1910-1914, but he was also to encounter many unexpected challenges. These he met with acclaim and credit to the office of First Citizen.

Chapter Seven
1914-1915

Observe the Sons of Ulster

The women's voices of despair, endurance and anger are quiet, and yet steadily they mount into a cumulative effect. Behind them is the backdrop of the war, always in the shadows.

From Charlotte Mews Poem *May 1915*

The press of the time portrayed Sir Crawford McCullagh as taking the lead in every facet of life in Belfast and Ulster and it is difficult to determine whether the number of offices held by the Lord Mayor came with the Mayoralty or with the man. Crawford appears to have held the chair of most, if not all, civic and philanthropic gatherings in Ulster. In his addresses, he mingled corporate, industrial, civic and Unionist endeavours as he extolled the virtues of Belfast and Ulster. The magnitude and the importance of the shipyards, the harbour, the tobacco works, and the rope works were mentioned in speeches to all visiting dignitaries.

One of his first acts after the outbreak of war, as President of the Industrial Association, was to have all shipping insured in London. Ireland was an island, not self-sufficient, and thereby was dependent upon shipping for all its imports. As well Ireland's prosperity, in large measure, was dependent upon its exports. He made sure that all vessels, both to and from Irish ports and those that travelled a circuitous route, while en-route to Ireland were fully insured. This was just one of the many instances where he demonstrated his commercial acumen. As well as running his department store in Castle Place he was also President of the Belfast Industrial Association, which included Retail, Drapery, and Allied Trades. He was chairman of the Linen Merchant Association, the Belfast and Northern Ireland Grocers' Association Ltd., and the Belfast Chamber of Trades. In 1914 he was elected President of the Association of Municipal Authorities of Ireland and in 1915 was appointed Recruitment Officer for the Northern Division in Ulster.

The Association of the Municipal Authorities of Ireland

In 1912, Crawford was approached by the Lord Mayor of Dublin, Lorcan Sherlock, to attend a conference in the Mansion House, Dublin. The driving force behind the foundation of the Association of the Municipal Authorities of Ireland was Robert Finlay Heron a member of the Church of Ireland, a Unionist and a Dubliner who was Town Clerk of the then independent Urban District Council of Blackrock, County Dublin.

The purpose of the AMAI was to establish the interests of all the municipal authorities in Ireland. Heron was anxious that it would be a non-political organisation, which would draw its support from the entire country and from all political persuasions by concentrating on municipal affairs, and strictly avoiding party controversies. As a southern Unionist working for a municipal authority with a large Protestant and unionist population, Heron feared that the increasing political polarization would be fatal for the future of his community. This viewpoint was articulated in the *Irish Times*, then a newspaper of unionist sympathies, which was to warn that the new municipal association should avoid the fate of the General Council of County Councils and steer clear of political entanglements.

Finlay Heron's qualities of diplomacy and efficiency enabled him to win all-party support in the establishment of the AMAI, and the inaugural conference was held in Dublin City Hall on 11 and 12 December 1912. The Lord Mayor of Dublin, Alderman Sherlock of the Irish Parliamentary Party hosted the conference and acted as

Chairman of the proceedings. Sherlock was subsequently elected first President of the AMAI (1912-1915). At the time there were 124 municipal authorities in Ireland and 55 sent delegates to the conference. The Lord Mayor defined the objects of the AMAI as "securing greater powers for municipalities and urban district councils to deal with every day subjects affecting their localities". He also echoed Finlay Heron's sentiments by emphasising that the Association should steer clear of party politics, in order to maximise its potential as a pressure group for municipal councils.

In 1914, the renowned Scottish polymath and town planner Patrick Geddis came to Dublin and was asked by Lord and Lady Aberdeen (the Lord Lieutenant and his wife) to organise a civic exhibition in Dublin. This was held in the Linen hall Buildings, Constitution Hill, and the adjoining grounds of the Kings Inn between 15 July and 31 August 1914. It was reported as being a great success and recorded that almost every Irish municipal authority exhibited along with a wide range of other Irish bodies and organisations.[1]

Interestingly, the author, whilst reading through the Lord Mayor's correspondence in PRONI (Public Record Office of Northern Ireland) came across a letter to Sir Crawford McCullagh from the Countess of Aberdeen requesting the Lord Mayor of Belfast and the Corporation to attend the opening of a civic exhibition by the Lord Lieutenant in Dublin. The reply reads:

'The Council greatly regret that the unsettled state of the country renders it impossible for those holding different political opinions to meet together without such meeting being misinterpreted and as the citizens of Belfast cannot at this juncture run any risk of their settled views on the present situation being misunderstood, we respectfully decline the invitation'

The Corporation did in fact contribute to the exhibition although it does not say in what capacity.[2]

---

1.   PRONI LA7/2EB/53

2.   PRONI LA7/2EB/53

The 1915 annual conference (the fourth) was held on 21 and 22 September 1915 in Dublin City Hall and in his opening speech, Lorcan Sherlock voiced strong support for the war effort, much to the approval of the delegates. Lady Aberdeen, who was in attendance, was warmly greeted and Sir Crawford McCullagh was unanimously elected second President.

In 1916 the Easter Rising (24-30 April) produced no official response from the AMAI, although symbolically (in view of the impending collapse of nationalist-unionist co-operation as practised by the Association), the Linenhall Buildings, site of the 1914 Civic Exhibition was destroyed in the course of the fighting. At the suggestion of Sir Crawford, the fifth annual conference was held on 26 and 27 September 1916 in Belfast City Hall (the first occasion that it was held outside Dublin City Hall) and doggedly followed its usual practical and non-political path. Items on the agenda included the necessity for reducing municipal expenditure as a result of the war, utilization of water power for industrial and municipal purposes, the necessity for a single Act of Parliament to govern municipal authorities, social housing, the fight against tuberculosis, income tax, the effect of dental treatment on national health and physique and municipal trading.

The principal source for the history of the AMAI is the series of annual reports of the annual conferences that have appeared since its foundation. The first five (1912-1916) are currently lost, except for that of 1913, a copy of which was in the University College, Dublin Library's Special Collection.

It is perhaps worth noting that the formation of the AMAI coincided with the most acute stage of the Home Rule Crisis (the Ulster Covenant was signed on 28 September 1912, the AMAI was founded on 11 December 1912 and the Ulster Volunteer Force established on 13 January 1913).

Asquith's attempt to appoint a Military Governor in Belfast

As a precaution against civil disorder, the War Office in London assigned Sir Nevil Macready as General Officer Commanding the Belfast District and gave him authority over the police force, which in effect meant taking over from Brigadier Gliechen, a grand-nephew of Queen Victoria, who was responsible for law and order in Belfast. Major General Macready had already seen active service in the 2nd Boer War and was twice mentioned in dispatches. On return to England he had been appointed Assistant Adjutant General in the Directorate of Personal Services at the War Office and was instrumental in forming the Territorial Army. A man with marked Liberal tendencies he believed in the right to strike and was a firm supporter of Irish Home Rule.

Sir Crawford has written an account of the situation himself which demonstrates his stubbornness in the face of authority:-

"One afternoon a man walked into City Hall asking to see the Lord Mayor. My secretary Major May came into my office with a distinguished looking man in uniform. He informed me that he had been appointed Military Governor of Belfast by the Prime Minister Herbert Asquith and was to take charge without further delay. I rose up from my chair and told him: 'Two men cannot ride this Belfast horse, and certainly I am not going to ride behind. I will not let you, or anyone else, even the Prime Minister, usurp my position as Lord Mayor.' He introduced himself as the acting Military Governor Sir Nevil Macready and explained the usurpation was not of his making. He was only a crown servant fulfilling his duties to his Westminster and Whitehall superiors who apprehended rioting and bloodshed. To prevent such disasters was the British Government's responsibility. At any rate he had his scheme cut and dried, I think it included bombardment from the sea, if necessary. With all the determination I possessed, I solemnly assured him that to adopt such provocative and repressive measures would be to create disaster and a massacre. If strife occurred over the passing of the Home Rule Bill, I could use the Police. If they were not effective, I would have the military take action. Only then would it be his time to assume command of the situation.

He found my Ulster doggedness much more solid than soft soap for he changed his tactics. Would I give him a written pledge to that effect? Without a momentary hesitation I agreed to this proposal. Then, after partaking of some hospitality, my unusual visitor departed for London. Meanwhile I arranged for the military to be reserved in readiness at both Victoria Barracks and Holywood in County

Down. A couple of days later Sir Nevil returned to the City Hall to tell me he had spoken to Mr. Asquith. The reaction of the Prime Minister to my guarantee was if the Lord Mayor of Belfast is so damned foolish to take responsibility, it is his look out. Nevertheless Sir Nevil was still uncertain of our character and apprehensive of a massacre. At any rate, throughout the night the Home Rule Bill was before Westminster, my uninvited guest and I kept vigilance in the City Hall until morning. Nothing eventuated to disturb the stillness; and we did not find it necessary to extend our arms overhead to prevent the magnificent dome of the City Hall from crashing around our ears! Withal I found my unwelcome companion a charming conversationalist, and a very gallant officer he proved himself in the war a few months later"

The amended Home Rule Bill was passed for the third time on the 25 May 1914 and in Belfast the streets were quiet and without disruption. The reply of Ulster to the passing of the Home Rule Bill was a series of parades by the U.V.F. The guns brought in by Frederick Crawford to Larne and Donaghadee were now seen for the first time in the hands of the Volunteers at which many battalions were presented with colours. Carson arrived in Belfast at Whitsuntide and showed considerable concern at the blatant display of arms.

Civic Entertainment at City Hall

By now Margaret McCullagh had been catapulted into her husband's demanding civic life. Her busy existence around the many responsibilities helping Crawford in Castle Buildings and her other role in the quiet enclave of Helen's Bay as wife and mother was suddenly turned upside down when she found herself having not only to accompany her husband to municipal functions but also to host them herself.

On Friday 15 May 1914, Maggie, acting for the first time as Lady Mayoress, was to hold her first engagement at City Hall. As the wife of the new Lord Mayor of Belfast and partner in one of the most prestigious department stores in the city, she now felt it more suitable to call herself Margaret in her new role as Lady Mayoress.

There is no doubt that Crawford was proud of his wife. She was at this time a very attractive woman and although she had put on some weight since her children were born, she carried herself well and dressed in feminine clothes that suited her fuller figure. The pictures in the press at the time show her looking happy and relaxed in her new role and Crawford did all in his power to make her feel confident and secure in herself.

On one of his buying trips to Paris, Crawford purchased a magazine called *Gazette du Bon Ton*, a unique Parisian fashion journal. One of the couture houses he frequented was owned by the Callot Sisters who were famous for their exclusive and trend-setting styles. These innovative designers with their unique and flattering lines were famous for twisted lace around the edges of blouses and camisoles and the use of antique fabrics and lace in afternoon tea dresses and exotic evening gowns. Their gossamer silk lingerie creations were embellished with bands of exquisite lace and bouquets of silk flowers. Trend setting designers like Martha Callot and her sister were influential in changing women's attitude to dress, and the corset, for so long a symbol of incarceration for woman, was being phased out in order to make creations more comfortable for the modern women. It was now time for the emphasis on the waist and hips of the hourglass silhouette to change. These new designs allowed the waistline to remain just below the bosom, creating a new 'empire line' and so there was a slight raising of the hem at the front.

Motivated by Margaret's need to dress according to her new status as Lady Mayoress Crawford purchased from the Callot sisters a selection of evening gowns, tea dresses, afternoon frocks, hand made blouses and silk lingerie embellished with lace. As she hosted her first formal engagement as Lady Mayoress, Margaret did indeed look confident and every bit the perfect hostess as she stood at the top of the City Hall's grand marble staircase with her husband and her daughter Helen. Her beautiful afternoon tea gown of honey-coloured silk was layered with French tambour lace and her hair was fashionably swept up under a hat of Tuscan straw massed with white ostrich feathers, the brim softened with the same lace that matched her dress. Helen, a pretty teenager of thirteen with pale skin and soft fair curls was dressed in saxe-blue ninon with a straw hat to match, wreathed with tiny pink roses.[3]

Crawford's private secretary Mr. Frederick Moneypenny had been grooming Margaret for her role as civic hostess and would also ensure that in the future Margaret would be given every assistance in entertaining her guests, making her feel comfortable and secure in her new role as Lady Mayoress. A string quartet played music on the landing as some fifteen hundred guests were entertained by the Lord Mayor in the Banqueting Hall. Stained glass windows displayed the royal arms, the arms of Belfast and the arms of the city's founders. It was a most successful evening and the first of many banquets and civic receptions that would be hosted by the new Lord Mayor and his wife.

William Gibson's Last Will and Testament

A month later on the 26 June 1914, Crawford was called to London to give evidence in a court case involving the last will and testament of his close friend and mentor William Gibson.

For many years Crawford and Margaret were invited to holiday with William Gibson and his wife at Villa Lisnacrieve, a beautiful French country retreat which was situated in the Mimosa Hills above Cannes in the South of France. William and his young wife always had a steady stream of guests staying at the villa including famous film stars and wealthy businessmen. Crawford mentions in his memoirs bumping into Gordon Selfridge at Le Touquet airport where they enjoyed a memorable lunch before both flying to the South of France to holiday at Villa Lisnacrieve. The owner of a famous silver and jewellery business in Regent Street, London, William always had a 'collection' of fine jewellery which he kept in a safe at the villa for those who wanted to buy something special for their wives while on holiday.

---

3.   *Belfast Evening Telegraph* May 1914

Crawford recalls in his memoir how after lunch one day the house party departed for the Casino. William had asked Crawford to accompany him on a walk, as he did not want to join the others at the gambling tables. As they walked up the Mimosa Hills together he told Crawford that he wanted to alter his will, and that he intended to leave his fortune to the farmers of County Down to buy seed. Crawford pointed out that, like himself, he had relations who most probably would benefit from a small legacy, as there was scant poverty in Co. Down compared to what had been in his youth. William, however was determined to leave his money to the farmers, he said he had done enough for his relations, particularly his nephew Robert. He then made the remark "You know my desire is not to leave too much money to young people, I do not believe in that. I like to help them who help themselves". Prophetic words from a wise man whose will was contested by his nephew stating that his uncle was not of sound mind. Later on in the day when they arrived back at the Villa his solicitor arrived from Brighton and a new will was made.

When Crawford returned home to Belfast a solicitor called in to see him in Castle Place and showed him a diary which Mrs. Gibson had kept at the villa. She had written that her husband had had a private conversation with Crawford regarding his new will. The solicitor wanted to know if he had any information on the matter as the will was being contested. Crawford was subsequently summoned as a witness when the case was heard in London and was examined by F.E. Smith on 26 June 1914. He was directed to tell the court what had transpired. He informed the court of the conversation, adding that he was a friend and business associate of the testator, that William Gibson told him that he wanted to build a technical college for farmers in Ulster to enable them to till the lands with scientific skills. He finished by saying he was a man of acute business ability who to his knowledge had never shown any sign of mental infirmity. After giving his testimony plaintiff's counsel had no further questions, whereupon the Judge dismissed the case.

William Gibson died on the 1 November 1913, at the Prince's Hotel, Hove, Brighton leaving a gross estate of £305,601.15s.3p an enormous sum of money in those days. Villa Lisnacrieve was left to his wife with an annuity of £3,000, plus property in Castle Place. £10,000 was bequeathed to The Queen's University, Belfast, £1,000 to the Victoria Hospital and £500 to the Unitarian Church, Dromore. Substantial annuities were bequeathed to relatives and various donations of lesser amounts to friends and employees. The residue of his property which amounted to £150,000 was to be applied in perpetuity 'for the purpose of assisting poor and deserving farmers, resident and holding farms in County Down and County Antrim, 'by grants of money, or annuities, for the purchase of stock, seed or implements'. The persons to benefit by this fund are to be nominated as worthy objects of this bequest by the Lord Mayor of Belfast (Sir Crawford McCullagh). There was to be no provision for his nephew Robert James Gibson as he had made suitable provision in his lifetime.

On his return from London Crawford held his first garden party as Lord Mayor in Botanic Park. The month of June had developed into long days of unbroken sunshine and Edward Carson and James Craig were his principal guests. Crawford, throughout his entire mayoralty, entertained from his own pocket and was a most generous host. No expense was spared in the lavish preparations and entertainments that were laid on for over five thousand people. The long list of guests had been drawn up by Crawford and his diligent secretary Sir Frederick Moneypenny, secretary to successive Lord Mayors, and one familiar with social protocol. Guests included city councillors and their wives, business colleagues from the drapery trade, friends including the McConnells and the Mackies, learned professors from Queens University, Trinity College Dublin and the new Technical College. Men with vision and enterprise who worked hard to make Belfast the most advanced city in Europe in terms of industrial might. The gardens were at their most beautiful, flower beds blooming with geraniums and chrysanthemums, delphiniums and agapanthus. It made people forget the ever present tension that surrounded the city. Little did they know that one present danger would make way for another and that in six weeks time they would be at war with Germany.

The following month, on the 8 July, the Home Rule Bill was amended yet again by substituting the permanent exclusion of the whole province of Ulster, for the proposed county option with a time limit. The Bill as amended passed the 3rd reading on the 14 July. The Ulster crisis came close to reality when a few days earlier Edward Carson had come over from London for the 12 July celebrations. He arrived on the 10th by Liverpool steamer to a cheering crowd, women waved handkerchiefs and men threw their caps in the air shouting 'King Carson' all the way from Belfast and in every village on the road to Newtownards until finally reaching Mount Stewart where he was staying with his good friends Lord and Lady Londonderry.

Carson had come to attend a meeting of the Ulster Unionist Council, which was sitting for the first time as the Provisional Government. To the Lord Mayor and the assembled committee he explained the extreme gravity of the situation. The Home Rule Bill now looked imminent and in that event nothing remained for them but to put into operation the terms of the Covenant. Next day there was a parade of three thousand Ulster Volunteer Force troops at Larne, with Carson urging them to preserve their self-control. As it happened, the 12 July passed without incident despite immense gatherings of excitable men all over the province.

When Carson and Craig returned to London the Prime Minister Herbert Asquith informed them that the King was to call an all-party conference at Buckingham Palace on 21 July. In essence it was a plea for compromise from the opposing parties. The discussions that followed centred around areas that would be included in the province of Ulster. For the next few days the conference, in Churchill's words, 'toiled round the muddy by-ways of Fermanagh and Tyrone' without reaching any compromise. As a last resort the Prime Minister proposed the definite exclusion of the six north-eastern counties which now form Northern Ireland, but Carson would not accept this, and inevitably, the conference came to a disappointing conclusion. Civil war in Ulster was only averted by the events that occurred in Europe over the next few days. A chain reaction began with the assassination of Archduke Franz Ferdinand, heir to the Austro-Hungarian throne, in the Bosnian city of Sarajevo. On 1 August, Germany declared war on Russia. On 3 August, German troops crossed the Belgian frontier and on 4 August 1914 the United Kingdom was at war with Germany.

Recruitment In Northern Ireland

From the outbreak of hostilities Crawford McCullagh, as Lord Mayor, used his public platform to constantly and consistently avow his own and his country's allegiance to the throne and empire. He urged all citizens to set aside any differences of religion or politics and to come together in an all out war effort. He continually called upon all citizens to respond to the times with true patriotism and sacrifice, knowing "Britain expects everyone to do his duty". By his encouragements, his devotion to duty and by his example, Crawford and Margaret inspired the people of Belfast and Ulster in the ensuing war effort. On 7August 1914, three days after the declaration of war, a meeting was convened in City Hall Belfast for the purpose of organising assistance to the government in the face of this international crisis. The Lord Mayor aided by his secretary, Sir Frederick Moneypenny, called together representatives of the civic, professional, commercial and industrial life of Belfast and the province of Ulster.

The first to give assistance was the First Battalion Young Citizens' Volunteers. Approximately two hundred of them attended, filling the City Hall, the only women present being members of the Ulster Volunteer Nursing Corps. The Lord Mayor proposed a motion that "a fund be raised to give assistance to the dependents of those who may volunteer or serve in the reserve, and that steps be taken to further encourage and promote volunteering in Ulster". Numerous speeches endorsed his proposal thus setting in motion the enormous war effort put forth by the citizens of Ulster. Recruiting began on 4 September 1914. The volunteers came in large numbers and soon the requested twelve thousand men were 'In Colour'. Then came a demand from Lord Kitchener for an Ulster Division to be formed from the Ulster Volunteer Force. Recruiting officers took over a building in Victoria Street, close to the Old Town Hall where the 36th (Ulster) Division was kitted out with the standard British army uniform of tin hat and puttees. To this regular uniform, the Division was granted permission to add the badge of the Red Hand of Ulster, a significant public concession to their separate identity by the London administration. Training began with recruits billeted under canvas, before moving to regular camps at Clandeboye, Ballykinlar, and Newtownards in County Down, and at Finner on the coast of Donegal. After training and before departing to the front, the 36th (Ulster) Division marched through the streets of Belfast on 8 May 1915 with all the buildings decked in flags and bunting. Hundreds of people had flocked to the city from all over the province to wave goodbye to these brave men — some would return severely wounded, many would not return at all. With bands playing and colours flying, the volunteers stopped in front of the City Hall where the salute was taken by General Sir Hugh McCalmont. The Lord Mayor, his wife, the Lady Mayoress, and members of the Corporation and guests gathered to review the troops. Before they moved on, Crawford addressed the parade, praising and encouraging them. He assured them that all Belfast's prayers and best wishes were with them. When the Division reached England, King George V reviewed the men. A cinematograph film of His Majesty and the men was made and brought to Belfast and used for recruitment.

On the 10 May the *Belfast Evening Telegraph* described the parade at the City Hall:

On, like a restless flood, four deep, tramp, tramp, tramp, passed the saluting base, where every head turns like well oiled machinery, down Chichester Street the long line goes. The sight sends the blood rioting through one's veins and stirs the spirit like a trumpet call.

Crawford was appointed Honorary Director of Recruitment for the Northern Area during the autumn of 1915. Recruitment meetings, rallies, concerts and other recruitment tactics were conducted regularly under his direction. Soldiers from the front visited and military bands from various units played at most public events. Officers held public meetings and men who had won medals were publicly acclaimed. All these efforts were used to swell the military ranks in a number of recruiting campaigns. As Lord Mayor, Crawford requested colleagues and businessmen of the city to implore their employees to join up and 'to inform them that if they joined the army, their places in business would be kept open for them until they returned'. By January 1916, eight hundred employees from the Corporation of Belfast had joined up. Crawford arranged for the families of civic employees, who were lost at the front, to receive half pay for six months.

Concern was expressed that men from the country were coming to Belfast to obtain positions in the Corporation and city businesses, vacated by 'those who chose to serve their country'. Initially, only men who had been in Belfast three months were hired, later this was changed to six months before they could be employed. It was estimated that there were over 75,000 men between the ages of eighteen and forty in Ulster. With 20,000 men in the shipyards and munitions, there were 54,000 men of military age, of whom 27,000 ultimately enlisted. They formed one complete Division with reserves as well as five battalions in the 10th and 16th Divisions; four Battalions in the Iniskillings and Irish Fusiliers and two Battalions in the Royal Irish Rifles.

England, Scotland and Wales introduced registration and compulsory service from January 1916. However, all service remained on a voluntary basis in Ulster. Crawford McCullagh said "Men were under no legal obligation to join, but they had their consciences to reckon with, and they must decide for themselves". Men of military age received forms and telegrams urging them to join up. Those in the shipyards and munitions resented receiving the recruitment material since they were declared 'essential to the war effort and were not allowed to leave their posts'. However, these men were urged to complete the forms so that a complete registry could be set up to properly determine who was eligible for service.

On one occasion, a Victoria Cross winner from Cork passed through Belfast unannounced. Word of his arrival spread rapidly and Crawford, hearing of it, arranged for a reception at City Hall. Many were rounded up and the occasion was used to encourage men to enlist. Crawford held a special service to present the Captain and crew of the vessel *Howth Head* with a solid silver salver. They had rescued the crew of the *S.S. Dunsley*, which had been sunk by a German submarine. Again this occasion was used to reiterate Ulster's loyalty to the Crown in the face of the terrible outrages being perpetrated by the Germans, and men were encouraged to join in the war effort. Early in the war the Employer's War Munitions Committee was formed to organise all skilled labour and to convert machinery to ammunitions manufacturing. Again the Lord Mayor was at the forefront of this endeavour. All the trades and the Technical Institute rallied round this effort. At one point, Belfast was turning out 50,000 grenades a week along with various types of shells.

Throughout the war Crawford kept in close touch with the authorities, both in Britain and at the front. He was greatly concerned for the wounded and their families and raised money to buy beds and equipment for hospitals and nursing homes. He worked effortlessly and diligently through his first year as Lord Mayor, oblivious of the arduous demands placed upon himself and his wife. He attended all corporate, civic and philanthropic events, and met these demands and responsibilities with acclaim and commendation. As first citizen, he fulfilled his role of Lord Mayor so assiduously and conscientiously during his initial term of office that at the beginning of 1915 he was unanimously re-elected to a second term of office.

Chapter Eight
1915-1916

Keeping the Home Fires

The devastated landscape looked terrible-but covered
in snow, it was beautiful. We heard the Germans singing
'Silent Night', and they put up a notice saying 'Merry Christmas',
so we put one up too. Then a German jumped on top of the
trench shouting 'Happy Christmas', Tommy!', so we jumped
up. A sergeant-major shouted, 'Get Down'. But we all went
forward to the barbed wire ... and shook hands.

Private Frank Sumpter, London Rifle Brigade,
The Western Front, 25th December, 1914

On the 15 May 1915 the Right. Honourable Ivor, Lord Wimbourne, Lord Lieutenant of Ireland and Lady Wimbourne arrived in Belfast to bestow on Crawford McCullagh the honour of knighthood for his services to the War Effort. Their Excellencies, along with their two daughters and entourage had arrived by train from Dublin the previous evening. When they arrived they were given a warm welcome by the Lord Mayor and prominent citizens of Belfast, they were escorted to Belfast Castle and entertained as guests of Lord Shaftesbury.

That evening Sir Crawford and Lady Margaret McCullagh hosted a reception with over 2,000 select guests in the City Hall. There had been no social events since the outbreak of War, so there was great excitement and the event was naturally heightened and increased by the visit of such important dignitaries. The City Hall was elaborately decorated with a simulated lake, palm trees, immense floral arrangements, exotic and tropical plants, beautiful carpets and luxurious easy chairs and settees; many of the latter borrowed from private homes.[1]

A lavish buffet was served during the entire evening in the large Banqueting Hall together with a selection of champagne and fine wines. As on previous occasions, Crawford paid for this event himself. The Lord Mayor and Lady Mayoress along with the Lord Chamberlain, Sir Frederick Moneypenny received all the guests. A large crowd gathered outside City Hall to glimpse the arrival of visiting dignitaries and glamorous ladies in beautiful evening gowns. A musical interlude was provided by the band of the 5th Battalion Royal Rifles. The following morning, May 16th, Lord and Lady Wimbourne were escorted by the North Irish Horse battalion and mounted constabulary to the newly decorated Ulster Hall in Bedford Street where they were received with full honours by the Lord Mayor, Lady Mayoress, the Corporation and other dignitaries representing the churches, academic and professional life, religious and philanthropic institutes and commercial, industrial and agricultural interests. Crawford chaired the proceedings. This was followed by the Corporation's address and twenty-five other addresses. Lord Wimbourne, after acknowledging the 'exceedingly great part that Belfast was taking in the struggle for national existence', said he had been instructed by His Majesty King George V to confer the honour of knighthood upon the Lord Mayor of Belfast for his unstinting work in civic, social and national services. In his reply, Crawford said he regarded the distinction with pride, not so much personally, but as an honour bestowed upon the city and the enterprising citizens of Belfast. The official party left for the Royal Victoria Hospital followed by a luncheon for three hundred at the City Hall hosted by the

1. *Belfast Evening Telegraph* 15 May 1915

Lord Mayor, where a personal tribute was paid to Lady McCullagh by Sir Robert Anderson.

Margaret McCullagh's Contribution to The War Effort

In the presence of Lord and Lady Wimbourne and the assembled gathering he complimented Lady McCullagh on her charm and remarkable powers of benevolence and philanthropy. Her labours on behalf of the various funds in relation to the War shed fresh light on northern civic life. Sir Robert Anderson added, 'she has been untiring in her exertions on behalf of National Relief in the broad sense, and on behalf in part of the care of wounded soldiers and the local funds for caring wives and families and rendering more effective the ambulance at the front. Her own special funds have, in the readiness of response and the amounts realised, given an impetus that seems almost to exhaust the possibilities of a situation far reaching in every respect, but demanding to the end the aid and service of men and women of all classes. His Majesty has on several occasions sent his personal thanks to Lady McCullagh whose devotion and self sacrifice in the best of all causes has won her universal admiration.'[2]

Margaret McCullagh had always worked alongside her husband when building up the drapery empire. She was an astute and eager businesswoman who threw herself into her husband's affairs and did all she could to promote his interests, something she did all her life. When Crawford became Lord Mayor she continued in her role with pride and diligence. With typical enthusiasm she immediately began a round of social and philanthropic activities. She was quoted in the press as saying that she felt, that, as Lady Mayoress, she belonged to the city and to its people – that, after her own family, they had first claim upon her, and she must take an interest in every worthy enterprise. The papers at the time reported that she had a 'kindly disposition and gifted with infinite tact', she was described as a 'quiet, self-possessed person with a simple modesty and a natural grace. She

---

2.   Alfred S Moore, *A Merchant Prince*

was always solicitous for the comfort and enjoyment of guests and was seen as a friend of all grades of society'. In his memoirs Crawford describes her as easy going and cheerful, devoted to her home and family. She was especially fond of her roses which grew in abundance both in the garden and in the greenhouse and guests would comment on the wonderful scent which greeted them on entering the house.

Crawford was immensely proud of his wife and grateful to Frederick Moneypenny, the Lord Mayor's Private Secretary who taught and guided her as she worked to meet the demands of her position. Her husband said she must have had an inherent organisational ability in order to have met the tremendous civic and social demands, and to have done so with acclaim. She had a pleasant speaking voice, making her speeches agreeable and this must have stood her in good stead as she occupied the Chair on many committees. Considered a strong leader and noted for overcoming obstacles, she was a zealous advocate and energetic promoter of benevolent endeavours. Her enthusiasm instilled confidence in and support for many philanthropic, civic and military causes.

When hostilities broke out she plunged headlong into helping with the war effort in whatever capacity she felt was most worthy. With the help of her husband she organised the Prince of Wales National Relief Fund and immediately raised £50,000. She raised a further £14,000 for the Ulster Volunteer Force Hospital fund which provided 266 beds along with complete surgical and nursing staff. The Soldiers' and Sailors' Help Society was established to assist the returning wounded from the Front. When a request came for assistance Margaret helped raise £10,000 to build and equip ambulances. Initially twenty-two ambulances were sent, all built in Belfast. Later two more ambulances were completed and dispatched which were all sent as gifts from Belfast. Each was equipped to take four stretchers, or if seated could accommodate ten to twelve slightly wounded soldiers. Each ambulance had the 'Red Hand of Ulster' and 'Presented by the City of Belfast' painted on its side.[3]

Margaret, assisted by the Rotary Club, conducted many fund raising events, including a 'Flag Day' when flags of all the Allies were sold. The Society was also concerned with collecting money for men who were maimed for life and whose pension would be too meagre to live on. A request to support the Red Cross Societies of Great Britain, Belgium and Russia 'moved the Lord Mayor with characteristic energy, to set about devising ways and means to inaugurate a movement which would enlist the sympathetic cooperation of many willing workers and rebound to the credit of the city, generally'.

A greater than ever outlay was required to assist the wounded from the Dardanelles expedition. Margaret was ultimately credited with raising £12,500 for the British, Belgian and Russian Red Cross Societies. She held benefit concerts in City Hall and in December 1916 she received a letter and certificate from Petrograd, Russia, thanking her for her contribution to their flag day movement. The certificate and letter are still in a display cabinet in Belfast City Hall.

As president of the Royal Ulster Horticultural Society, Crawford suggested that a 'Chrysanthemum Day' replace the Annual Chrysanthemum Show, suspended due to the War, and incorporate 'Our Day', which marked the first anniversary of the amalgamation of the British Red Cross Society and the Ancient Order of St. John of Jerusalem in order to unify and strengthen their efforts. On 1 October 1915 the Chrysanthemum Day street collection in Belfast raised £4,000. Crawford chaired the newly formed committee and Margaret as Lady Mayoress chaired the executive branch of the committee.[4]

In November 1916 Margaret opened The Sailors' and Soldiers' Rest Home at 19 Castle Place, a place she said "where our convalescent

3.   Alfred S Moore, *A Merchant Prince*

4.   Alfred S Moore, *A Merchant Prince*

wounded, after temporarily coming out of hospitals, on pass, can call and enjoy rest, recreation and refreshments". The Lady Mayoress was supported, in this endeavour by the owner of the premises the directors of the Scottish Temperance Assurance Company, the Committee of Irish Temperance League and many other civic groups. Throughout the war years almost 160,000 wounded passed through Belfast and as injured men whilst in hospital received no pay the rest home was of great advantage. Previously these men would have wandered the streets while out on pass. [5]

Throughout their mayoralty, a New Year's Eve party was given to over 1,500 of the city's poor and needy. These were gatherings uniquely free from pomp and ceremony and any semblance of charity atmosphere. The Lord and Lady Mayoress and their children Daisy, Helen and young Boysie received their guests with the same cordiality as at a society reception. Traditional Christmas fayre was presented followed by plum pudding and tea. There was also a cinematograph show and concert. When the evening had finished every man received a packet of tobacco and every woman a parcel of tea accompanied by a personally signed New Year's good wish from the Lady Mayoress. Returned and wounded soldiers had similar treats.

In 1915 Crawford received a letter from a widow who had lost her son at the Front. In it she donated a pair of socks. This was for an auction which had been set up to raise funds for a disabled home for soldiers and sailors. In her note she severely criticised the farmers in her area who, she felt, refused to support the war effort either monetarily or by joining up. Aware of this anomaly, Crawford on several occasions had expressed concern over the lack of support from the agricultural community with respect to the war effort.[6] Recruitment from the rural areas lagged far behind urban involvement. If there had been a notable increase in farm produce, this might have been understood; however, in his opinion this was not the case. From a

5. Alfred S Moore, *A Merchant Prince*

6. PRONI LA7//2E

country background himself he was sympathetic to farmers but prag-
matic in wanting more effort for wartime supply from them. At one
point Crawford advocated the removal of fences in order to increase
productive land. As ambassador for Belfast he had visited Belgium,
France and Germany where he observed that fences did not take up
land, as they did in Ireland.[7]

At this time during the war Crawford made a point of inspecting
at City Hall the veterans from the Battle of Stormberg in the Boer
War. He also received a Canadian Trade Mission and a visit from
the Premier of Queensland. As Chief Magistrate, the Lord Mayor
chaired all meetings of the magistrates. On 9 April 1915, the magistrates assembled '… for the purpose of considering a memorial with
reference to the drinking traffic'. The memorial, signed by thirty-
three magistrates, stated that:

> the drinking traffic was seriously interfering with the fitness of men in the army,
> of the quantity and quality of the out-put of armaments and supplies generally …
> and that our city should do its part in reducing the temptation to drink by closing
> all drink shops from 6.00pm until 10.00am the next morning, and all day Sunday
> … further they appealed to all government leaders to unite in passing the meas-
> ure drastically reducing the hours liquor could be sold.

Crawford advised the assembly that they lacked the power to make a
closing order earlier than 9.00pm. A recommendation must be made
through the City Commission to the Lord Lieutenant and proper
authorities. Representatives were appointed to further the matter,
chaired by the Lord Mayor, Crawford McCullagh. Eighty magistrates
met again. Crawford reported that at the ensuing meeting between
the representatives and the members of the licence trade, the latter
asked for an adjournment to a later date. Meanwhile, the Chancellor
of the Exchequer brought in new proposals. At a second meeting the
licensed trade stated that 'Lord George's proposals would be ruinous

---

7.   PRONI LA/7/59

to their trade'. Thus 'they were where they left off, and no further'. This seemed to end the matter.[8]

Both publicly and privately Crawford advocated for a variety of causes. At the beginning of the war, he stressed the need to stabilize prices and admonished against hoarding to prevent the development of shortages. Several times he suggested the weekly half-day holiday be changed from Wednesday afternoon to Saturday morning so young people from the country could go home for weekends.

The outbreak of war saw anti-German sentiment and when the Lusitania passenger liner was torpedoed by a German submarine off the coast of Cork on 7 May 1915 resulting in the death of 1,000 people, anti-German feeling in Britain and Ireland became widespread. Sir Otto Jaffa who had been Lord Mayor of Belfast from 1899-1900 was subjected to racial hatred not because he was a Jew but because he was born in Germany, even though he was loyal to the Crown and his son Arthur and nephew were serving in the British Army, Sir Otto was accused of being a German spy but in a letter to the *Northern Whig* newspaper in May 1915, he stated;

"how anyone who has any knowledge of me and my life would think that I could approve of the horrible and detestable actions of which she [Germany] has been guilty is almost beyond my comprehension".

Sir Otto subsequently resigned his post as Alderman of Windsor Ward for Belfast City Council in June 1916 when he was almost 70 years of age and took up residence in London where he died in 1929.

Although Crawford was neither anti-semitic nor anti-German his loyalty would have been to the citizens of Belfast at that time and at a monthly meeting of the city council held on 1 December 1915 it was resolved that the following addition be made to Standing Order no. 59.

8.   PRONI LA/7/2

'That no contract shall be entered into with any person of German or Austrian Nationality; or any firm or company whose subscribed capital is held or controlled by persons of German or Austrian Nationality or who acts for or represents - directly or indirectly any German or Austrian firm, merchant, traveller and any such contracts now in existence should be terminated as soon as possible'[9]

A year later in February 1916 Sir Crawford chaired the inaugural meeting of the Belfast Anti-German Union in the Ulster Hall. He gave a rousing and patriotic speech in support of Britain and the Empire and against the Germans who "were wont to supplant British workmen and dump their goods on our land". Those attending determined to develop present and future attitudes towards Germany. They would set up a defensive policy to protect their industries and trade by establishing a Custom Union with their allies with four degrees of duties: first and highest for Germans and their friends, second for neutrals, third for allies, and fourth for the Dominion with a view to a self-supporting empire.[10]

Women's Role During The War

Before the outbreak of war those in power in Belfast were becoming increasingly self-protective. Mounting labour unrest threatened Unionist solidarity; the loss of the *Titanic* in 1912 had been a major blow to the morale of Harland and Wolff and from 1910 it looked as if nothing less than open rebellion could prevent Westminster from breaking the Union.

When War was declared, and after the outbreak of hostilities in 1914 the skills of both men and women in industrial Belfast were urgently required, not only in the shipyards, but in the rope works, and the linen mills. Women played increasingly important and dangerous roles during the war years. Many of the young women who served as nurses and signed up as volunteers had never had first hand experiences of dealing with men who were just off the battlefield. It is difficult to imagine the pressure and the trauma that women must

9.   PRONI LA7/2E/59

10.   Alfred S Moore, *A Merchant Prince*

have put up with on the front line in the surgical units. The hospitals were overcrowded, operating very often with a shortage of medical supplies and food. Typhus and cholera took heavy tolls, and sometimes there was no way of separating the wounded from the sick. The training consisted of a three-month course in first aid, they were shown how to bandage a limb, give an injection, take a temperature and clean a wound. They were told how and when to administer various drugs and before they realised it they were on the front line. A harrowing account was written by Emma Duffin a nurse waiting to treat the wounded at Le Havre:

> I had not been on night duty very long when the big push began and the trains came and came, and the boats did not come fast enough, and we worked all night and came on duty again after breakfast and prayed and looked for the boats, especially the *Asturias* as she was the biggest. I was sent on duty on the station platform; if the hospital had not made me realise the war I realised it that night; under the big arc lights in the station lay stretchers 4 deep … at the end of the station were the walking cases; they were past walking, and the majority had laid down huddled together, their arms in slings, and their heads bound up, the mud from the trenches sticking to their clothes and the blood still caked on them. I was up and down all night feeling I was in a bad dream … attempting the hopeless task of trying to make men with their legs in splints a little more comfortable, feeling the pulses of the men who felt faint, rearranging a bandage that had slipped and watched for haemorrhages.[11]

It was not just on the 'Western Front' that women were making their mark in the First World War. On the Home Front in Britain and Ireland, women were to set the foundations that would shape the development of their social roles in the 20th Century. The catalyst to women's legacy in Britain and Ireland has its origins in areas such as the munitions sector and on the land. Work that was traditionally done by men was now being performed by women. These brave women worked in factories in dire conditions with little protective clothing and as such they were exposed to the many dangers that making munitions brought with it. In Belfast alone seventy-five mil-

11.   Emma Duffin PRONI D2109/13

lion artillery shells were produced in factories such as James Mackie's. Davidson's and Company, and the Falls Foundry.

There was now a new world order in which familiar boundaries had been removed and replaced with something strange and unfamiliar. The next decade especially for women, would bring radical changes in the home and in the work place. Many girls born into domestic service were now finding that they were given a wider choice of options and, for these women, nothing was ever going to be the same. Although the workforce at Harland and Wolff had been severely depleted due to enlistment, shipwrights and boiler workers worked to full capacity in the shipyards, building, refitting or replacing battleships, hospital ships and 'standard ships', simplified cargo vessels urgently needed to replace losses at sea. The smaller shipyard of Workman Clark built patrol boats, boom defence vessels, sloops and cargo ships. The linen industry was now in full swing and women in their droves went to work in the mills in order to fulfil the demand for sheets, bandages, tents, stretchers, sheets and aeroplane fabric needed for the ravages of war.

All the traditional export industries prospered, the Belfast Ropeworks, for example, producing 50 per cent of the Royal Navy's cordage requirements. There were new industries too. In 1917 Lord Pirrie volunteered to open an aeroplane works, starting with six de Havilland machines, followed by one hundred Handley Page V/1500 heavy bombers for raiding Berlin, and three hundred Avros. He built an aerodrome on the site of a 170-acre farm he bought at Aldergrove in Co. Antrim,[12] now Belfast International Airport.

Many of Crawford's friends had lost sons and close relatives in the slaughter of The Great War. He was intensely aware of the sacrifices Belfast people had made and he and Margaret worked tirelessly for bereaved families of all denominations. It is unsurprising then that Crawford was given a knighthood for his war work but he often re-

---

12. Alfred S Moore, *A Merchant Prince*

marked that those who should really be honoured were the wounded and fallen of that conflict.

Ernest McCullagh

Ernest McCullagh who was still living with his uncle at this time had continued his religious studies with a tutor and after successfully matriculating he was accepted by Trinity College, Dublin to study theology. While at Trinity he shared a room with Tom Marshall from County Down and the two became great friends. After graduating with a B.A. Honours the two fellow countrymen emigrated to Canada, entering Presbyterian College, at McGill University, Montreal. They arrived in Canada on 24 September 1913 the day before Ernest's 22nd birthday. When War was declared in 1914 he enlisted in the first McGill reinforcements of the Princess Patricia Light Infantry Regiment, 23rd Military Battalion. Ernest landed in France in May 1915 with the 2nd Battery Royal Canadian Artillery, the 1st Canada Division as a gunner with the 2nd Field Battery. On 22 April 1915 the Germans had launched a major attack on the Western Front at Ypres lasting until 25 May. There was heavy fighting at Gravenstafel, St. Julien, Frezenberg, Bellewaarde, Aubert and Festubert. It was during the Battle of St. Julien that the Germans used poison gas for the first time on the Western Front. For those witnessing the awful results it must have been harrowing, especially as most of these men would have been friends. Some victims were lucky and death would have come came relatively quickly, but others would have endured a horrible slow death while their lungs collapsed and filled up with liquid. Blindness, skin lesions and respiratory problems were other symptoms. It wasn't just men who died, but hundred of horses died from the effects of gas poisoning as well. In an effort to minimise the anguish suffered by bereaved families, the reports by officers of deaths in action usually intimated that death was instantaneous or else that pain and suffering were minimal.

Throughout the war Ernest McCullagh kept in touch with his Uncle Crawford and wrote to let him know that after the Battle at Vimy

Ridge on 9 April 1917 he had been wounded during the conflict sustaining a shrapnel injury to his right hand. Ernest kept a diary of his experiences at the front and wrote of the intolerable conditions and the horrors of living in the trenches. The lack of sleep, the quality of food, the rats and lice, the noise from the constant bombings, and

No. R.L.2-1-26/Cas.7817.
(In replying, please quote above No.)

To Mrs.C.Donaghy,
6 Main Street,
Lemavady,Ireland.

Canadian Record Office,
Green Arbour House,
Old Bailey, London, E.C. 4

Madam,   August 7th , 191 7

I regret to have to inform you that a report has this day been received to the effect that (No.) 85148 (Rank) Gunner (Name) McCULLAGH,E.C. (Regiment) 1st.Brigade,Canadian Field Artillery is ill at No.10.Canadian Field Ambulance suffering from Shrapnel Wound Right Hand.

I am at the same time to express the sympathy and regret of the Militia Council.

Any further information received in this office as to his condition or progress will be at once notified to you.

I am, Madam,
Your obedient servant,

For Lt.Col.Officer in Charge of Records.
Lieut.
C.O.M.F.

Form A 3. R. 105.

the rain which gave the men trench foot and made walking any distance extremely painful was all brought to life in his account of the war. He related in his letters how they would lie in rain sodden, rat infested dug outs for days methodically cleaning their rifles where each one was stripped, cleaned, greased, checked and then checked again, every bullet placed carefully into its magazine. A normal period in the trenches at that time was four days in without a break and then four days out in the reserve trenches. In the days out the men had to go up to the line quite often, particularly at night, to carry out repairs, to mend barbed wire entanglements, or to carry up ammunition, bombs or supplies. Some of the trenches they had been in could not be dug out properly as they filled up with water very quickly so they put up sandbags. Although pretty much bullet proof, the sandbags were fairly fragile and required constant fixing; in most places duckboards were provided on which to stand, although they were submerged regularly during heavy rain. He wrote of the mud and how it never seemed to stop raining and that everyone was fed up with being constantly cold and wet and how it took days to dry out their clothes. He said he dreamt of the wonderful meals he had enjoyed at his uncle's house and how they were all sick of eating corned beef out of tins and bully beef stew that was made in horse drawn carts, by not very expert cooks, and drinking strong black tea made in large dixies. There were no plates but mess tins were used and apart from the officers nearly everyone drank their tea from tin mugs. Most letters home contained requests for warm clothing, but he also asked for toilet rolls, tobacco, sweets, handkerchiefs, and 'muscatol to keep the flies away'. Ernest served in France, Germany and Italy as a Bombardier and then as a Corporal, part of the time. Remaining in France after the armistice, he served with the Army of Occupation in Germany, receiving a discharge from the Occupation Forces on 1 June 1919. The last entry in his pay book was 12 August 1919. When granted leave he came home to Ulster spending some time with his mother and step-father in Limavady then going to see his aunt and uncle and cousins at Lismara, Whiteabbey where the family had moved in 1915[13] [see appendix 3].

Lismara, Whiteabbey

The McCullaghs moved from Helen's Bay to their new home Lismara, Whiteabbey in 1915 and the transition at this time proved to be a lot easier than had been anticipated, not only from Margaret's perspective but also from the children's point of view. Margaret had come from humble beginnings in a district where she was now going to return to and was acutely aware of the fact that she would now be seen by her peers as superior on account of her newly acquired status as 'Lady'. The situation was softened when it was agreed that her eccentric sister Ellen would come and live at Lismara with them. Ellen was a tiny short sighted spinster who wore very thick steel rimmed spectacles, her father once said to her 'you needn't have to worry dear, nobody would clamber over a brick wall to get at you!' She was often

---

13. Private correspondence to Sir Crawford McCullagh from Ernest McCullagh belonging to the estate of Sheilagh Hearnden McCullagh (deceased)

to be seen walking through Whiteabbey village with one odd shoe on each foot. She remained at Lismara until her death in 1947.

From an early age the three children had been looked after by nannies and housekeepers however it would appear from letters and personal accounts that life in Helen's Bay although insular was happy. Boysie was educated at home by Miss Hamilton, the Reverend Hamilton's sister, whilst Helen and Daisy attended The Miss Boyce's Academy for Girls. The school was held in a house called Seahaven at the bottom of Church Road situated across the road from Helen's Bay beach. Some of the senior girls came to school on their ponies and were allowed to have them tethered at the back of the house while they attended lessons. Helen and Daisy who were brought up living close to many of the girls at the school, played tennis on the grass courts at Tordeevra and Rathwyre and swam off the Horse Rock at Helen's Bay beach. Boysie's main interest was wildlife especially birds and in later life it became his life long passion, eventually becoming an eminent ornithologist and owning the largest aviary in Ireland. They were very friendly with the Mackie children particularly Isobel and James and the idea of moving to a beautiful house that would be adjacent to theirs in Whiteabbey made the move that more appealing. Moving to Lismara required that arrangements be made concerning the second stage of the children's education. Unfortunately for the children this left little time or energy for more than perfunctory parenting. It was agreed that the girls would be sent to board at Alexandra College, Dublin while Boysie attended a small private establishment in Whiteabbey called The Ladies School.

Sir Crawford had always wanted to move to Co. Antrim and especially to a home that would be more fitting for Belfast's First Citizen. His aspirations were not constrained by set boundaries and he never made any secret of the fact that he wanted to live the life of a 'Merchant Prince'. One house in particular had always been in the back of his mind and when it was advertised for sale he was delighted to be in a position to purchase the property. The house in question was a magnificent residence on the shores of Belfast Lough called

'Lismara' situated on the County Antrim side of the Lough in a small village called Whiteabbey. It was a house they both knew from their courting days as they had walked passed it many times. Crawford had visions then of living in such a house and now his dream was to be fulfilled.

The two-storey 'Italianate Style' mansion was made of fine sandstone with a front entrance that had a projecting square portico with pillars and three steps leading to the front door. A black and white tiled vestibule led into the hall where two white marble classical statues on plinths stood in arched niches. The ground floor had five imposing reception rooms including dining room, morning room, drawing room and billiard room. All these rooms had high ceilings with rich plasterwork on cornices and were furnished with ornate Italian marble fireplaces and south facing views over the Lough from bow shaped windows. The kitchens were well away from the family's living quarters and were a labyrinth of small rooms with pantry, larder, scullery and a cold room for hanging meat and storing perishables. When they moved to Lismara they employed a cook, a butler, a parlour maid and housemaid with the staff sleeping downstairs in bedrooms convenient to the kitchen. The family slept upstairs in spacious bedrooms overlooking the gardens, there were also two bathrooms on the second floor. The house was approached from the main road by a driveway that led from an impressive gate lodge complete with 'porte cochere' ending at the front of the house in a wide semi circular sweep. The extensive grounds comprising 19 acres had been landscaped with fine trees, herbaceous borders and flowering shrubs of hydrangeas, rhododendrons and azaleas. At the rear of the house the manicured lawns ran down to the shores of Belfast Lough commanding spectacular views of the Holywood Hills. A large green house hugged an old stone wall and was home to peach trees, camellias and exotic plants. There was also an old coach house where in later years young Boysie would keep his menagerie of injured birds and rabbits and where he would first become interested in the mating habits of ducks.

In years to come Margaret planted a rose garden containing a wide variety of roses surrounding a fountain and sun-dial. Various fruit trees were also grown and a narrow winding path was developed in the woods that ended in a beautiful clearing where on fine sunny days the family would picnic and hold swimming parties while watching boats sailing up and down Belfast Lough.

The Lismara estate lies on the Carrickfergus Road, later renamed Shore Road between the villages of Whitehouse and Whiteabbey. The name Whiteabbey is derived from the ancient abbey of the Dominicans or White Friars which had existed in the vicinity. The estate was created from land previously in the possession of the owners of the neighbouring estates of Hazelbank which came into the possession of the McTear family in 1796, and Abbeylands owned by the powerful McCalmont family since the beginning of the 19th Century. Hazelbank at this time was the home of the Mackie family.[14] Lismara House was originally built by John Finlay, a flax and tow merchant in 1850 and designed by Charles Lanyon, Lord Mayor of Belfast (1866-1868), the leading architect and engineer of the time who was responsible for transforming Belfast during the period 1840-1860. Lanyon designed other landmark buildings including Queen's University, The Custom House and Crumlin Road Jail and Courthouse.

Upon the death of John Finlay in 1860, Lismara was sold to James Hind who was also engaged in the linen industry in Belfast as a flax spinner and mill owner. James lived at Lismara until his death in 1883. The house then passed into the hands of Herbert Owen Lanyon, youngest son of Sir Charles Lanyon and his wife Amelia (daughter of James Hind). They lived at Lismara from 1883 to 1890 when it again changed ownership and was purchased by Edward Robinson of the famous Robinson and Cleaver Royal Irish Linen Warehouse for £6,250, a sum which included all the furniture.

---

14. Kathleen Rankin, *The Linen Houses of County Antrim & North County Down*, p.28

Edward Robinson was born on 17 February 1849 in Ballymena and became one of the most prosperous linen merchants in Belfast at that time. He commenced business with his partner John Cleaver in 1870 as a retailer of Irish Linen and Tweed products. Within a very short time the firm of Robinson and Cleaver had built up an extensive customer list in Britain and Ireland and in 1879 had to move to larger premises in High Street, Belfast. Several Royal Appointments were granted to the firm and following negotiations to purchase land at Donegall Square and Donegall Place to build even larger premises, The Royal Irish Linen Warehouse of Robinson Cleaver was officially opened on Friday 27 August 1888, featuring electric lighting throughout and an hydraulic lift to all eight floors. Edward Robinson later became a magistrate for County Antrim and an Alderman of the City Of Belfast. He died on 6 March 1906. The family continued to live there until 1915 when his son Major Harold Robinson sold the house to Sir Crawford McCullagh.[15]

Having settled into their new surroundings Crawford and Margaret joined the congregation of Whiteabbey Presbyterian Church. Crawford would have been familiar with a large number of parishioners, many of whom played an important part in keeping the wheels of industry in Belfast turning. One of their neighbours was his friend from Helen's Bay James Mackie who lived in the adjoining estate of Hazlebank, he and his family worshipped at Whitehouse Presbyterian Church. During these particularly hard times these leading citizens and entrepreneurs showed an enduring public spirit in religious, social and philanthropic affairs and by example were an inspiration to the citizens of Belfast.

When the Reverend W. B McMurray was installed in Whiteabbey Presbyterian Church on the 21 April 1914 the Great War was looming like great dark clouds over the people of Ulster. In his memoirs he writes:-

---

15. Kathleen Rankin, *The Linen Houses of County Antrim & North County Down*, p.62 & p.63

'When that terrible tempest arose and broke in fury upon the world in August 1914, the young men of our congregation did not timidly search for a refuge, in which they might shelter from its stormy blast. On the contrary, at the blowing of the trumpet they rallied round their country's flag in large numbers. No less than one hundred and two of them answered the call, and these fifteen paid the supreme penalty for their patriotism. During those grim and ghastly years our hearts went out to God in anxious prayer for our brothers on the battle front and on the dangerous seas, and our women laboured to make some provision for their comfort. When at last the storm had blown past, and peace and quietness reigned once more, our people raised a memorial to the men who had fallen, and showed their appreciation of the courage and endurance of all our men who wore the King's uniform by the installation of a pipe organ in the church, and the erection of a suitable tablet in the porch, at the cost of some £1,500' [16]

16.   Rev. W. B. McMurray, *Whiteabbey Presbyterian Church, A Record of the first 100 years 1833-1933*

Chapter Nine
1916-1918

Battle of the Somme

When shall their glory fade?
O, the wild charge they made!
All the world wondered.

Tennyson

Throughout the war in Europe Sir Crawford kept in close touch with the authorities both in Britain and at the front. He was greatly concerned for the grieving families and the wounded. The terrible toll that the Great War had on families could be seen on the faces of people all over Ulster. The Battle of the Somme, which began on 1 July 1916, was really a series of savage engagements with the enemy, which lasted intermittently for the next four and a half months and resulted in enormous losses on both sides. During the first thirty-six hours, for example, the famous 36th Ulster Division suffered 5,500 casualties in the neighbourhood of Thiepval. It has been described by many as the bloodiest day in the history of the British Army. British forces attacked in waves towards the German wire, much of which was undamaged, despite a huge preparatory bombardment. Regardless of the heavy losses sustained on the first day, Field Marshal Sir Douglas Haig decided to press on with the attack and the conflict continued until 18 November 1916. There were major battles at many places including Albert, High Wood, Delville Wood, Pozieres, Guillemont, Ginchy and the Ancre. Armoured vehicles were used for the first time on 15 September at Flers-Courcelette and on 27 September the village of Thiepval was taken. Many of the officers who were killed were either friends or acquaintances of the McCullagh family.

A visit to the Reform Club or the Ulster Club became a familiar ritual of commiserations and heartfelt sympathy for the loss of so many lives. Families had to come to terms with not only losing one son but in some cases the dreaded telegrams came with the news that another son had been wounded or gone missing. Sometimes news about a death on active service reached the bereaved family quickly while on other occasions a considerable period of time might elapse. When a family was informed that a relative was missing in action the following explanation was included:

> The term 'Missing' does not necessarily mean that the soldier is killed or wounded. He may be an unwounded prisoner or temporarily separated from his regiment. Any further information received will be at once sent on to you.

There was always the risk that the authorities would get it wrong and cause unnecessary distress if someone who was missing in action was reported killed in action too soon and subsequently turned up alive. Due to such cases there were times when news of a death reached a bereaved family unofficially in a letter written by a surviving comrade before the family heard the news officially. Sometimes a full year or more elapsed between a 'missing in action' report and the dreaded 'killed in action' official intimation.[1]

Newspapers were read avidly by soldiers at the front and by those who were recuperating in military hospitals. When a soldier was posted as missing in action and no more letters from him were received, the family at home requested information from readers of these papers – both those serving at the front and those recuperating in military hospitals. *The Times* reports on the 3 July were headed 'The Great Battle', 'The Glory of Ulster', 'Great Traditions Upheld'

---

1. Barry Niblock, *Remembering Their Sacrifice in the Great War. The War Dead of North Down and Ards*, p.18

and 'Unparalleled Acts of Heroism'. The *Belfast News Letter's* daily column, 'Ulster and the War', went from an average of two columns to five. The headlines in the press told their own story; for days after the battle they read, 'Ulster's Sacrifice' and 'Ulster's Sacrifice for the Empire', and the losses at the Somme drew the close-knit community together in grief. Jonathon Bardon in his book *A History of Ulster* gives a moving account of events which occurred on the first day of the battle:

> "At 7.10 a.m. on 1 July, concealed by a smoke barrage and lingering mist, troops of the Ulster Division climbed out of their trenches and formed up in no-man's-land. It was the anniversary of the Battle of the Boyne; some men wore orange lillies and at least one sergeant draped his sash over his uniform. Here, in front of Thiepval Wood and astride the River Ancre, the six-day allied artillery barrage reached a horrific climax. 'As the shells passed over our heads,' John Stewart-Moore observed, 'the air hummed like a swarm of a 100 million hornets.' At 7.30 a.m. the guns suddenly stopped firing, officers blew their whistles, and the men advanced at a steady marching pace towards the German first line"[2]

The newspapers in Belfast, as elsewhere on 3 July, reported the opening of the Somme offensive, and spoke of brilliant successes. It was several days before the casualties were known, as day by day the lists in the papers grew longer, a hush of mourning fell upon the whole of the province. No division was more closely knit, because its core was the U.V.F. and, besides, the Ulster community was small and compact. In the trenches, writes Captain Falls, 'the talk, not only of men from Belfast and the larger towns, but of those from the country villages, would be of streets ... of farms and lanes of which those present had known every detail of childhood'[3]

In small communities like Whiteabbey, where the McCullaghs now lived, the villagers and townsfolk would have heard news about the war from itinerant preachers. These preachers travelled to local towns and villages on bicycles preaching the gospel. They played a pivotal role in public awareness at the outbreak of war in August 1914 as

---

2.   Jonathon Bardon, *A History of Ulster*, p.454

3.   A.T.Q. Stewart, *The Ulster Crisis*, p.241

they were a great source of information for current affairs and political matters around the country. The radio had its early beginnings around the turn of the twentieth century but even by 1914 it still wasn't readily accessible to the majority of people at that time. Because of this, and the fact that newspapers cost money, which many could not afford, the best way to hear about local news was to convene in the market square, where you would often find itinerant preachers belting out the latest news along with the Good News.

It was in this way that much of rural Ireland heard about the outbreak of war against Germany, and the impact that preachers had by announcing such an event cannot be overlooked. As a result of hearing an itinerant preacher, many men of varying ages felt a sense of calling to war. Such was the sense of excitement and enthusiasm which was generated throughout many communities in Ireland. Friends would sign up together and gradually the sense of camaraderie, coupled with the incentive of adventure brought a great number of men to the recruiting offices to enlist in the army. Sir Edward Carson also had a huge influence on young men at this time and writing from his home in London sent a message to the Ulster people:

> 'I desire to express, on my behalf and that of my colleagues from Ulster the pride and admiration with which we have learnt of the unparalleled acts of heroism and bravery which were carried out by the Ulster Division in the great offensive movement on 1 and 2 July. From all accounts we have received, they have made the supreme sacrifice for the Empire, of which they were so proud, with a courage, coolness and determination, in the face of the most trying difficulties, which have upheld the greatest traditions of the British Army. Our feelings are, of course, mingled with sadness at the loss of so many men who were to us personal friends and comrades, but we believe that the spirit of their race will at a time of such grief and anxiety sustain those who mourn their loss, and set an example to others to follow in their footsteps.'[4]

On 3 July, a distinguished English Staff Officer writing at the front to Lt. Col. Frederick Crawford told *The Times* that

> 'the Ulster Division has been through an ordeal by fire, gas and poison. It has behaved marvellously and got through all the German lines. Our gallant fellows

---

4.   *The Times*, 3 July 1916 - The Glory of Ulster, Message to the Ulster People

marched into a valley of death, shouting "No Surrender" and "Remember the Boyne". He said he wished he had been born an Ulsterman, but was proud to have been associated with the most gallant men in the world. Many a family will have lost a son or a father out there. I do not believe men ever passed to another world in so glorious a light. After the day before yesterday I hope I may be allowed the rest of my life to maintain my association with the Ulster Province'[5]

Many of Crawford's friends lost family and close relatives in the slaughter and he was intensely aware of the sacrifices of Belfast people of all denominations and both himself and Margaret worked tirelessly for bereaved families. When Crawford received his Knighthood in 1915 for his war work he often remarked that those who should really be honoured were the wounded and fallen of that conflict.

Crawford was particularly distressed by the news of Sir Daniel Dixon's son Major Daniel who was killed in France on 1 July. Other brave men that the McCullaghs knew from well-known families included Lieutenant Dermot Neill, son of Sharman D. Neill (Jewellers) of Donegall Place. Dermot was 29 years old and had been a Director in his father's firm for some years. He was a keen member of the Ulster Volunteer Force and was one of the first to join the 13th Royal Irish Rifles (1st County Down Volunteers) when it was formed. Afterwards he was transferred to the Machine Gun Corps. He was a great sportsman and sailor. What made this tragedy even more poignant was the death of his younger brother who served with 5th Royal Irish Rifles (Royal South Downs) and had been killed in action a year earlier on 9th May 1915 at Fromelles in France. In the small village of Helen's Bay the death of Jerome Lennie Walker on 6 May 1916 was received with much sadness. His death was reported in the local newspaper under the headline, 'Helen's Bay Lieutenant killed' and the report carried details of Jerome's experiences. They had escaped from Belgium where Jerome's father Franklin Walker directed the company of Reilly and Walker Flax Merchants. The family had been well-known by the McCullaghs when they lived in Helen's Bay.

---

5.   *The Times*, Monday 3 July 1916 - Staff Officers Tribute

Yet another young man cut down in his prime on Tuesday 24 October 1916 was Captain Leslie Porter. Recognised as one of the most skilful motorists in Ireland he was a prominent figure in motoring circles. He founded the 'Northern Motor Company' in 1899 and later set up his own firm 'Leslie Porter Ltd, Automobile Engineers and Agents'. He drove a Wolseley car in the 1903 Paris to Madrid motor race and in 1908 he came fourth in the Tourist Trophy race in the Isle of Man. He was a great airman and member of the Royal Flying Corps and he could often be seen looping the loop between Holywood and Bangor. He married a daughter of George Herbert Brown of 'Tordeevra' in Helen's Bay. The *News Letter* reported 'the death of Captain Porter adds another name to the roll of heroic young Ulstermen who have made the supreme sacrifice whilst serving in the Royal Flying Corps'[6]

Crawford was also saddened to hear of the death of Lord Basil Blackwood on 4 July 1917. He was the third son of the First Marquess of Blackwood and Ava of Clandeboye Estate, Clandeboye. Lord Basil was private secretary to Lord Wimborne at the time Crawford received his Baronetcy.

The 5 Minute Silence

At the beginning of 1916 Crawford had been unanimously elected Lord Mayor for a third term. Taking on responsibility for the people of Ulster, he saw it as his duty to the bereaved citizens of Belfast to do something significant to honour Ulster's soldiers. A decision was made by the Grand Lodge of Ireland and the Orange Institution to cancel the 12 July celebrations. In his appeal to the citizens and Orangemen of Belfast he said:-

> "These times are exceptional, and nothing great can be accomplished apart from self-sacrifice. The men of Ulster have responded nobly to their country's call and it is up to those who remain behind to strengthen their hands. There is hardly a home in the province that has not experienced the loss of a member who had fallen in the fighting line, and in these solemn days it is therefore a fitting thing

6.   *The Belfast Book of Honour*, p.534

that we should be hushed and sober. In the presence of the tremendous issues with which the country is faced, silence is golden."

On 12 July 1916, the anniversary of the Battle of the Boyne, the Lord Mayor requested that all businesses be suspended for the duration of five minutes, from noon till 12.05pm. The request was not to be confined to employers and employees in the industrial, mercantile and commercial concerns, but applied to the citizens in general, who were asked to discontinue their household duties for the period stipulated. He asked that street traffic be at a complete standstill for five minutes, so that the city's tribute to the heroes of the Ulster Division would thus be impressive and universal. It was also suggested that both business and private house blinds should be drawn for the same five minutes. Trains stopped in their tracks the city's trams came to a halt and the Police Courts were adjourned. As men and women on factory floors, in hospitals, in shops and in homes all over Ulster bowed their heads in respect of the men of the 36th Ulster Division who had fallen at Thiepval, silence echoed through the streets of Belfast as the usually bustling city came to a complete standstill.

Many men from Northern Ireland who were on active service in the Great War and survived the experience came home suffering from serious physical and, or mental infirmities. For many of the survivors, gas poisoning, lost limbs, lost fingers and toes from frostbite, the effects of malaria and other tropical diseases, shell shock, blindness, deafness and nightmarish memories made working impossible and severely curtailed their quality of life after the cessation of hostilities. These men were living memorials to the sacrifice made by those who died. Some survivors died prematurely from causes attributable to service and other survivors spent the remainder of the their lives in institutions then called 'lunatic asylums'[7]

Many homes across the province were turned into hospitals and care homes for the wounded soldiers returning from the Front. The McLaughlins were a well known family who lived and worshipped in

---

7.   Barry Niblock, *Remembering Their Sacrifice in the Great War*

Whiteabbey. William McLaughlin was a partner in McLaughlin and Harvey one of the most successful and established building companies in Belfast. Their most famous commission was the building of the new City Hall, opened in 1906. The McLaughlin's lived in a house called Macedon situated in the neighbouring district of Whitehouse. When War was declared the they offered a portion of their home for the convalescence of wounded soldiers and had it equipped with skilled medical and nursing attendants. Tragically, they too suffered the tragic loss of their son, who was killed while serving at the Front. Colonel James Craig and his wife donated their residence 'Craigavon' to the Neurasthenia Hospital.

Mount Stewart the estate belonging to Lord and Lady Londonderry on the shores of Strangford Lough was taken over by the Red Cross in WWI and used as an Auxilliary hospital. Further research reveals attic rooms connected to the estate's house were used as a convalescent ward during both the First and Second World Wars. During the difficult period immediately after demobilisation, when returning servicemen flooded the labour market, Ulster landlords were asked to employ as many as possible. Twenty ex-servicemen were assigned to Mount Stewart where they helped level and clear the site of what is now the Italian Garden that stretches along the south front of the house. During WWII the house was requisitioned by a Royal Engineers Bridging Company, whose job was to tarmac Newtownards Airport runway. Recent work on the Mount Stewart estate, now owned by the National Trust has revealed carvings made by Royal Air force airmen dated 1940 and is thought to have been made by soldiers based at the estate during the Second World War. The inscription humorously reads: 'Victory Hours R.A.F'[8]

The Duchess of Abercorn established the Ulster Volunteer Hospital in Pan, France, at the beginning of the War. The initial forty beds were later increased to one hundred and the hospital moved to Lyons. French soldiers, as well as those wounded at Verdun were

---

8.   Rachel Martin, *Newtownards Chronicle* February 2016

treated there. The hospital was serviced by volunteers from Belfast. The Belfast Boy Scouts raised £600 in a bottle drive to build a recreation hut at the Front. It was set up by the YWCA and then called the Belfast Boy Scout Hut. Baden-Powell accepted the hut in May 1916 and said it would be returned to Belfast when the war ended. [see appendix 4]

Unionist and Nationalist Politics

Ireland in 1916 was a hotbed of political activity both North and South. Although the question of Home Rule was supposed to have been put on hold for the duration of the War, circumstances occurred which prompted the Irish Question to be thrust to the forefront of politics.

John Redmond, after a split in the movement, committed the Irish National Volunteers to fight for King and Country. Initially Nationalists were as enthusiastic as Unionists to join up. However the delay in granting Home Rule caused problems within the Irish Parliamentary Party and diminished the standing John Redmond had built up with the nationalist population.

The common cause which the war had given both Unionists and Nationalists began to unravel on the Nationalist side by 1915 with casualty lists growing and no appreciable advance on the Home Rule issue. In Dublin on Easter Sunday, 23 April 1916, an insurrection broke out led by the Irish Republican Brotherhood, a small underground revolutionary group under Patrick Pearse. This force was strongly separatist in outlook and being mainly Sinn Feiners, were imbued with a deep dislike of constitutional ways, and were unsympathetic towards John Redmond and the Irish Parliamentary Party.

The small IRB group in control of volunteers thought they could now be led in rebellion and the leaders signed a Proclamation declaring themselves to be the 'Provisional Government of the Irish Republic' and took over key Dublin buildings. For five days the Irish capital was in turmoil until the insurgents were subdued and arrested. Throughout the struggle for Home Rule, the Irish Volunteers had been aided by an Irish American organisation called Clan na Gael who provided money and arms. The expected weaponry from Germany, however, had been intercepted, leaving the insurrection with little prospect of success. In the week of the rebellion the lives of four hundred and fifty people were lost, while the number of those wounded reached over two thousand. The centre of Dublin had been severely damaged with over £2,000,000 worth of property destroyed. After the rebellion the majority of the military leaders were shot by firing squad. Only Eamon de Valera and Countess Constance Markievicz were spared.

The 16 executions that followed the insurrection profoundly affected Irish and Irish American opinion. The United States had great sympathy with Nationalists and their fight for independence. Moreover, the majority of southern nationalists, who had been indifferent during the Rising, were appalled by the long and protracted manner in which the executions were carried out. Subsequently, opinion radicalised as the leaders became martyrs for the cause. The Government now found themselves in the position of having to placate American opinion in order to persuade President Wilson to bring his country into the War on the Allied side. The British Cabinet immediately sent the British Prime Minister Herbert Asquith to Dublin and Belfast to consult the civil and military authorities.

According to correspondence in the Public Record Office, Sir Crawford had received a letter from Prime Minister Asquith prior to his visit to Belfast on 15 May 1916. The letter is dated 8 May 1916 and relates to the proposal that all arms in Ireland should be surrendered to the Crown. In replying Sir Crawford wrote that he deplored the suggestion, as he felt that any such proclamation would be looked upon by the population of Belfast and Ulster as a punishment for the offence of the Sinn Feiners in Dublin with whom they had no connection. He wrote:-

'So far as the safety of the country is concerned there is no necessity for anything of the kind and I sincerely trust that in the steps taken to put down the rebellion nothing will be done which would interfere with or reflect in any way upon the loyalty of those who stand for the King and constitution … I am writing from the point of view of the peace and stability of the city and the district, and I feel satisfied that the peace which now exists will not be helped forward by an interference with the peaceable and law abiding subjects such as is rumoured'[9]

A few days later on 15 May, Asquith returned to Belfast and spent four hours in the city chambers with the Lord Mayor. Sir Crawford then issued this press release:-

'Mr. Asquith, accompanied by his private secretary, Mr. Bonham Carter, arrived from Dublin by motorcar this afternoon. He was entertained to lunch by the Lord Mayor in the Parlour of City Hall, and met, at his (the Prime Minister's) request a few citizens, with whom he had a full and frank discussion as to the present state of affairs. He returned to London this afternoon, accompanied by his secretary'.

The Times commenting on the visit, said:

'Never before had a Prime Minister of England visited Belfast while in office, let alone a man who had engineered placing the Home Rule Bill on the statute-book, however, the general feeling was one of calm and quiet confidence in the strength and determination of Ulster, and a hearty contempt for the hopeless journalistic ignorance which suggested that any individual statesman, in the course of a flying visit, could weaken or alter the fixed conviction of the Unionists of the North'.

When Asquith returned to London he announced that the Government had asked Lloyd George to negotiate a settlement with the Irish leaders, although the rising of 1916 and general war weariness was making the offer of Home Rule inadequate to the wishes of most Nationalists.

Business As Usual

In November 1916 Crawford was once again proposed for Lord Mayor but the *Northern Whig* reported that:

'The Lord Mayor on his own behalf and on behalf of the Lady Mayoress expressed warm appreciation of the proposed honour but added that as he was strongly of the opinion that the honour of Mayoralty should go round the Council,

---

9.   PRONI D1507/A/16/8

he preferred in the circumstances that some other member should have the opportunity of filling the chair rather than accept office himself for a third period'.

These words were sufficient then to facilitate the election of his friend Councillor James Johnston as Lord Mayor in 1917.

In truth one of the reasons for his stepping down was the decline in his wife's health. Margaret had stomach problems, possibly brought on by lengthy banquets and tight fitting gowns. While Crawford's main concern now was his business interests he tried to spend as much time as possible with his wife and they took frequent trips to Europe to take the waters at Baden Baden in Germany which had wonderful spa treatments.

Although Crawford had continued to perform the many responsibilities that were called upon him as Lord Mayor during those difficult years of the war, he did not neglect his business in Castle Place. In May 1916, he bought Castle Market (formerly Montgomery's Market) and Castle Lane. He had to wait to build on this site due to a shortage of steel in war-time. The press at the time stated that 'as one of the largest businesses in Belfast, it was in his interest to ensure a well run city'.

An article, mourning the passing of Montgomery's Market concerning the purchase and conversion of Castle Market appeared in the *Belfast Telegraph* titled 'The Passing of Castle Place'.

'Not only will the market disappear but the cobble foot path and Castle Lane, the Irish Temperance League Café, grain, furniture and fruit dealers, restaurants, Mr. Dargan's bookshop, Mr. Rannigan's Hairdressing house and the lock-up shops of the market property. Thus with the forthcoming development of Castle Place will vanish a very interesting part of old Belfast.'[10]

In his business, as in City Hall, Crawford always had a loyal and hard working team of men and women who dealt with his busy schedule. Major May, his secretary in City Hall, attended to his mail and diary engagements which were at that time exceedingly comprehensive. Presiding over the deliberations of the Council were not only ardu-

10. *Belfast New Letter* - May 1916

ous and tiring but frequently protracted. The meetings starting at 12 o'clock noon, often not finishing until 8.45 p.m. and then adjourning until the following day, when they sat from 3 p.m. until 6 p.m. There were two special meetings later in the month – on the 10th and 19th respectively. If an Alderman wanted to speak, his name was put down on a sheet of paper, and he was allowed to speak in his proper turn.

Shortly after Crawford vacated his office on 23 January 1917, his successor Alderman Sir James Johnston convened a public meeting in the City Hall of the citizens of Belfast at which a resolution was cordially adopted placing on record "the citizens warmest appreciation of the admirable and valuable services rendered to the city and the Empire by Sir Crawford and Lady McCullagh". It was proposed that Sir Crawford would be presented with his portrait in oils for the City Hall and further portraits of himself and Lady McCullagh as personal gifts for their home. The resolution proved exceedingly popular and in a very short time a sum of almost twelve hundred pounds was subscribed. At a subsequent meeting commissions were entrusted to Mrs. Ernest Normand (Henrietta Rae – the portrait painter) for a full-length portrait of Lady McCullagh; to Mr. James S. Sleator, A.R.H.A., for a full length portrait of Sir Crawford McCullagh for the City Hall; and Mr. W. G. Mackenzie for a full-length portrait of Sir Crawford for his residence Lismara. The presentation of the portraits was held in the City Hall with Lord Mayor Sir James Johnston presiding.

In accepting his decision to retire at the beginning of 1917, generous tributes were paid to his services by the Council in general. Further as a token of the gratitude of the citizens of Belfast it was unanimously agreed that:

'The smallest compliment the city can pay our respected Lord Mayor – as some slight mark of the general appreciation of his manifold services – is that the roll of Honorary Burgesses be extended by the inclusion of the names of Sir Crawford and Lady McCullagh.

In thus seeking to honour our civic heads Belfast would be but honouring itself, and there will be but one opinion, that no compliment was ever more deservedly earned.'

Elected Honorary Burgesses of Belfast

The Roll of Honorary Burgesses is one of the most precious of the City's records, registering the signatures of forty-seven men and women who have given distinguished service to Ulster's capital and province, or have distinguished themselves abroad. The Book of Belfast is bound in red and each page is an artistic masterpiece with beautiful lettering and colouring executed by local artists. The name of each Burgess appears at the top and underneath is recorded the service for which the honour was bestowed. Viscount Pirrie is the first entrant and the list includes the Marquis of Londonderry, the first Marchioness of Dufferin and Ava, Sir James Henderson, a former Lord Mayor of Belfast, the ninth Earl of Shaftesbury, Sir John Lavery and six Field Marshalls. Sir Edward Carson had been nominated, as a Burgess of Belfast, by Sir Crawford and confirmed by the City Council on 4 August 1914, 'for his unswerving devotion to Ulster'; however, due to the sudden outbreak of war he was not honoured until 1917. Sir Edward was then a Cabinet Minister and First Lord of the Admiralty. He considered Ulster his 'spiritual home' and strongly endorsed and supported the aspirations of the Unionists. Sir Edward and Lady Carson stayed with Crawford and Margaret at Lismara during their visit from England and the McCullaghs held a huge garden party and other social events in honour of their visit. Other Honorary Burgesses included Mr. Henry Musgrave, D.L. of Drumglass House, Malone Road, associated with Queen's University and the Royal Victoria Hospital, and Sir William Quartus Ewart, of Glenmachan a well known linen merchant and Knight of the Order of St. John of Jerusalem in England. Both were confirmed as they had 'given great impetus to outstanding industries and added to the name, fame and progress of the city'.

Sir Crawford and Lady McCullagh were both honoured, singly, for their civic, philanthropic, and war efforts. Each recipient received a casket containing the certificates conferring the Freedom of Belfast. The casket for Sir Crawford McCullagh bears his crest on the front, in enamel painting, with the motto 'Vi est animo', also in enamel. Beside this is a view of the City Hall, and, on the other side a view of his residence 'Lismara'. Other special incidents are also recorded in enamel – 'The march past the Ulster Division 1915' and 'the conferring of Knighthood on Councillor Crawford McCullagh by his Excellency the Lord Lieutenant, 1915'. The badge of Ulster and the Union Jack appear at the ends of the box; containing the inscription 'This casket contains the certificate of the election and admission of Councillor Sir Crawford McCullagh, J.P. Lord Mayor of Belfast, 1914-1916, as an Honorary Burgess of the city and County Borough of Belfast'.

The casket for Lady Margaret McCullagh has in front, the monogram 'M.C.M'C in varying enamel colours with views of the City Hall and Lismara. On the other side there are two very interesting plaques. One is a copy of the Badges of Queen Mary's Needlework Guild and the other is a 'Red Cross' showing a wounded soldier and sailor, indicating Lady McCullagh's great involvement with the war effort. The inscription on the casket reads: 'This casket contains the certificate of the election and admission of Lady Margaret Craig McCullagh (Lady Mayoress of Belfast 1914-1916) as an honorary burgess of the city and county borough of Belfast'. In responding for both his wife and himself, Sir Crawford McCullagh said, "…these beautiful caskets will be treasured by both of us and we shall hand them down as cherished heirlooms. They will remind us of happy and busy days associated with the mayoralty of the city and as a token of the regard and good wishes of the city"[11]. The caskets were donated to the people of Belfast by the family and now reside in City Hall.

---

11. *Belfast Evening Telegraph*, Friday 20 July 1917

Although Crawford's role as Lord Mayor and Belfast's Chief Magistrate, terminated in January 1917 after three years, he did not give up his commitment to the community. Together with Lady McCullagh he strenuously and enthusiastically continued in every way possible to ensure the welfare of the Empire and her fighting forces. Nor were his municipal activities relaxed as he was still a councillor. Elected as such in 1906, he was now a senior member of the City Fathers and remained on City Council for 40 years, seventeen of which he was to serve as Lord Mayor – proof of the remarkable regard in which he was held by his fellow citizens.

Chapter Ten
1918-1919

End of War

---

*Five great intellectual professions have existed in every
civilised nation; The merchants to provide for it; the
soldiers to defend it; the pastors to teach it; the physicians
to keep it in health; the lawyers to enforce justice in it;
and the duty of all these men is, on occasion to die for it.*

Ruskin

The Irish Convention

Although officially retired as Lord Mayor, Crawford still continued to play an active role in municipal activities and it came as no surprise to Lady McCullagh when her husband received a letter from the British Prime Minister, David Lloyd George requesting his attendance at a conference in Dublin.

Dear Sir Crawford McCullagh,

I have the honour to invite you to be a member of the Irish Convention.

The terms of reference to the Convention are set forth in the following passage from a letter on the subject which we recently addressed to the leaders of the principal Irish Parties in the House of Commons:

"Would it be too much to hope that Irishmen of all creeds and parties might meet together in a Convention for the purpose of drafting a Constitution for their country which would secure a just balance of all the opposing interests, and finally compose the unhappy discords which would have distracted Ireland and impeded its harmonious development?

I further referred to this matter in the House of Commons in these words:-

"The Government therefore, propose to summon immediately on behalf of the Crown a convention of representative Irishmen in Ireland, to submit to the British Government a Constitution for the future government of Ireland within the Empire".

I trust it will be possible for you to accept this invitation to take part in a work of the highest National importance. It has been arranged that the first meeting of the convention will take place in Dublin on the 25 July, and I shall be very much obliged if you would kindly let me have an early reply to this letter.

Yours sincerely, David Lloyd George

In December 1916 a second coalition Government had been formed with Lloyd George as Prime Minister and throughout the winter of 1916 to 1917 there had been discussions within the British Cabinet on how to resolve the Irish Question. On 16 May 1917 Lloyd George offered the Nationalist Leader John Redmond the enactment of Home Rule for the twenty-six southern counties. Three electoral by-election wins by Sinn Féin alarmed both the Irish Party and the British government. Therefore four days after the death of Redmond's brother Major Willie Redmond on the war front, Lloyd George proposed to call a Convention of all Irish Parties and interests which Redmond agreed to, hoping it might yet produce a deal which would secure the future of constitutional nationalism. Lloyd George for his part was trying to appease both American opinion and gain both theirs and Irish support in the war.

Although Crawford found himself and the other delegates to the Irish Convention regularly travelling to meetings in Belfast, Dublin and Cork it did however, give him an opportunity to see his daughters Helen and Daisy who were attending Alexandra College in Dublin. The Russell and Shelbourne Hotels accommodated many of the delegates on their visits to Dublin. Entertainments and hospitality were part of the life of Dublin society which developed around the convention and it was hoped this would break down the isolation of the Irish political groups. When the convention met in Belfast delegates were similarly invited by Lord Londonderry to Mount Stewart his estate near Greyabbey.

The Convention comprising around 100 delegates had its first meeting at Trinity College, Dublin on 25 July 1917 under the chairmanship of Sir Horace Plunkett. The meetings lasted until 5 April 1918 and consisted of individuals from wide-ranging backgrounds including Bishops, business and professional men, university dons, politicians, land-owners, Lord Mayors and aristocrats. The Ulster Unionists were represented at the Convention by Hugh Thomas Barrie MP for Londonderry, who acted as their Chairman. Also Lord Londonderry, acting as both Lord Lieutenant of Down and secretary of the Ulster Unionist Delegation. The aim was to address the 'Irish Question' and other constitutional problems relating to an early enactment of self-government for Ireland. Also to debate its wider future and come to an understanding on recommendations as to the best manner and means this could be achieved.

A letter written by Sir Edward Carson to a distinguished member of the Unionist Council shows the Ulster frame of mind. The letter headed 'confidential', and dated 18 May 1917 contains the following:-

'The functions of the Ulster representatives in the Convention may be stated as follows:-

(1) To secure a position for Ulster which shall be compatible with the principles for which we stand.

(2) To secure the acceptance by the other side as ample safeguards as possible for the Unionist minority under the Irish Parliament.

(3) In view of the fact that the principle of Home Rule for Ireland has now become the law of the land to endeavour, if they think fit, to secure that the form of Home Rule which is to be put into operation shall be the best possible in the interests of Ireland and of Great Britain, and free from the many defects of the Home Rule Act of 1914, apart from the obnoxious principle of that Act which is beyond recall.[1]

---

1.   Henry Maxwell, *Ulster Was Right*, p.193

The conference opened with the delegations outlining their positions. Lord Londonderry spoke first for the Ulster Unionist Council, stating that they had come to the convention in 'friendliness' and with an 'open mind' to reach 'some general kind of agreement of what is the best for the government of this country'. He took pains to explain how Ulster Unionists believed that their economic prosperity was attributable to the union and the empire, and how they viewed the British Isles as a common unity, and not as a colonizer and colonized.[2]

Other delegates spoke for the Ulster Unionists at the opening meeting and again stressed economic arguments against Home Rule. Although the debates were largely concerned with finance, many other matters were discussed including completion of land purchase, housing, transport and the war effort. The Convention also laboured under long internal wrangles, which resulted in electing committees, sub-committees, reports, interim reports and minority reports. By late 1917 the issue of an All-Ireland Parliament brought clashes between unionists and nationalists. These were no longer over partition but rather over taxing powers and defending a customs union. Matters eventually came to a head over the question of fiscal autonomy when a clause in one of the reports was submitted by the Roman Catholic Bishop of Raphoe, the Reverend O'Donnell. This clause giving Ireland the powers of a Dominion included the right to control Customs and Excise and this caused widespread anger amongst the unionists. This proposal struck at the very root of Belfast's existence and prosperity as a southern majority formed from a largely rural electorate would dictate to the profit making minority in the industrial north. Belfast depended on its wide and varied export trade and as the only industrial community in Ireland had unions with headquarters in Britain so permitting free flow of labour. This interchange and uniformity of law was essential to Ulster's industrial

2. N.C. Fleming, *The Marquis of Londonderry: Aristocracy, Power and Politics in Britain and Ireland*, p.53

life and was why Ulster was opposed to their inclusion in the policy of an all Ireland system.

As a delegate representing his fellow Ulster businessmen, Sir Crawford addressed the conference insisting a common system of finance with one Exchequer was a fundamental essential both for Ireland and for Great Britain. Moreover, he stated "It is only by full community with the economic life of the great industrial people with whom we have so much in common – and from whom we refuse to be divorced – that the development of our resources can be best furthered".

The Convention dragged on until the spring of 1918 with little satisfactory outcome. Lord Londonderry had to leave the Convention at this time due to ill health, allegedly a victim of the notorious Spanish influenza epidemic. John Redmond who had been ill for a good part of the Convention's proceedings died at a London nursing home on 6 March. His place was now taken over by John Dillon, the new leader of the Irish Parliamentary Party, who was less consensual than John Redmond and more sympathetic to the aspirations of Sinn Féin.

At the same time the situation on the Western Front deteriorated dramatically eliminating any hopes of an agreement. The German offensive of 21 March threatened to over-run the Allied armies and there developed a manpower crisis which forced the cabinet on 28 March to extend the spectre of conscription to Ireland. At the same time the final Convention report, previously agreed on 5 March by forty-four votes to twenty-nine, arrived in Downing Street. Its key recommendation called for either Home Rule with a federal United Kingdom or Dominion status within the Empire. The Cabinet ministers grasped the opportunity to make a totally illogical decision, drafting and agreeing on 5 April a 'dual policy' of conscription and devolution. It signalled the death knell of a political era. With it the strategy of Irish political constitutionalism was killed by being connected to the military draft. The War, its duration, the suspension of the Home Rule Act and particularly the conscription crisis drastically increased support for Sinn Féin, with the numbers of people joining its branches rising rapidly. For the Unionists, the War confirmed all their pre-war suspicions that the Irish Nationalist could not be trusted, contrasting the Easter Rising with the Battle of the Somme, the conscription crisis providing a watershed for Ulster Unionists to withdraw securely into their northern citadel.

The Spanish Flu

When Crawford came home to Lismara after the Convention, the Spanish flu pandemic had circled the globe. The source of the pandemic is still disputed but undoubtedly The Great War, with mass movements of men in armies and aboard ships aided in its spread and outbreaks occurred in North America, Europe, Asia, Africa, India, Brazil and the South Pacific.

In most influenza outbreaks it is juveniles, the elderly, or already weakened patients who are most at risk. However the 1918 pandemic predominantly killed previously healthy young adults. Researchers believe that infection by the particular strain of virus which caused Spanish flu set off an overreaction of the body's immune system known as a cytokine storm. The bodies of young adults with strong immune systems were quickly ravaged by this reaction often leading to death whereas the weaker immune systems of children and older adults gave them a greater chance of survival.

The severity of the infection was such that by the end of 1919 the Pandemic had killed somewhere between fifty and one hundred million people across the world. It has been cited as the most devastating epidemic in recorded world history. More people died of influenza in a single year than in four years of the Black Death/ Bubonic Plague from 1347 to 1351.

By the summer of 1918 this horrific virus had found its way into Belfast and was affecting homes all over Ulster. At first people thought that they were dealing with a common cold, but it soon became clear when symptoms became virulent that the infection was deadly. Schools and public libraries were closed for a time and many people, especially those that could afford to, stayed at home or went abroad in the hope that they might escape the deadly infection. Picture houses and theatres stayed open. Although a breeding ground for germs, they were sprayed with a mixture of Phenol and Lavender to keep them germ free.[3]

Armistice – November 1918

The viral infection was still raging across the province when news of the Armistice reached Lismara. The barracks at Enniskillen in County Fermanagh had picked up a faint radio message at 6.30am and the military troops there spread the news by launching rockets and shouting the news in the streets up and down the town. The McCullaghs celebrated with their friends and neighbours after attending a church service in the village of Whiteabbey, and in Belfast the ending of the War was proclaimed with the sounding of ships' sirens and the firing of fog detonators at the railway stations across the city. The Irish News reported people pouring out of the mills, city-centre stores and workshops, producing 'a display of enthusiasm, amounting almost to emotionalism, on the part of the public such as has never been witnessed in this city'.

Crawford made sure he was at Castle Buildings before noon and very wisely, gave his staff the afternoon off. He closed the store to prevent looting but his faithful manager Mr. Hogg refused to leave the store declaring that he would stay behind so that he could call the police in case any trouble did arise. Mill girls swept down the Falls Road 'to the accompaniment of lively choruses while Irish Flags of green and gold mingled with the Stars and Stripes and flags of the Allies'. Trams were forced to a halt as women streamed onto the streets to link arms with soldiers from the Victoria Barracks, and someone upended a pony cart that was carrying a load of kindling and started a bonfire in the middle of Royal Avenue. After raiding several shops, some

---

3. Jonathan Bardon, *A History of Ulster*, p.460

shipwrights broke into the Panoptican Cinema around 1pm and according to the *Irish News*:

> They proceeded to wreck everything they could get their hands on. Pictures were smashed; several arc lamps were shattered, scores of seats were pulled up from the floors and thrown through the windows on to the street. Gas brackets were torn from the walls, so that the gas was allowed to escape in great volume.[4]

In Castle Place people played a game of ring o'roses, while bands of all descriptions, many accompanied by torchlights, added to the general din. Great crowds gathered around the City Hall, singing, shouting and throwing ribbons and bunting around the statue of Queen Victoria. It was well after midnight when the manager of Castle Buildings finally got home to his family. After witnessing an afternoon and evening of rioting and revelling he was able to tell Crawford the next day that thankfully there had been no damage to the shop. In his memoirs Crawford recalled giving his manager the day off and told him to take his wife to the pictures, not knowing that the Panoptican Cinema in High Street not far from Castle Buildings had been completely vandalised.

Patriotism comes with a price on its head, and all over Ulster, families still grieving over the loss of so many loved ones were very much aware of the voluntary contribution that their men had made in support of the war effort. The Ulster Division alone won nine Victoria Crosses in addition to seventy-one Distinguished Service Orders, four hundred and fifty-nine Military Crosses, one hundred and seventy-three Distinguished Conduct Medals, one thousand two hundred and ninety-four Military Medals, one hundred and eighteen Meritorious Service Medals, to say nothing of the foreign decorations awarded to the Division and numbers specially mentioned in dispatches. With the War in Europe now effectively over, the people of Ulster wanted peace and a quiet time to reflect on their losses so recently inflicted on their families. The *Belfast Telegraph* reminded its readers,

---

4.   Jonathan Bardon p.461

'it would be ungenerous not to think of... the greater army which mourns at home, wives for husbands and mothers for sons who are today beneath the sod in France, and Flanders. For those lonely ones, the gladness of this hour is chastened by the thought of the vacant chair'.[5]

In March 1919 Margaret McCullagh received her C.B.E., (Commander of the Order of the British Empire) from Lord-Lieutenant French of Vimy on Behalf of King George V for her unswerving duty and contribution to the war effort. Crawford held a grand party at Lismara in her honour, inviting close friends, neighbours and colleagues who had actively supported his wife in her endeavours. It was a decoration she richly deserved. As Lady Mayoress she had supported her husband and her country through difficult times and as a result her health and demeanour would suffer considerably in the coming years.

The signing of the Peace Treaty, (Treaty of Versailles) took place in London in July 1919. There were numerous celebrations including a river pageant, a day of thanksgiving and the lighting of bonfires nationwide. Ulster had two Peace Day celebrations, one on the Twelfth of July which commemorated the Battle of the Boyne and the First World War and the other on the 9 August 1919.

The Twelfth of July celebrations in 1919 were reflective of the atmosphere that the War had helped to generate among Ulster Unionists. New arches were erected, covered in images of gallant Ulstermen fighting for the Empire and angelic nurses ministering to the wounded, and inviting the people to 'Remember our fallen heroes of the 36th Ulster Division'. Banners portraying the stoical men and women of the 1689 siege of Derry were carried alongside contemporary banners depicting the new heroes of Ulster, the men who had given their lives for the cause of the empire.

Significantly Nationalist Veterans of World War I took little part in these Peace Day celebrations as for them the war's end brought only the prospect of partition. To those who had volunteered to achieve

---

5. Jonathan Bardon p.461

an all Ireland Home Rule their sacrifices and heroism now rang hollow. After the Peace Day celebrations the people of Belfast went back to their homes. The way they had lived their lives before the war had been irrevocably changed. It was seen in all households across the Province and not just Ireland but world-wide.

There was now a new world order in which familiar boundaries had been removed and replaced with something strange and unfamiliar. The next decade especially for women, would bring radical changes in the home and in the work place. Women had done much to keep things going while the men had been away, working in factories; as bus conductors, working on the land and keeping the country fed as well as nursing the sick. Many girls born into domestic service were now finding that they were given a wider choice of options and, for these women nothing was ever going to be the same again.

Chapter Eleven
1919-1922

The Troubles

The Troubles came; by 1922 we knew of and accepted violence in the small streets at hand.
With curfew tense, each evening when that quiet hour was due, I never ventured far from where I knew I could reach home in safety.
At the door I'd sometimes stand, till with oncoming roar, the wire-cage Crossley tenders swept into view.

John Hewitt - Kites in Spring.

Ulster was now thriving in the aftermath of the war. Ships that had been destroyed in the conflict had to be replaced but although long hours and the suspension of normal trade union rights were tolerated during the war, when the hostilities in Europe ended the skilled workers, recalling promises made in the war years, demanded a reduction in their working hours from 54 hours a week to 44. In early January engineers in the shipyard, the gasworks and electricity station went on strike. Thousands of workers were involved in the strike and on 25 January 1919 going on the rampage in Belfast they smashed the windows of shops. There was an element of cross community support for the strike. Charlie McKay, a prominent strike leader was a Catholic.

Department stores remained closed and Crawford ordered all his employees to go home until the strike was over. Thousands of linen workers found they couldn't go to their factories. There were no trams or streetlights, and many homes found themselves without lighting and cooking facilities. Picture houses closed their doors, the shipyards and the Belfast Ropeworks had their gates barred, and by the end of the first week simple provisions like bread, milk and coal were in short supply.

The influence of revolutionary socialists in Germany and Italy were initially blamed for the action, then local moderates feared that the strike represented the rising of the workers against the capitalist system. In fact the strikers were mostly workers who had no interest in socialism per se; they simply wanted better working conditions. The Lord Mayor Sir James Johnston and councillors including Crawford held a meeting in City Hall at the end of January which resulted in troops being called from Dublin and on 14 February soldiers took over the gasworks and the electricity station and the strike quickly collapsed.

The strike greatly alarmed the ruling classes of Belfast but not as much as the prospect of an all-Ireland parliament separate from imperial control.

Local Municipal Politics

On the 14 December 1918, just a month after the armistice had ended the fighting in World War I, a general election was held in Britain and Ireland. The election, also known as the Khaki Election due to the immediate post-war setting, was won by a coalition of the Conservatives under Andrew Bonar Law, most of the Liberals under David Lloyd George, and a few independent and former Labour MPs, and produced a government which retained Lloyd George as Prime Minister. It was the first to be held after the Representation of the People Act 1918, which meant it was the first United Kingdom general election in which nearly all adult men could vote. This increased the Irish electorate from around 700,000 to about two million. All men over 21 and military servicemen over 19 gained a vote in parliamentary elections without property qualifications. Significantly on 6th February a Bill granting limited female suffrage passed its second reading and six million women in Great Britain over the age of 30 who were householders, the wives of householders, occupiers of property with an annual rent of £5, or graduates of British universities were now on the electoral register for the first time.

The election of December 1918 had resulted in a complete polarisation of the Irish representation with the overwhelming defeat of the Irish Parliamentary Party (IPP) which had dominated the Irish Political landscape since the 1880's, and a landslide victory for the radical Sinn Féin Party led by Eamon de Valera who was still held in an English prison. The Ulster Unionist representation had 26 seats and a few survivors of the Irish National Party under John Dillon took only 6.

On the 11 March 1919 the British Government formally introduced in the Commons a Bill entitled the Local Government (Ireland) Act. This provided that the Irish Local Government Board be required by order to divide the boroughs into wards containing not less than six members apiece and equal in population. However, borough councils were enabled within three months of the passing of the Act to submit schemes of their own for the approval of the local Government Board. In spite of the turmoil which gripped the whole of Ireland during the year, only three of the six county borough councils and five borough councils subject to the order failed to submit a scheme within the subscribed time.

Belfast Corporation submitted a scheme dividing the city into nine wards, co-extensive with the nine parliamentary divisions established by the Representation of the Peoples Act, 1918. The Act also repealed the provisions of the Municipal Corporations (Ireland) Act 1840, prescribing that one half of the Aldermen should go out of office every third year and one third of the councillors annually. Henceforth aldermen and councillors would serve for an equal term (three years) and the aldermen would be those candidates who were first elected in every ward. The campaign in Belfast did not get under way until January 1920 when 147 candidates were nominated for the 60 seats.

Polling day was on 15 January and out of 135,548 voters on the register, 89,031 polled, a turnout of 65.7 per cent, well above the norm for local elections.

The results produced a council more balanced politically and socially than before or since. A Unionist councillor was returned for the Falls Ward (together with two Sinn Féin, two Nationalist and one Labour), a Nationalist alderman in Victoria Ward, and only in Cromac, Ormeau, St. Annes and Woodvale did the official Unionists secure the majority of seats. Sir Crawford McCullagh was elected Councillor for Cromac Ward. Among the new members were Denis McCullough, Sinn Féin Councillor for Falls and one time member of the inner circle of the Irish Republican Brotherhood, Sam Kyle, Labour Alderman for Shankill, and Thomas Gibson Henderson, independent Unionist Councillor for Shankill.

Whilst municipal politics continued to be a matter for discussion and debate in Ulster it was a time when the people of Ireland were reflecting on other issues that concerned the country as a whole. After the election the Sinn Féin candidates, although entitled to sit as MP's in the British parliament, chose to boycott the Westminster body and instead assembled as a revolutionary parliament they called Dáil Éireann: Irish for 'Assembly of Ireland'. However Unionist and members of the Irish Parliamentary Party refused to recognise the Dáil. At its first meeting on 21st January 1919 the Dáil issued a Declaration of Independence and proclaimed itself the parliament of a new state called the Irish Republic.

In early 1920 the British Cabinet had succeeded in passing a new Government of Ireland Bill, this Bill repealed the Act of 1914 and would give Ireland two Parliaments; There was no other feasible course, for as the Prime Minister Lloyd George explained, the position was:

(1) Three-fourths of the Irish people are bitterly hostile and are at heart rebels against the British Crown and Constitution

(2) Ulster is a complete contrast, which would make it an outrage to place her people under the rest of Ireland and
(3) no separation from the Empire can be tolerated, and any attempt to force it will be fought as the United States fought against secession.

Hence, the new Government of Ireland Act received Royal Assent on 23 December 1920. This Proposal would give Ireland two parliaments (each with a Prime Minister), one for the Unionists and one for the Nationalists. Six north-eastern counties (Londonderry, Tyrone, Fermanagh, Antrim, Down and Armagh) to be under the Unionist parliament, with the citizens agreeing to the creation of 'Northern Ireland' by way of a referendum. The other twenty-six counties to be under a Nationalist Parliament and known as Southern Ireland. It subsequently became known as the 'Irish Free State' with the Sinn Féin leader, Eamon de Valera as the first Prime Minister. There was also the assumption that Nationalists would find two Home Rule parliaments less offensive than a straightforward exclusion of the north-east. These proposals soon produced a catalogue of violent acts culminating in the ambush and subsequent murder of two local Irish members of the Royal Irish Constabulary in County Tipperary, by members of the Irish Volunteers. This course of events soon drove the Dáil to recognise the volunteers as the army of the Irish Republic and the ambush as an act of war against Great Britain. The Volunteers therefore changed their name, in August, to the Irish Republican Army. This effectively marked the beginning of a reign of terror culminating in what would become known as the War of Independence.[1]

The 'Troubles' as they were called were only just in their infancy with an occasional report in a local newspaper telling of a police inspector being shot or a local magistrate being attacked. But now that the IRA had stepped up their activities, Dublin had been transformed once again. Armoured cars toured the city's streets. Dublin Castle and the

1. Budge and O'Leary pp. 137-139

Mansion House, the Lord Mayor's residence where Crawford had spent many convivial evenings with heads of state, had sentries at the gates and rolls of barbed wire coiled menacingly around the railings.

It was at this crucial time that Daisy and Helen McCullagh returned home from Alexandra College as Crawford and Margaret felt it was no longer safe for them to be boarding in Dublin. Ironically only a year before they had spent a leisurely family weekend in the Shelbourne Hotel, taking the girls to fashionable Jammets for lunch then shopping in Switzers department store in Grafton Street. The green lawns, the duck pond and lush foliage and flowers of St. Stephens Green seemed tranquil and serene as the afternoon sun faded and the family took afternoon tea in the elegant drawing room of the hotel. In the evening they went to see a production of The Mikado at the Abbey Theatre where Crawford in his memoirs recalled seeing Countess Markievicz, who had recently won a seat in the House of Commons as a Sinn Féin representative.

In the month of June the violence escalated with special police constables being killed by the IRA in Belfast and Newry, then ten Catholics were shot in reprisal by the Specials. Sporadic fighting erupted continuously in the York Street area, leading to the driving out of families from the New Lodge Road and Tiger Bay. The violence continued well into July and reached a crescendo when Special Constables joined Protestant mobs in Belfast over the Twelfth parades. Sixteen Catholics and seven Protestants were killed and over two hundred Catholic homes were destroyed.[2]

This crucial time in Ireland, both North and South was to have a profound effect on the lives of virtually every person who lived in this small island. From January 1919 until a truce came into effect on 11 July 1921, a state of undeclared war existed in some areas of Ireland between the Irish Republican Army, representing the independent aspirations of militant Irish nationalism and the forces of the British Crown who were charged with restoring law and order.

2.   Jonathan Bardon, *A History of Ulster*, p.482

The Black And Tans

From the outset, the IRA campaign was mainly directed at the Royal Irish Constabulary and by June 1920, fifty-five policemen had been killed, sixteen barracks destroyed another twenty-nine damaged and over four hundred abandoned buildings had been burnt to the ground. As a result its conviction rates, recruitment levels and morale all fell sharply. In response the British Government transformed the force into an auxiliary army, by equipping it with motor vehicles, rockets, bombs and shotguns . The British Authorities also responded to this situation by advertising in England for British ex-servicemen firstly, and then later for ex-officers, to join the RIC and bring their recent experience of weapons and warfare to what had formerly been a distinctly Irish police force. Known respectively as the 'Black and Tans' and the 'Auxiliaries' so named because of their distinctive khaki uniform with black Glengarry caps and armbands, these two elements of the RIC became infamous for utilizing their experience of war to terrorise the civilian population of Ireland, especially the Catholic Irish in the southern counties. Of the eighteen companies eventually formed, four were located in Dublin, another four in County Cork, with the others being distributed in counties in the centre, west and south of Ireland. Their presence in the loyalist stronghold of Ulster was not considered to be necessary. However, when some Black and Tans appeared in Belfast they were swiftly dealt with by the IRA. Jim McDermott in his book *Northern Divisions* recalls an incident on 21 March 1921 when two IRA men shot and killed three Black and Tans in the middle of Belfast. It was reported in the *Irish News*:

Three uniformed Black and Tans were shot in Victoria Square. They were motor drivers posted from Gormanstown for special duty and were to return again to Gormanstown that night. They had stopped to talk to a girl beside Finlay's Soap factory when four or five men attacked them with revolvers. Two of the Black and Tans were killed almost instantly. The third was injured and staggered down the street.

He died of chest wounds the next morning. In the shooting a Protestant shipyard worker was struck by a stray bullet and he too was killed. He left behind a widow and eight children.

The IRA group made a safe escape down Telfair Street.

Although it was highly unusual for Black and Tans to be in Belfast, they had a bad reputation among Nationalists for their use of brutality in systematically breaking up the ranks of Sinn Féin and before long the full resources of IRA propoganda was immobilized against what they recognised as the most formidable menace to their activity which they had yet encountered.

The Swanzy Riots – Violence in the North and South of Ireland

On the 12 July 1920 Edward Carson addressed his followers at Finaghy outside Belfast. His speech contained the message that the Ulster people would not tolerate Sinn Féin, and if the Government would not protect them from the machinations of Sinn Féin then the Ulster people would take matters into their own hands.

Crawford's own sentiments were relayed in his memoirs when he regarded the boycott of Belfast goods, initiated by Sinn Féin during the summer of 1920, as the chief cause of growing political and religious feeling. A unionist deputation from Enniskillen proclaimed that the boycott was the culmination of a campaign against them and which had included raids on their houses, threatening letters and damage to property.[3]

On 21 July, the first day after the 12 July holidays, notices were placed in the shipyards calling for Protestant and Unionists workers to meet at lunch-time outside the gates of Workman Clark's shipyard. It was the day of the funeral of Colonel G.F. Smyth, an RIC divisional commissioner from Banbridge, shot dead in Cork four days previously. The call to drive out 'disloyal' workers was enthusiastically supported. At the end of the meeting hundreds of apprentices and rivet boys from Workman Clark marched into Harland and Wolff's yard and ordered out Catholics and Socialists. Some were kicked and beaten, others were pelted with rivets, and some were forced to swim for their lives as one Catholic remembered:

3.   Crawford Memoirs

The gates were smashed down with sledges, the vests and shirts of those at work were torn open to see if the men were wearing any Catholic emblems, and woe betide the man who was. One man was set upon, thrown into the dock, had to swim the Musgrave Channel, and having been pelted with rivets, had to swim two or three miles, to emerge in streams of blood and rush to the police office in a nude state.[4]

DASTARDLY LISBURN CRIME.

August 22nd 1920

District-Inspector Swanzy Murdered

SINN FEIN ACT OF VENGEANCE.

Murderers Make their Escape.

TRAGEDY CAUSES GREAT DISORDER.

A terrible crime was perpetrated at Lisburn yesterday, the victim being District-Inspector O. R. Swanzy, who was shot dead while returning from the morning service at Christ Church.

The murder was committed by a party of men who are said to have travelled to Lisburn in a taxi-cab which they hired in Belfast. They are believed to have been strangers to the district.

Large numbers of people were in the immediate vicinity when the fatal shots were fired, but the miscreants succeeded in making their escape.

Subsequently widespread disorder broke out, and many shops and houses were wrecked and looted.

A scene in Bridge-street.   Saving belongings from a threatened house.

The riots at Lisburn following the murder of Inspector Swanzy have left scenes of wreckage everywhere. General Macket Pain (inset) has arrived, and it is expected the town will be placed under military control.—(Daily Sketch Exclusive Photographs.)

Following the expulsion of Catholics from the shipyards there were further attacks on local mills and factories. Trams carrying shipyard workers were stoned that night and for the next three days and nights there was inter communal warfare, as loyalists attempted to burn Catholics out of their homes and businesses. They were driven from the Sirocco Works, Mackie's, McLaughlin and Harvey's, Musgrave's and Coombe Barbour's. After three days seven Catholics and six Protestants had died violently.

A committee headed by the Catholic bishop, Dr. Joseph MacRory, estimated that ten thousand men and one thousand women had been expelled from their work.[5]

4.   Jonathan Bardon p.471

5.   Jonathan Bardon p.471

One of the pivotal actions that precipitated the violence in Belfast at this time was the murder of Tomas MacCurtain. As well as being Lord Mayor of Cork, MacCurtain had been OC of the No. 1 Brigade of the IRA. One of the men involved in the killing was District Inspector Oswald Swanzy of the RIC. On Sunday 22 August 1920 DI Swanzy was murdered by the IRA in Lisburn, Co. Antrim. The IRA would have seen the Swanzy shooting as a well-executed and justified execution. To the loyalists in Lisburn it was a murderous outrage. In the next three days Protestants attacked and burned sixty Catholic-owned public houses and business premises, set fire to a priest's house and some Catholic houses and finally driving out almost all the Catholic residents, many of whom took refuge in Dundalk.[6] The *Irish News* reports of 23 August states that:

> For a considerable distance the burning buildings could be viewed and the crash of falling masonry could be heard even on the outskirts of the town while huge tongues of flame and myriad sparks lit up the sky for miles.

The *Newsletter* said that 'several large establishments were a seething mass of fire[...]it looked like a veritable inferno'. Fred Crawford noted in his diary that the shooting of DI Swanzy upset both him and his fellow Unionists and that 'feeling against the rebels is running very high [....] Lisburn is like a bombarded town in France'. By 24 August 1920 violence and upheaval to the city had escalated to a very serious level. In East Belfast Ballymacarratt shops were destroyed by unruly mobs who engaged in looting and stone throwing battles. Catholic properties, including houses and business were burnt and looted. The destruction continued day after day as reprisal after reprisal resulted in widespread casualties and extensive damage to both Protestant and Catholic properties.

The last weekend in August 1920 was marked by the intensity of arson on Catholic-owned property. On Monday 31 August there was a full-scale battle around the York Street area. At around 8am shipyard workers going to Workman Clarke's yard were attacked. The shipyard

---

6.   Jonathan Bardon p.472

workers left the trams intent on causing as much trouble as possible and within a short space of time the whole length of York Street was involved in a running battle. The *Irish News* reported that:-

> 'the battle ebbed and flowed down the side streets and York Street was given over absolutely to the crowds and the tram car services were stopped. Most people took another route home as the Co-Operative stores were severely smashed up'.

The *Belfast Telegraph* reported that:-

> 'A Sinn Féiner was seen to come out openly into the middle of York Street and fire a number of shots towards where a large crowd had gathered at the junction of Donegall Street and Royal Avenue ... snipers were busy practically all afternoon around Little George's Street and they inflicted many casualties on people in the various thoroughfares. There was also revolver fire, and several men were seen to fall very seriously wounded.

The *Daily News* on the same day also reported that in York Street the riots had reached epic proportions:-

> Fully a thousand men were engaged at one time, and thousands of pounds of damage was done, mainly to plate glass windows. Women fought ferociously and supplied the men with ammunition torn up from the cobbled paved side street. The Orangemen fought around two immense Union Jacks.

The rioting was finally broken up with the arrival of the military who responded with machine gun fire. However, the violence had now reached such a crescendo that it simply moved on to North Street and again firearms were used. The military and police tried to keep the situation quiet. Those workers who did return to the shipyards the next day were protected by force and considerable steps were taken to avoid the same trouble happening again. A Curfew was proclaimed and anyone found on the streets without a permit between the hours of 10.30pm and 5am was to be arrested. This curfew was to be enforced, with intermittent lapses until 1924. By the end of August a total of 22 people had been killed, 169 civilians seriously wounded, more than 180 fires had been dealt with and reported and nearly £1 million worth of damage. Crawford advised his wife and daughters to avoid Belfast city centre at all costs and Sir Wilfred Spenders wife Lillian had written in her diary:

'You see the Sinn Féiners have a way of hiding in the side streets and firing at random into the main thoroughfares which is rather upsetting, one just keeps out of the bad areas until order is restored'.

She felt it was a great pity that the Government did not recognise the UVF as a legitimate force and

'allow the responsible ones among them to be armed. Order would soon be restored then. As it is the Sinn Féiners are well armed and every morning they fire on the unionist shipyard workers as they go to work, the latter retaliate as best they can with sticks and stones. Then the soldiers fire on them both. The Unionists are furious'.

Senior Ulster Unionists were alarmed that their cause would be ruined by further assaults on the Catholic population. Craig simultaneously threatened and warned the Government of this in a memorandum on 1 September 1920:

The Loyalists in Ulster believe that the Rebel plans are definitely directed towards the establishment of a Republic hostile to the British Empire, and that they are working in conjunction with Bolshevik Forces elsewhere towards that end ... the situation is becoming so desperate that unless the Government will take immediate action, it may be advisable for them to see what steps can be taken towards a system of organised reprisals ... partly to restrain their own followers ... unless urgent action is taken, civil war on a very large scale is inevitable.[7]

On 7 September 1920 a deputation from the Ulster Unionist Council met Bonar Law and other prominent government ministers in London. The following day a Council of Ministers, presided over by the Prime Minister, decided that the Chief Secretary should take the necessary steps to organise a force of special constables in the six counties and appoint a Permanent Under-Secretary of Belfast who was to be a representative of the Irish Government in Belfast. Sir Ernest Clarke was appointed additional Assistant Under-Secretary in the Irish Office and was responsible for creating the Ulster Special Constabulary with particular administrative responsibility for the area which was to form Northern Ireland. Sir Ernest recognised the urgent necessity of creating an armed force to deal with the rapidly deteriorating situation. Using powers available to him under

7.   Jonathan Bardon p.474

the Special Constables Act (1832) he set about his task enthusiastically and energetically. Within five weeks of his appointment on 22 October 1920, he published details of the new Special Constabulary which was to comprise three categories:-

1. 'A' Specials – These were to be paid and full-time but would only serve within the divisionswhere they were recruited.

2. 'B' Specials – These were to be part-time and unpaid, apart from a small allowance for service and wear and tear of clothes. Their arms were to be determined by the police county commander. They were to do 'occasional duty, usually one evening per week exclusive of training drills, in an area convenient to members, day duty being required only in an emergency'.

3. 'C' Specials – These were to be a reserve force and were only to be called out in case of emergency.

Initially recruitment, which commenced on 1 November 1920, was confined to Belfast and Co. Tyrone but was soon extended to all the counties which were to form Northern Ireland. By the end of 1920 the Special Constabulary totalled nearly 3,500 'A' constables, 16,000 'B' constables, and over 1,000 'C' constables.

As Councillor for South Belfast Crawford witnessed first hand the birth pangs of this new state of Northern Ireland. Parliament's task of maintaining law and order at this time was extremely arduous in the face of constant interruptions from the Southern Republicans whose determination to drive the British from Ireland was savage in its extreme. Property and life in the city was held under menace. Not only police and soldiers but private citizens were marked out as victims. Northern Ireland seemed to be teetering on the brink of anarchy.

Robert McElborough, a gas worker, described conditions in east Belfast in the spring of 1922:

'I was taken off meter work and was told by the superintendent to keep the lamps in Seaforde Street and the Short Strand in repair ... anyone who lived in the area remembers the cross-firing that was kept up day and night. No one would venture out and trams passed this area at full empty, or with passengers lying flat on the floor I can't tell you how I got the cart into this area. I ran with it and got safely into Madrid Street ...with rifles cracking overhead... It was the snipers on the roofs and back windows who were the danger. Anyone seen on the streets within the range of their   guns was their target, and they found out later through the press what side he belonged to. I had seen men who were going to work shot dead as a reprisal for some other victim. My only dread was when I was standing on the ladder putting up a lamp, bullets that I suppose were meant for me went through the lamp reflector'.[8]

The IRA carried out a series of arson attacks on prominent manufacturing businesses and warehouses in the city, moving into the countryside targeting mansions and castles belonging to wealthy landowners. Masked men march on the undefended house of Lady Una Ross at Strangford, forcing Lady Una and her maids into the garden, and made them watch the burning of the house and all its contents. Nearby Castle Ward, the home of Lord Bangor and his family was defended by the B Specials. Shane's Castle on the shores of Lough Neagh was targeted as was Garron Tower on the Antrim Coast, Glenmona House in Cushendun and Crebilly Castle near Ballymena. Railway stations and flax mills in rural areas were also set on fire. The killings continued without restraint. On 18 May three Catholics were murdered in the city centre and the following day three Protestants were murdered in Little Patrick Street.

For Crawford and Margaret McCullagh one of the worst murders at this time concerned the gunning down of the their friend and colleague William Twaddell. W.J. Twaddell was a Labour MP for Woodvale, a well known Orangeman and a leading member of Belfast Corporation who had consistently supported Crawford throughout the debates in Stormont regarding housing subsidies. He was also in the drapery trade and owned a large shop in North Street. On the morning of 22 May he was on his way to work unaware that he was being followed by three men. He was walking down Garfield Street and was only about 50 yards from his shop when the men opened fire, fatally wounding him. Seven shots were fired with all the rounds

8.   Jonathan Bardon p.488

hitting his body. The assassins then fled into Lower Garfield Street opening fire on their pursuers. A constable opened fire on them but his revolver jammed and the criminals disappeared. During this exchange of fire a woman was struck in the arm by a stray bullet and several other persons had narrow escapes. William was taken to the City Hospital but died shortly after he was admitted. His death was a great blow to his many friends and fellow Orangemen on the Shankill Road, and his murder led to the immediate policy of internment. The first two hundred men arrested were Catholics and, after being held in Belfast, Larne and Newtownards were transferred to a ship moored in Larne Lough.

Although Belfast was subject to a Curfew Order in August ordaining that every person in the city, with certain recognised restrictions, should remain indoors between 10.30pm and 5.00am and that at 9.00pm all places of entertainment closed and the tramway system suspended the killing and destruction continued. During the month of May a total of forty-four Catholics and twenty-two Protestants were murdered in Belfast. Between 1 April 1921 and 31 March 1924 over one million pounds was paid in compensation for malicious injuries suffered during the 'troubles'. The rattle of fire engines summoned to an incendiary outbreak could be heard every hour.

Although prominent among the many critics of the Black and Tans was the King, George V, who in May 1921 told the Chief Secretary's wife, Lady Margaret Greenwood, that 'he hated the idea of the 'Black and Tans', the same can't be said of Winston Churchill, who writes in his book *The World Crisis*

It has become customary to lavish abuse upon the Black and Tans, and to treat them as a mob of bravos and terrorists suddenly let loose upon the fair pastures of Ireland. In fact, however, they were selected from a great press of applicants on account of their intelligence, their characters, and their records in the War ...... they acted with much the same freedom as the Chicago or New York police permit themselves in dealing with armed gangs. When any of their own men or police or military comrades were murdered they 'beat up' the haunts of well-known malignants, or those they considered to be malignants, and sharply challenged suspected persons at the pistol's point. Obviously there can be no defence for such conduct except the kind of attack to which it was a reply'.

In England, meanwhile a London based Anti-Reprisals Association was formed in 1920. They petitioned politicians and other prominent citizens in Britain to join in a campaign to embarrass Lloyd George's government over the misdeeds of the Black and Tans. So adverse was the publicity subsequently generated in the British and world press, that it was later hailed by Sinn Féin's Director of Propaganda, Desmond Fitsgerald, as having "been most damaging to England's prestige". Eventually Lloyd George came to realise that the Black and Tans were getting out of control and threatening the Government they had been sent to Ireland to support. By mid-1921 the British Government had become more amenable to a political settlement with the IRA.

The Anglo-Irish Treaty was established in 1921 and made provision for the continuation of the Council of Ireland after the Irish Free State was established. Under the Treaty, if Northern Ireland chose to opt out of the Irish Free State (as it subsequently did) the Council was to continue but the Council's powers could then only be applied to Northern Ireland and not the Irish Free State. While its functions only applied to Northern Ireland, its membership continued to be 40:20 selected by each of the Parliaments of the Irish Free State and Northern Ireland respectively and one by the King's representative. Therefore, after the Treaty, it was no longer the all-Ireland body originally envisaged as its powers applied only to Northern Ireland. Instead, it was a body in which the Irish Free State might influence the affairs of Northern Ireland and consequently was increasingly distrusted by the Government of Northern Ireland. The Council was duly established on 3 May 1921. On 23 June, the House of Commons duly elected its thirteen chosen members to the Council: Sir R.N. Anderson, Rt. Hon. John Andrews, Mr. J. Milne Barbour, Rt. Hon. Sir R. Dawson Bates, Mr. William Coote, Rt. Hon Sir James Craig, Bart; Captain Herbert Dixon, Mr. W. Grant, Dr. Robert. J. Johnston, Sir Crawford McCullagh, Mr. Samuel McGuffin, Mr.

Robert McKeown, and Major David G. Shillington. The House of Commons of Southern Ireland was a body which although established, never functioned and never elected members to the Council. In fact the Council of Ireland never met.

The new Parliament was initially housed in Belfast City Hall, but later moved to the Presbyterian Assembly buildings, Botanic Avenue from 1921-1932 while a Palladian style Parliament building was constructed at Stormont on the Castlereagh Hills outside Belfast. Sir Crawford was elected to the first Parliament of Northern Ireland as one of four representatives for South Belfast from 1921-1925. On 15 September 1921 the proceedings on the resumption of Parliament were discussed and the order papers of the cabinet settled.

With political storms still brewing between the two islands and where loyalty was combined with strict security King George V came to Belfast on 22 June 1921 to inaugurate the Northern Ireland Parliament. It was a ceremony fraught with very critical issues not only for Ulster and Ireland but for the entire British Empire. As a member of the new Parliament the importance of this unique event accentuated the responsibility Sir Crawford had to his King and his constituents in South Belfast.

The Royal Yacht *Albert and Victoria*, was escorted from Holyhead by a flotilla comprising two great battleships, two light cruisers and ten destroyers. A Royal salute of 21 guns marked the start of the Royal procession from Donegal Quay. Their majesties, together with the Irish Viceroy, Viscount Fitzalan, occupied a State coach drawn by four magnificent grey horses preceded by an outrider. Hundreds of people came from the surrounding Ulster countryside. They lined the historic High Street and central thoroughfares where the pavements and lampposts were painted red white and blue to welcome the King and his consort Queen Mary. They waved flags, sang the national anthem and shouted greetings to the royal visitors until they were hoarse.

Outside the City Hall the King inspected the Royal Ulster Rifles who furnished the Guard of Honour. Inside the municipal palace the reception hall served as the House of Commons while the inner sanctum of the Council chamber provided the appropriate atmosphere for the Senate House. The Lord Mayor's suite of apartments was occupied as the Regal retiring chambers and the City Hall was a majestic setting for the Premier's luncheon.[9]

The King in his speech from the Throne selected the moment for one of those humane acts which, as expressive of the deepest sentiments of a whole people are the best justification of constitutional monarchy. He addressed only the Unionists MPs. Nationalists and Sinn Féiners held to their pledge 'not to enter this north-eastern parliament', in words which by their manifest sincerity delighted his subjects in both islands, His Majesty issued an appeal for both peace and reconciliation

> "This is a great and critical occasion in the history of the Six Counties, but not for the Six Counties alone, for everything which interests them touches Ireland... I speak from a full heart when I pray that my coming to Ireland today may prove to be the first step towards an end of strife amongst her people, whatever their race or creed".

They were taken to the Ulster Hall were the King told Sir James Craig who was newly elected Northern Ireland Prime Minister how glad he was to have come to Ireland but that his entourage had grave doubts about his safety and were very much against the visit.

His entourage had every reason to be nervous, the following day the IRA blew up the train carrying the King's cavalry escort from Belfast back to Dublin, killing four men and eighty horses.

---

9.   The gilt chairs that were used for the Royal Visit belonged to Sir Crawford and came out of Lismara. They were give to City Hall by the McCullagh family.

Chapter Twelve
1922-1927

Silver Lining in Troubled Times

In any great matter it is not in the beginning but in the continuing of the same, until it be thoroughly finished, which yielded the true glory.

Francis Drake

Helen McCullagh

Shortly after Daisy and Helen McCullagh returned home to Lismara from boarding at Alexandra College, Dublin in the summer of 1920 Helen became engaged to Andrew Wilson.

Andrew Calwell Wilson was the son of John Wilson J.P. owner of The Whitewell, Dying, Finishing and Laundry Works. He had two sisters Minnie and Gladys Evelyn and four brothers John, Bob, William and Fred. They lived in Faunoran, a grand house in Greenisland, near Carrickfergus with beautifully landscaped gardens, stables and a tennis court. When John Wilson died in 1913 he left the house, land and businesses to his sons William, Andrew and Fred. His wife Sarah remained living in the house after her husband's death.

Wilson and Sons had their offices in Cornmarket, in the centre of Belfast and were well known in social and business circles. Helen and Andrew were introduced when they were still in their teens and were inseparable according to their daughter Maureen. It came as no surprise to the family when they announced their engagement. Helen was 20 years old and ready to settle down in her new home.

Both families approved of the match, and they married a year later in Whiteabbey Presbyterian Church on 26 April 1921. They spent their married life in Annaghmore on the Upper Road, Greenisland not far from Faunoran. Helen was born with a weak heart and having contacted TB as a child was in constant poor health. Nevertheless as a young girl she often accompanied her parents to functions in City Hall. In later years she undertook a considerable amount of civic duty when her mother was unable to fulfil her municipal role as Lady Mayoress. In 1926 Helen gave birth to a daughter Maureen who developed a great love for horses keeping them at Faunoran. She turned out to be a great horsewoman competing at shows all over Ireland and winning many prizes for show jumping. When she retired from the sport she presented a silver trophy 'The Maureen Wilson Cup' which is still awarded to the overall show jumping winner at The Balmoral Agricultural Show.

During the war years Faunoran hosted the Greenisland Horse Show. This was a major social event with competitors travelling from all over the country to compete for substantial prize money. There were riding, jumping and novelty competitions. One regular competitor who Maureen Wilson taught to ride was Patricia Curran, daughter of Judge Lancelot Curran. Patricia was brutally stabbed to death on the evening of 13 November 1952 in the wooded grounds of her family home, The Glen, Whiteabbey. She was only 19 years old.

Andrew Wilson died in 1958 and Helen and Maureen moved from Annaghmore to leafy Fortwilliam Park on the outskirts of Belfast. Helen by this time was spending most of her time in bed as a result of a weak heart. Although only 56 years old her health had now deteriorated to the extent that she became permanently bed-ridden spending the remaining years of her life propped up by a mountain of pillows being looked after by Maureen. Helen died in 1968 and Maureen eventually married John Blair, the man she had been in love with for most of her life. They lived together in Harberton Park in the Balmoral area of South Belfast. Maureen died of cirrhosis of the liver in 1979.

Daisy McCullagh

After Helen's wedding, Daisy was sent to board at Selwyn College, a private school in Richmond, Surrey. She was attractive, sociable and popular at school. Her diaries reveal her feelings at being free from restraint for the first time in her life and how liberated she felt with her new friends. They also reveal how she was often reprimanded for staying out late. Sir Crawford would visit his daughter when staying in London and recalls in his memoirs how she told him that her punishment for failing to return to school at the appropriate time was to buy expensive soap for the house mistress!

Her best friend at Selwyn College was a girl called Mabel Rayner. She had a wonderful voice and as a young girl became understudy to Charlotte Josephine Collins (Jose Collins) an English actress and singer celebrated for her performances in musical comedies and early motion pictures. Family legend has it that Mabel's mother was Lottie Collins who popularised the song 'Ta-ra-ra-Boom-de-ay!'. Mabel and Daisy were very much a product of their time. Parents disapproved and tried to maintain the decorum and discipline of the decaying Edwardian era, but social mores were changing and it seemed that there was no controlling these young people who smoked and drank to excess, frequenting clubs in London where eligible young men in Oxford bags danced the night away with girls who bobbed their hair and wore dresses with little or no undergarments.

In the 1920s illegal or unlicenced drinking clubs had sprung up all over London serving alcohol or 'hootch' in tea cups. When Daisy's best friend Mabel reached 21 her wealthy parents bought her a two seater Daimler. A few years later while she was driving to Henley to play a squash match, a bus came out of a side road and ploughed into the car killing her instantly. It was a tragedy that affected Daisy considerably and according to her brother Boysie this precipitated the start of her excessive drinking and wayward behaviour.

There were occasions when she would accompany her father on buying trips to Paris where he indulged her passion for expensive couture gowns. With her perfect reed-thin figure and striking looks she suited the clothes of that era and loved wearing wide-legged trousers and dropped waist fringe dresses with long strings of pearls. While in London she had her dark hair cut short and shingled as was the favoured style of the time. Margaret McCullagh in common with most mothers at this time considered a touch of lip salve and a little powder sufficient for any young lady – Daisy consequently laid in a store of theatrical make-up brought back from London including bottles of clown white and powdered rouge which she used liberally. In the 1920s fashion was defined by a totally new body awareness, which manifested itself not only in ideals of beauty but also went hand in hand with a more permissive society. This was a golden era for extravagance and, above all, for outrageousness. She adored cocktails and champagne and writes in her diary how she incurred the wrath of her mother when she came home drunk from a party. This now became a recurring habit with their rebellious daughter. Crawford and Margaret did not drink alcohol and they disapproved of the louche behaviour of these young men and women who often stayed over at Lismara. They would party into the night with the record player blasting out the latest dance craze drinking cocktails so potent that the maids when coming to clean up the mess in the morning would very often find some of Daisy's friends asleep on the chairs and sofas. On a number of occasions she disappeared to London and Paris on shopping sprees with Crawford's niece Pat.

To everyone's surprise the man who captured Daisy's heart was an unlikely choice for such a wayward spirit, but Victor Henderson was perhaps the only person who could indulge her whims and at the same time steady her excesses. They were from similar backgrounds, had know each other since childhood, were both extravagant and when they became engaged in 1922 Crawford and Margaret approved of the match believing that Daisy would settle down and be looked after in the manner to which she had become accustomed.

Victor Henderson lived in a splendid house called Parkville, in Whiteabbey village. His parents, Andrew and Annie Henderson had three sons and three daughters. They were well known in the community having established themselves in the area of Carnmoney (there is still a village in the area called Hendersonstown) about 1750 with a flax and corn mill using the water power of Cully's Burn. Victor's family owned Whiteabbey Bleaching Company and Bleach Green which was established in 1860 by Andrew Henderson, or 'Andy of the Green', as he was affectionately known in the neighbourhood. It used this same water source as the mill and was at one time the largest bleach works in Ireland. When Andrew died his eldest son Frederick took over the running of the Bleach Works with his two sons Stanley and Seamus who had been educated at Sedburgh. They were wealthy, sophisticated and well travelled. Although they spent their winter holidays skiing in St. Moritz, the boys' favourite sport was fishing, and in the summer months they would head off to fish at Lackagh in County Donegal.

Victor and Daisy were married in Whiteabbey Presbyterian Church on 10 July 1923 and took up residence in their new home called 'Danehurst', a large red brick house in Fortwilliam Park off the Antrim Road. Victor was deeply in love with Daisy and completely spoiled her with jewels, furs and extravagant holidays. They spent their honeymoon in the South of France. The Henderson's loved to ski and every winter they took a suite of rooms in the Suvretta House Hotel in St. Moritz. She was as indulged by Victor as she had been by her father. The birth of her first child Lionel Victor Crawford on 17 June 1926 seemed to calm her natural exuberance for high living and she settled comfortably into motherhood much to the relief of all those who loved her.

In 1924 Boysie finished his schooling at Campbell College at Knock on the outskirts of Belfast and subsequently joined the family business in Castle Place. He bore more than a passing resemblance to Edward Prince of Wales and to some extent emulated the pampered lifestyle. When he left school his father bought him a Crossley 20/70 sports car, one of only 100 made at the time costing £840. He would drive recklessly around the lanes of Whiteabbey terrifying the locals and then through the streets of Belfast dressed in his favourite Prince of Wales check tweeds and plus fours.

His father was keen for him to settle down and follow in his footsteps. He consequently entered City Council in 1935 as Councillor for Clifton Ward in North Belfast and is was seen accompanying his father at Corporate Meetings, in fact according to the *Daily Express*, father and son were inseparable in their comradeship. However it would appear that the role of Councillor did not suit Boysie's temperament as he was often absent from council meetings.

Ever since Boysie was a small boy his abiding interest involved rescuing and healing small animals, particularly birds and he eventually left his municipal career to concentrate on his hobby. When his father died in 1948 Boysie married Elizabeth Green. He sold the original house and built a large house in the Lismara demesne which he also called Lismara to evoke and retain its name. He devoted the rest of his life to birds, building the largest aviary in Ireland in the grounds of his home. He was a member of the Northern Ireland and British Ornithology Association and in later years had the distinction of being the first person to successfully breed Eider ducks in captivity. He was Northern Ireland's foremost ornithologist and he left a legacy to Belfast Zoo where a birdhouse is named after him.

The Classic Cinema

In 1922 Sir Crawford formed a company called Classic Cinemas Ltd., The Directors were Mark and Isidore Ostrer, Hugh Turtle, A. W. Jarratt and Samuel Donald Cheyne. For many the cinema was the only means of escape from the drudgery of everyday life, and Belfast was no exception for the working class people upon whom the cinema relied for their patronage. For a few hours a week they could walk into surroundings they could only dream about and forget their problems and hardships of living in 1920s Belfast.

Sir Crawford's love affair with the silver screen began in 1910 when he visited the Electric Cinema in York Street. The following year he went to the Picturedrome which opened on the Mountpottinger Road and subsequently there was such a demand for 'talkies' that in that same decade Belfast saw the opening of no less than six cinema's including The Princess Picture House, The Willowfield, and the Popular, known as the 'Pop'.

Sir Crawford's first inspiration to build a cinema began on the evening of 16 December 1916. As Lord Mayor he was invited to open the new Royal Cinema in Arthur Square in the centre of Belfast. In his speech he described the interior as "a masterpiece as far as cinema houses is concerned". The cinema was lavishly equipped and sumptuous in its interior. Soon it became the most popular cinema in Belfast and it was this success that he wanted to emulate. In order to raise the capital required to build a 'Super Cinema' which would rival all others in the city, Sir Crawford first approached two old friends and business colleagues, Hugh Turtle and Donald S. Cheyne. Donald Cheyne was a partner in Kyle and Cheyne, Draper and Shirt Manufacturer. He was also a Property Developer, High Sheriff, Alderman, and Councillor and Justice of the Peace in 1917. Sir Crawford and Donald had been apprentices together in the Bank Buildings. Hugh Turtle was Chairman of the Belfast Savings Bank. Both Crawford and Hugh were accomplished businessmen with significant influence in the commerce of Belfast. They both saw the potential of the business proposal as a means of securing a high return on their investment, due to the phenomenal demand for such places of entertainment and Crawford, ever the shrewd businessman, was always looking for a land venture or business opportunity whereby he could expand his business and property portfolio

The influence – financial and otherwise – of William Gibson on the development of Crawford's business interests in Belfast was enormous. The name 'Castle Buildings' originally belonged to Gibson to delineate the buildings he occupied at 'Gibson's Corner'. It was only in 1905, that he allowed the name 'Castle Buildings' to be transferred to McCullagh's new emporium of that date. Through his friendship with Gibson (whose property portfolio included the area that the original Belfast Castle was built on) Crawford had secured some of the most lucrative real estate in Belfast City Centre. Adjacent to that which he had already acquired in Castle Place in the previous decade, not only did he secure the area covered by Castle Market with a direct transfer of ownership from Gibson to McCullagh in 1920 but also access rights to Cornmarket, primarily as a means of expanding his existing business interests found in Castle Place.

Backed by partners in possession of the valuable collateral gained over 20 years of trading in Belfast City Centre, the new Classic Cinema soon began to take shape on the unique triangular site formally occupied by Castle Market. The frontage onto Castle Lane required the demolition of several shops and a small hotel at No. 17 known as the Wellington Arms run by Andy Majury.

As with his unprecedented Art Nouveau masterpiece at Castle Buildings, and Modernist Movement style at 27-29 Castle Lane, Crawford employed the finest architects to design the new picture house. The exterior featured Ionic pillars from the first floor upwards rising to curved pediments at the top of the four storied building. The project from its inception was to be greater than anything that had gone before. The grand auditorium was to seat 1,804 patrons, a capacity that could not be matched by any of the Classic's predecessors. Crawford was determined that his cinema should become the showplace of the city, outshining the nearby Royal and Imperial Cinemas on Arthur Square and Cornmarket.

The Classic Cinema opened in a blaze of publicity on Christmas Eve 1923, with the premier showing of *Chu-Chin-Chow* a musical comedy written, directed by and starring Oscar Ashe. Oscar was a prolific Australian actor, director and writer, who produced many Shakespeare plays and successful musicals both on stage and screen. In 1923 movies were still presented in silent format and required musical accompaniment to complete the show. Small cinemas had often relied on piano accompaniment, but the Classic revealed on its opening night a 30 piece orchestra in full evening dress, into which they changed each evening at 5.00pm. The Classic and its presentation was perfect when it came to self-promotion. The impressive architecture of the façade was specifically designed to create a sense of awe even before the patrons made their way inside. Its black and gold colour scheme added to the ornate splendour of the palatial 'Baroque' interior of the auditorium with its gold leaf mouldings and paintings on the ceiling.

The cinema manager, Mr Noel Hobart, always in full evening dress, stood at the top of the steps leading from the semi circular main entrance and presided over immaculately presented usherettes who were trained to the highest standards. The same black and gold colour scheme was used in the design of the staff uniforms with the usherettes wearing trouser suits! With a minimum of four continuous presentations daily, and a varied programme typically lasting 3 hours, admission to the dress circle was 2 shillings (10p in current terms) whilst those choosing to sit in the stalls could gain admission for 1 shilling (5p in current terms)

The willingness on the part of the owners to invest in such a major project such as the Classic showed the degree of optimism and commitment by all the partners including Sir Crawford. By then there was a boom in the cinema trade in Belfast and the 1930s witnessed the opening of The Castle, The Astoria, The Ambassador and on 7 December 1935 Sir Crawford was asked to open The Strand Cinema on the site of the castellated Strandtown House, former home of shipping company owner Sir Gustavus Heyn. The cinema offered 1170 seats (900 in the stalls and 270 in the more expensive 1/6p balcony seats). After some uncertain years the Strand closed in 1983 but was rebuilt in 1994 and reopened successfully as a four-screen cinema.

The 1920s was a particularly troubled time in Irish politics and sectarian rioting was common on the streets of Belfast. In the council chamber of City Hall, Unionist dominance was being challenged, so Crawford as a City Councillor would have been acutely aware of the unstable situation in Belfast at that time. Perhaps it was because of the need for such escapism and entertainment that the Classic became such an immediate success. Not surprisingly people took solace in the world of the cinema where the fantasy created by Hollywood and European filmmakers usually came with a happy ending. The glamorous stories on the silver screen carried on as if all was well in the world at large, they were full of optimistic plots, plenty of singing and dancing, and lots of comedy. The cinema therefore took peoples minds off the troubles and if they had money for a seat they could choose from four screenings a day, except Sunday. Customers could also dine in the Silver Service Restaurant on the first floor of the building before or after the performance they were attending.

By way of maintaining its position as the biggest and best cinema in Belfast, the directors invested in a magnificent Wurlitzer Theatre Organ with Leslie Thompson opening the instrument in 1927. The Wurlitzer was positioned in the former orchestra pit and slowly rose up on a lift from the depths of the cinema during the interval. The audience were encouraged to join in, with the words to the songs being placed up on the screen. For many, the Wurlitzer recital was the highlight of a Classic visit. Audiences were enraptured with the organist's repertoire of classical and popular melodies and once again, the directors of the Classic were seen as being at the forefront of cinematic innovation. The Classic was also one of the first cinemas to introduce 'Ardente Deaf Aids' for hard of hearing patrons. The staff supplied headsets which could be plugged into sockets placed at the end of the seat rows in the balcony. The sockets were wired to the sound system and as a result allowed the patrons to overcome their hearing problems.

In August 1928 the Directors decided to align themselves with a national cinema chain called Provincial Cinematic Theatres Ltd., a London based organisation, in order to secure access to 'first run' films and distribution rights, another shrewd move from Crawford as it was essential for the Classic to maintain its competitive edge as the leading cinema of the city. Within the space of a year of the merger,

Provincial Cinematic Theatres Ltd., was taken over by Gaumont-British Picture Corporation Ltd., the control of this company had been taken over by Isidore Ostrer, a prominent UK entrepreneur and financier. The company was very much a family run business with Isidore's four brothers taking leading roles in the company's success. In 1930 there was a restructuring of the board of directors at the Classic with Mark Ostrer taking over as Chairman and Managing Director of the Company. Both Sir Crawford and Hugh Turtle remained on the board as local directors, although overall control was from the corporation's head office in Regent Street, London. The Ostrer Brothers built Lime Grove, Britain's first purpose built studios and production was prolific under the Ostrer's direction. As a result the Classic was able to secure 'first run' showings of many of the major British produced movies of the time.

In April 1932 five city hall councillors took their seats in the 1800 seat auditorium for a private screening of Frankenstein. The verdict of this body, named the 'Police Committee', was that the film was blasphemous and using the powers given to them, they promptly placed a ban of any further exhibition. The decision was later endorsed by the full Council claiming that the psychological effects of such a film lead to evil. The irony was of course that the recently appointed Lord Mayor of the city Sir Crawford McCullagh, as a director of the Classic, was powerless to stop the decision of one of the committees he presided over.

The Municipal Housing Scandal

As Chairman of the Improvement Committee Sir Crawford McCullagh was credited with two important achievements – the schemes for Slum Clearance and for Sewage Disposal. In 1918 he was called upon by the Housing Committee of Belfast Corporation to deal with the critical housing problem. Except for a relatively few residences erected by owner-occupiers, no appreciable building activity was manifest during the War Period of 1914-1918. Meanwhile the population in Belfast continued increasing. Attracted by the abundant employment offered by the shipyards, linen and ammunition factories, hundreds of families had settled in the city. It was obvious, therefore, in 1918 that there was a necessity for the provision of more dwellings. Hundred of families were enduring deplorable conditions and paying excessive rents for inferior accommodation. Simultaneously the over-crowding was a serious menace to the community's health. Before 1914 up to ninety-nine percent of Belfast's houses were produced by private enterprise. However, due to the war the high cost of labour and the shortage of materials made the policy prohibitive. The erection of working-class houses to let at weekly rents was no longer an attractive economic proposition. Furthermore, all classes of the community, and not only the working classes suffered from this problem.

When the Local Government (Ireland) Act came into operation in 1919 the Corporation was obliged to prepare its own housing scheme. Prior to 1919 the provision of housing for citizens was not part of the responsibilities of Local Government. According to Mr David Cook (Lord Mayor of Belfast 1978):-

'The Corporation was split as to whether it should take on that task (the progressive opinion) or should not (the voice of those who thought it a socialist or communist ruse to subvert the role and profits of private landlords and builders). In the early 1920s Local Government Administration was chaotically different to our own experience in which a competent and professional Municipal civil service has the space and confidence to view the antics of elected representatives with appropriate scepticism. The responsibility for building houses was assigned to the Corporation just as partition resulted in transferring powers from Local Government Board in Dublin to the Parliament and Government at Stormont.'

In 1919 The Corporation accordingly set up a Housing Committee of fourteen members under the chairmanship of Sir Crawford McCullagh with Thomas McConnell as vice-chairman. A Housing Department was established in the Town Solicitor's office and a staff of valuers and agents appointed. Crawford embarked on the role with energy and enthusiasm and was highly successful in terms of the houses actually built. The cartoons depicted in *Nomads Weekly* show him in working clothes with his sleeves rolled up and with trowel, cement and bricks actually building houses. One of the cartoons has the caption: 'The Bricklayers – The Belfast Housing Committee get a move on' and the atmosphere created by the captions as a whole is along the lines of 'Give us the tools and we will finish the job'.

Our Weekly Cartoon.

"THE BRICKLAYERS."—The Belfast Housing Committee get a move on."

In the beginning sixteen houses of various types, known today as 'Demonstration Houses' were completed. The Corporation decided to construct most of the houses by direct labour under the city surveyor's department, and the rest by outside contractors. The scheme eventually provided in total 2,562 houses – 1,029 'parlour type' and 1,533 'kitchen class' – with accommodation for approximately 13,000 persons.

One of the areas in need of new housing at that time was in Greencastle. Sir Crawford was approached by the Rev. Barton of Whitehouse Presbyterian Church and in his book *The God of my Life* he makes reference to a conversation he had with Sir Crawford.

'I suggested that there was need of new houses at Greencastle. Sir Crawford immediately acted on the suggestion and brought the matter before his committee, who received it favourably. Ground was taken on the Whitewell Road, streets were made, and about one hundred and thirty houses erected. The streets were called Whitewell Parade. Whitewell Crescent, Whitewell Drive, and Serpentine Road. The houses are built in blocks, with about eight in each block; the material used was concrete, and each block is of a different colour from the others. The houses have three bedrooms, a bathroom, two sitting-rooms and a pantry. When finished they were immediately filled with tenants, chiefly young married couples who had not previously been able to get houses of their own. They have mostly come from Belfast, and are nice people with young children'.

The Housing Committee continued building houses without attracting public attention until March 1925 when the auditor of the new Ministry of Local Government wrote to the Corporation, complaining that they were purchasing building materials, without advertising for tenders. The Council then asked two independent accountants to report on the purchase of building materials for the first six months of 1925. The report showed deficiencies both in the quality and quantity of the timber charged for in the accounts and also found out that from £13,977 paid out in the period, a total of £5,171.10s was overpaid. The Housing Committee fought a rear-guard action against the reports but on 1 September 1925 the Corporation formally petitioned the Governor to appoint a commission of enquiry. Robert Dick McGaw K.C. was appointed by the Minister of Home Affairs. He had been a parliamentary secretary in the Government of Lord Craigavon, but lost his seat in the election of 1925.

His report disclosed considerable negligence in the affairs of the City Housing Department. Namely irregularities in accounting, inferior materials being passed, and unexplained discrepancies both in quality and quantity of building materials being submitted. Certain firms had received contracts without tender and some members and officials of the Housing Committee, and even the city solicitor had financial interests in the sites. Megaw pointed out that the high cost of Belfast housing was due to the practice of direct instead of contract labour. This practice, in fairness to the Housing Committee, had been introduced at the behest of the Labour members of the Corporation. The auditor concluded his report by complaining of the 'disinclination of everyone concerned' to help with the Inquiry, the Housing Committee's failure to produce documents, unwillingness to give testimony by some members, and a quite unjustifiable air of complacency on the part of the Chairman. The Report not surprisingly caused considerable embarrassment to the Council and resulted in the resignation of both the city solicitor and surveyor. Also some others implicated in the housing contracts were prosecuted.

One of the irregularities submitted in the Megaw Report[1] concerned the disappearance of 66,000 bricks which were allegedly used to build a cinema owned by a member of the Housing Committee. It was inevitable given the circumstances of the enquiry that Crawford would be the recipient of covert insinuations by critics. Admittedly he was Chairman of the Housing Committee and accordingly accepted the accountability that the position incurred.

At the initiation of the scheme Crawford had advised the Corporation to appoint, as Special Housing Director, a fully qualified and experienced architect together with a qualified surveyor. Due to a plea of economy by the Corporation the recommendation by The Chairman and the Vice-Chairman was turned down. At a meeting of the Council in December 1928 Sir Crawford informed the committee that:-

> He had not the slightest pecuniary interest in any of the transactions which the Housing Committee carried through. He had no interest whatsoever in timber, slates, stones or other building materials. Further, the Corporation did not acquire from him any ground for building purposes. Either was he in any manner interested in the disposal of any ground taken from them.
>
> His conscience was, therefore, perfectly clean and he was eager to let the citizens of Belfast be judges of his career and his conduct. He had served the public for the best years of his life. He had no regrets over the Housing schemes. He felt it was his duty to take over the burden and do what he could for the people who were herded together in shockingly overcrowded conditions. In view of his past history and of the tremendous problem he had been called on to face, he felt satisfied that all unbiased citizens would give him the credit of having worked solely in the interests of the people amongst whom he had lived.[2]

As Chairman of the Housing Committee, Crawford had to take the blame for the Housing Scandal. It was no doubt proper that he should do so but at no stage in the report was it suggested that Sir Crawford was himself corrupt or benefited improperly from his Chairmanship. The problem arose partly out of the actual corruption of some members and officials of the Housing Committee. Megaw wrote,

1. Megaw Report PRONI
2. *Belfast News Letter* 30/12/1928

'that there was an undertaking, lubricated with an amount of give and take, be-tween certain members of the Housing Committee, the City Surveyor and (an official) as to the allocation of the contracts'.

In November 1927 the Lord Mayor, Alderman W.G. Turner, per-suaded the Council to set up a special committee (five Unionists and one Nationalist) to look over the whole system of municipal admin-istration and recommend accordingly. The Committee engaged the services of a London accountant with municipal experience (Arthur Collins) to conduct an enquiry for them. Collins's report claimed there were too many committees; they were encroaching on work that should be done by officials and there was undue participation by council members in the engagement and firing of staff.

Mr. Collins made over thirty recommendations intended to ensure Belfast government was similar to that of Birmingham, which he considered to be a particularly well-run borough. The Committee of Six accepted all Collin's recommendations and on receiving the report the Council listened to a plea by Alderman Turner, the Lord Mayor, for an end to the 'baneful influence and dry rot' of patronage for which he distributed blame between members of the Council and the weakness and acquiescence of the officials'. After a confused and disorderly meeting, all the main recommendations were carried, ex-cept the suggestion of indirect election of aldermen, and that a chief financial officer be appointed.

The Collins Report arose in connection with a major reform of Local Government administration carried out in the UK in the 1920's. Arthur Collins had already reformed Local Government Administration in Birmingham when he came to Belfast and his re-port in 1929 introduced the system of Committees and the rela-tionship between the elective representatives and the municipal Civil Service which, in principal, remains to this day.

In 1929, Sir Crawford stood again for his seat in Cromac Ward. He was opposed by W. H. Alexander a leading manufacturer and a member of the Reform Group in the Chamber of Commerce, stand-ing as an Independent Unionist. Alexander was dissatisfied with the

Collins proposals and campaigned on the slogan 'immediate reform or commissioners'. As chairman of the Housing Committee Crawford had to take the blame for the 1926 fiasco and his campaign was not helped by the fact that the General Purposes Committee had already designated him as the next Lord Mayor, in succession to Sir William Turner, then approaching the end of his sixth term. The other leading figure in the Housing Committee, Tom McConnell, also coming up for re-election was similarly opposed.

Alexander went on to defeat Crawford by a comfortable majority, however, in the 1930 election Crawford stood for the vacant councillorship of Woodvale and was returned. Following the 1931 election one of the last survivors of the Citizens Association, Sir William Coates, who had been elected Lord Mayor for 1929 and 1930, retired and Sir Crawford was elected to succeed him.[3]

3. Budge and O'Leary *Belfast Approach to Crisis,* p.150

Chapter Thirteen
1927-1932

The Great Depression

Four things a man must learn to do
If he would make his record true:
To think without confusion clearly;
To love his fellowman sincerely;
To act from honest motives purely;
To trust in God and Heaven securely.

Henry Van Dyke 1852-1933

Although Crawford continued to serve on Belfast City Council in the 1920s he was also heavily involved with his family business in Castle Place and building up his property portfolio. He was a keen speculator and would not shy away from individuals who needed support for changing trends especially in the world of technology.

For a short time in the mid-1920s, Belfast was at the forefront of the development of civil air transport in the British Isles. Spurred on by successful commercial flights to the RAF airfield at Aldergrove in 1921-23 in a far-sighted and adventurous move, Malone Air Park was established as the first municipal airport in the British Isles. Its greatest supporters were the then Lord Mayor, Sir William Turner and Belfast City Council. In January 1924 the Council determined 'in pursuance of the powers conveyed by the Air Navigation Act 1920 to establish and maintain an Aerodrome including the acquisition of suitable land and the erection of the necessary buildings together with proper apparatus and equipments' The sum voted for initial expenditure was £15,000.[1]

Captain Donald M Greig who took part in the airline project known as Northern Airlines, was encouraged to set up services to Liverpool, Glasgow, Carlisle and Stranraer.

Shareholders in the company included, the Baird family (proprietors of the Belfast Telegraph, Harry Ferguson Ltd (the firm belonging to Ireland's first aviator, who made his historic flight on December 31, 1909), Lord Londonderry (a keen airman and future Secretary of State for Air), Sir Thomas Dixon, Sir William Turner, local business-men such as Sir Crawford McCullagh and mill owners. The primary idea in the formation of Northern Airlines was to accelerate the de-livery of London newspapers in Northern Ireland, in which activ-ity Eason and Son Ltd took the leading part as the major wholesale and retail newsagents in Ireland. However, it was also intended to provide an airmail service and to carry passengers when the space was available. The service to Liverpool soon ran into difficulties with weather conditions often making flying almost impossible. Another route was established with a daily flight to Renfrew airfield, Glasgow in June 1924. Regrettably, the Renfrew-Malone link never developed as envisaged. In 1925 a schedule was opened with a newspaper flight from Malone to Carlisle on March 18. As with previous attempts at establishing a satisfactory route, the weather was a major limit-ing factor and an effort was made to identify an alternative which would ensure an unbroken service.[2] The service continued with regu-lar flights between Stranraer, Belfast and Londonderry. However the valiant efforts of Northern Airways came to an end on June 8, 1925. Weather conditions, inadequate weather reports, soft landing condi-tions due to the aerodrome becoming waterlogged and increasing op-erating costs finally forced the airline out of business, consequently,

1. Guy Warner, *Flying from Malone: Belfast's First Civil Aerodrome*, p.18.

2. 2 Guy Warner, *Flying from Malone; Belfast's First Civil Aerodrome*, p.50

the Air Ministry equipment at Malone was transferred to Aldergrove. The land once occupied by the airfield at Malone is now covered by the Taughmonagh housing estate and no evidence of its past use remains. Nearly a decade was to pass before a regular air service would link Northern Ireland with the mainland. Belfast Harbour Airport was eventually opened at Sydenham on 16 March 1938 by Mrs Anne Chamberlain, wife of the then British Prime Minister, Neville Chamberlain. Belfast City Airport as it became known was renamed George Best Belfast City Airport on 22 May 2006 to commemorate the life of International football legend George Best who was born and raised close to the airport.

Sir Crawford extolled the virtues of Belfast as being built on enterprise and foresight by law-abiding people. He possessed the keenest interest and confidence in every one he met which brought out the best in them. These qualities helped him in promoting the social and industrial prosperity of Belfast and Northern Ireland. He was involved in numerous commercial ventures, had enormous investments in property in Belfast and was a Director in many companies.

In 1927 Sir Crawford became a Director of Maguire and Patterson a company manufacturing matches such as Swan Vesta, Swift and the City Hall Match. The company was founded by Sir Alexander Herbert Maguire in 1897 as Maguire Miller and Co. It later evolved into Maguire, Patterson and Palmer with branch factories being built in Dublin and Belfast. The Belfast factory was on the Donegal Road, opposite Celtic Park, the home of Belfast Celtic F.C. In 1923 the firm amalgamated with Bryant and May - both brands were later produced on the Donegall Road along with Swan Vestas. Sir Crawford remained a Director with a yearly income of £50 until his death in 1948. The factory was subsequently damaged in 1971 in a terrorist attack and production of the Maguire and Patterson brands were transferred to Sweden.

Sir Crawford And The Belfast Hebrew Community

Having had a long association with the drapery and retail trade since his days as an apprentice in the Bank Buildings Crawford never forgot his long and sometimes arduous journey to being the self-made man he had become. He had a compassionate nature and was always ready to help anyone who needed support either socially or commercially. Over the years there emerged a strong Hebrew Community in Belfast. The Jewish business entrepreneurs became successful in many aspects of commercial trade in the city and in 1926 Crawford met a young man called Nat Goorwitch.

Nat Goorwitch was born in 1896 in Southern Imperial Russia, and as a sixteen year old he escaped from the pogroms to seek a better life in Europe. Arriving in London in 1912 he had only sufficient cash to rent a bed for one night, after which he had to sleep on a park bench. The boy was fortunate enough to be found by a stranger who, taking pity, offered the destitute young man a job in his tailor's shop. Hard work and determination led him to accumulate enough cash to make his way to the newly created Northern Ireland where he learnt to master the drapery trade. In 1927 he purchased Hall and Arbuckle, a firm of milliners and costumiers at 24-26 Castle Place. Nat settled in Belfast and bought an imposing house called 'Broome' at 126 Malone Road.

In 1927 at the age of fifty-nine, Crawford decided to sell Castle Buildings in order to invest in other business enterprises in the city. After 33 years in the drapery trade he finally sold the business to Swears and Wells, a leading department store specialising in furs with headquarters in Regent Street, London. The chairman of this company was Cyril J. Ross a leading member of the Belfast Jewish Community.

Over the next ten years the business of Nat Goorwitch prospered and looking for an opportunity to expand he approached Cyril Ross with a proposition to take over the lease of 11-15 Castle Arcade which had previously been owned by Sir Crawford. Goorwitch took over the lease and eventually acquired the adjoining premises with a total of three shops more than doubling the size of the sales floors. Nat Goowitch's Store soon became a household name with his largest shop at 38-44 Royal Avenue.

On 9 February 1929 , on the eve of the Great Depression, Crawford announced to the Press that he had bought the Metropole Hotel (or more precisely the site on which the Metropole Hotel stood) which extended from No. 95-101 Donegal Street and from No. 2-10 York Street. The first hotel to stand on this site was The Queens Arms Hotel developed by Thomas Cunningham in 1850. In 1898 it was purchased by Patrick and Frank McGlade. They refurbished the hotel and renamed it The Grand Metropole Hotel, no doubt to compete with The Grand Central Hotel, opened by John Robb on Royal Avenue in 1893. At the turn of the century the hotel was sold to Robert and Daniel McAlister, both magistrates of Belfast and established wine and spirit merchants of Bank Lane. They employed a young man by the name of Peter McAleese to manage the hotel. Peter McAleese later bought the hotel in 1916 during the first world war. A descendent of this family, Martin McAleese, married in 1979, Mary McAleese (nee Lenaghan) who became President of the Republic of Ireland in 1997.

The Metropole Hotel as it was now known was at the height of its success during the 1920s. The Grand Metropolitan Café with a separate entrance onto Donegall Street, was for two generations one of the leading restaurants in the city, a mecca for businessmen and commercial travellers. Although many people in Belfast will recall the Grand Central or Royal Avenue Hotels as having been the 'best' in the city, the Metropole was at this time a leading institution in city life. Despite the civil unrest which plagued the city well into the 1920s it was a favourite haunt of sporting and theatrical personalities as well as journalists from the *Belfast Telegraph* and the *Newsletter*. Although pressed to say what plans he had for the Metropole Hotel, Crawford refused to divulge any information, other than to say to the press that he and his wife would be going on holiday to the South of France and wouldn't be returning to Belfast until Easter.

The sum paid for the property was said to be substantial and while they were on holiday speculation was rife in the press that the property would be developed for retail use, since Sir Crawford McCullagh had no previous experience in hotel management. The press was kept guessing for another two years in which time the hotel continued to operate as 'The Metropole'. On 18 March 1931 the same year as he had been elected Lord Mayor of Belfast, Crawford made a further announcement to the press revealing that the Metropole had once again changed hands, Sir Crawford having sold the hotel to Alec and Mandy Berwitz, for a substantial sum.

The Berwitz brothers were from a prominent Jewish family with commercial interests in York Street, it was at these premises they carried on business as house furnishers and furniture manufacturers. The first family had arrived in Belfast in the 1880s having exiled themselves from Russia following the oppressive laws imposed by Tsar Nicolas III, a self confessed anti-semite. Trading under the banner of the Central Furnishing Company on York Street, the brothers' father Louis Berwitz, had achieved success for himself having settled in the Lower Antrim Road, near to the synagogue at Annesley Street, which had been opened by Sir Otto Jaffe, Belfast's only Jewish Lord Mayor.

On Friday 26 August 1932, an announcement was made in the Belfast Telegraph that the reconstruction of Belfast's landmark hotel was to commence the following Monday – plans having been lodged with Belfast Corporation by the architect Thomas D Purdy. Upon taking over ownership of the hotel, the Berwitz brothers announced they would be refurbishing the property in order to 'run it on more modern lines'. Sir Crawford, as a speculator, had purchased the property purely as an investment, and the rapid change of ownership must have been unsettling for the management and staff. Indeed the press announcement made directly after the sale, revealed that

Alec was already in London arranging finance for alterations which they hoped to make to the building.

For many years, and particularly with the steady growth in traffic in Belfast City Centre, Belfast Corporation had been wrestling with how to deal with the problems in traffic flow around certain major junctions of the city – one of which was Donegall Street and York Street. In particular, Donegall Street had become a 'bottleneck' and the Council was under great pressure to do something about the growing congestion. At this time the city planners began compulsory purchase of properties in the city centre in order to relieve the problem of traffic congestion. The Berwitz Brothers were shrewd businessmen – with no vested interest in the hotel industry – but with extensive retailing interests in York Street. Their aim was to acquire the prime site currently occupied by the Metropole where they would be in a strong position to compete with the Belfast Co-operative Society who had just commenced construction (1932) of their massive extension to the original 'Co-Op' at No. 12-20 York Street, opposite the Berwitz original premises. Although the brothers went through the process of submitting plans for the refurbishment of the property in 1932 the city planners turned down their application. Subsequently they sued Belfast Corporation for compensation, if they would have to tear down the building and erect a new one. In order to resolve the traffic congestion in that part of the city the Corporation were forced to pay out. The hotel was subsequently demolished in 1934. What was planned for the site was not a replacement hotel, but a modern four storey building, designed in the prevailing Art Deco style for retailing and taking full advantage of the corner site, so long occupied by the Metropole Hotel. The new building was set back from the original frontage line and the Berwitz Brothers continued to trade under the name 'Berriss' for their new enterprise. The family continued running the business until 1962 when it was taken over by Great Universal Stores Group.

Sir Crawford's Fourth Term As Lord Mayor

Sir Crawford McCullagh had been Chief Magistrate during the war years and now fourteen years later he was again unanimously elected Lord Mayor of Belfast on 5 December 1930. He had fulfilled his many responsibilities during those very critical First World War years, so, in again appointing him to be Belfast's First Citizen, his fellow councillors were fully confident that their action mirrored the wishes of the entire community.

At his re-installation in January, Sir Crawford was touched by the grateful references made to his wife Lady Margaret. In acknowledgement he said he could promise, on her behalf, that she would give of her best to aid him in his efforts for the advancement of the City and its varied interests. He believed 'she was the proudest lady in Belfast that day, not only because they had conferred on him that very high honour but because she was returning to City Hall by the unanimous wish of the people'. Indeed Lady Margaret was only too pleased to see her husband reinstated as Lord Mayor. She loved supporting her husband in any capacity and had in fact made it her life's work. Her duty was always to Crawford not only in the years when she was helping him build up his business empire but also in her role as Lady Mayoress. In addition her involvement in the numerous charities that she supported took up an enormous part of her life. This was to the detriment of her family as she wasn't always there when they needed her. This neglect would manifest itself in the form of alcohol abuse of which her children, particularly Daisy and Boysie were prone.

At his installation in the City Hall on 22 January 1931, Sir Crawford said he deeply appreciated the complete unanimity of the request. It was characteristic, also that in return he requested that members of the City Council aid him in upholding the dignity of that body:

> "He had always felt that they should have less suspicion of one another. Let them recognise more fully that every individual in that assembly, no matter to what political party he belonged, represented a constituency of the citizens to whom he was responsible and whom he was endeavouring to serve.

If these facts were kept in view their deliberations would be more harmonious and the honour and prestige of their beloved City would be enhanced. For himself, he did not assume infallibility. His rulings might always appear to be right, but they were given with a sincere desire to be fair to all parties and absolutely without bias".[3]

On taking office Sir Crawford told the Council how Belfast had suffered greatly from "trade depression during the past year and the citizens were groaning under the heavy burden of rates and taxation". He said the duty of the Corporation was to keep expenses as low as possible and look to prosperity in the future. Rather than reiterate events of the past year and forecast future policy, as had been the custom in the past, he said he would forego this and called for "all to work zealously for the progress of their city and happiness of the people".

In the past there had been a great deal of acrimony between members of the council. Sir Crawford addressed this by admonishing members;

"to help in upholding the dignity of council ... if they were less suspicious of each other and more in sympathy to one another – recognising that every individual, no matter what political affiliation, represented a constituency of citizens to whom he was responsible and who he was there to serve - if each kept this in mind, their deliberations would be more harmonious and the honour and prestige of their beloved city enhanced".

In order for Sir Crawford to gain control and manage the Corporation, in the best interest of Belfast he developed the 'City Hall Party', a permanent structure monopolizing all offices within the Unionist Council. This created a highly disciplined organisation with party leader, secretary, treasurer and regular meetings. The consequence was a more intensive control of the Council by the ruling party. Apart from appointments, in respect of which the Chairmen of Committees formed an 'advisory' committee, all offices within the council itself were monopolised by the Unionists. No longer did they feel, as in the period immediately before the First World War, the

3. *Belfast Telegraph* 1931

need to placate the Nationalists, who, though few in Belfast, were powerful at Westminster and disagreeably inclined to interfere in local legislation. The City Hall Party developed without any encouragement from Unionist Headquarters in Glengall Street which saw it as an alternative focus of power. To this day Glengall Street takes no official recognition of the existence of the City Hall Party[4]. It is ironic, therefore, that one of Sir Crawford's closest friends on the Council was the Nationalist Councillor Joe Devlin. [see appendix 5]

While Sir Crawford appears to have been on amicable terms with the Government leaders at major social and civic events, he did not mince his words publicly, when in the chair, or when addressing local groups. A proposal was put forward by Government to promote Northern Ireland as a centre for new industry and to give grants from public funds to undertake the manufacturing of goods, or commodities not previously produced in Northern Ireland. The proposal offered a wide range of suitable sites for factories. Foremost, a group of nine sites, forming a portion of the Harbour Estate, of up to 200 acres. As Northern Ireland is an integral part of the U.K. its trade with Great Britain was accordingly free and unhampered by tariffs[5]. In an address to chartered accountants in 1931, responding to remarks by the Prime Minister (Viscount Craigavon), he said

"whatever the Prime Minister has said about free sites for new industries in Ulster, newcomers in Belfast's industrial sphere could not expect freedom from rates.

We in the Corporation have already had application for particulars about sites for new industries. We have advertised in foreign Journals. We have offered foreign manufacturers all the facilities we can to come here and set up factories. From the Prime Minister we have had a statement about free sites.....

What would a firm, which has been struggling on all through these bad times paying rates, say, if we were to give new-comers freedom from rates? Well, we in the Corporation know that we would lose our seats!

---

4. Budge and O'Leary, *Belfast: Approach to Crisis; a study of Belfast Politics 1613-1970*, p.155/156

5. PRONI LA/7/3A/3

Some people expect we are going to have a boom. I hope we won't. A boom is not good for anybody, because it leaves a train of reaction behind it. Let it go on as it is! Things are going on nicely. Trade is improving, there is no doubt about it, and it will continue to improve"[6].

In 1931 the Ulster Industries Association was formed to promote agriculture and encourage the demand for locally produced goods. In October the Empire Marketing Board launched an appeal called the Buy Ulster Goods Movement in which the women of Ulster were urged to give Ulster made goods a trial and diminish unemployment in the Province. In December 1931 H.R.H Prince Henry, Earl of Ulster launched British Empire Week. Sir Crawford was requested by the Empire Marketing Board to make an appeal in the form of a letter to the press with a request to the public, the retailers and traders throughout Northern Ireland to "buy first the produce of the Home Country and next the produce of the Empire overseas"[7].

The term of office which began for Sir Crawford McCullagh with his re-election of the Lord Mayoralty in 1931, was to continue practically uninterrupted for a decade and a half, and was one of the most economically depressed in Belfast's history. Sir Crawford had now considerably less power than he had in 1914-1917. He was now Lord Mayor of the capital of Northern Ireland, rather than the Lord Mayor of a provincial city of Great Britain. Thus, in the years ahead, he had to counter much stronger opposition than he formerly experienced. As Lord Mayor, he automatically became a member of the Northern Ireland Senate, but this did not afford him his former power. The relationship between the Government and the Corporation, despite differences, was a close one. The Governor, Prime Minister and Sir Crawford were pictured together at almost all major functions, such as banquets, memorials and royal visits . Over the years, Sir Crawford met with and entertained Northern Irish and British government officials. As he did previously, he continued to use his position to promote cordial relationships between all facets of the community and

6. PRONI LA/7/3A/3
7. PRONI LA/7/3A/1

the Corporation, encouraged optimism despite the depressed times, and continued to acclaim the virtues of Belfast.

It was unquestionably a time for testing the spirit of the community and its leaders and how they responded is recorded in the commercial records of the city. The local press summed up Sir Crawford's hold on the gravity of the situation in the year ending 1931:

> Belfast has been fortunate in having had a long line of distinguished Lord Mayors and our present Chief Magistrate, Sir Crawford McCullagh has very ably maintained the high traditions of the City both in its civic business and in its social activities ... he has conducted the affairs of the Corporation with much wisdom; while he is always considerate in controlling discussions from irrelevancies, he is equally firm in arriving at decisions.

> As usual, Sir Crawford has lent his influence to many charitable institutions, particularly the coal fund which each winter brings appreciated warmth and brightness into many poor homes. Lady McCullagh is also as highly and universally esteemed for her unselfish service on behalf of the poor and suffering as for her graciousness as hostess at the various civic receptions.[8]

It was characteristic of Crawford's individuality that no matter how immense the stress and strain of the times his optimism always restored to the citizens of Belfast what they badly lacked – confidence in themselves and in the future. Courage and confidence were much needed. Increasing unemployment and widespread distress made a devastating impact on the city's finances. From 1921 to 1935 the shadow which persistently hovered over Great Britain and Northern Ireland was cast, not by warmongering amongst the nations, but by unemployment.

Correspondence received by the Lord Mayor's office at this time is indicative of the desperation felt by the majority of Belfast's citizens. Receipts from donations reveal that Sir Crawford and Lady McCullagh sent personal cheques to a very large number of charities and societies. These included the Samaritans, St. Vincent de Paul, Agnes Street Presbyterian Church, Belfast Association for the Employment of the Blind, Church Army Labour and Lodging Homes, the Cripple

8.   *Belfast Evening Telegraph* 1931

Institute and the Belfast Society for the Relief of the Destitute and Sick. On 23 November 1932 Sir Crawford sent a cheque for £105 to the Protestant Churches Relief Fund. Lady Margaret also had flowers sent on a regular basis to the Ulster Hospital for sick children and women. In July 1933 a meeting was held in Celtic Park for the coal fund where £500 was raised by the City Hall Relief Fund. The year before a record sub-list of the Coal Relief Fund was obtained, the amount being £3,438.18. This enabled the committee to supply coal in 24,516 cases with a total distribution of 3,037 tons of coal[9].

His attention was not only drawn to the plight of the unemployed and destitute, many letters of complaint and protests found their way into the Lord Mayor's office. In July 1933 he received a letter from the manager of the Ulster Bank in Dublin. He complained that owing to the ban on Easter Commemoration Ceremonies by the Northern Government a republican customer who lodged over £300 per week had closed his account. He said the same thing happened the year before. He wrote 'How long will this continue? Do you want me to be sent back to swell the unemployed?' he signed off 'One of your own'. There were also complaints regarding the Connswater River prompting Sir Crawford to order an enquiry into the allegations of debris and offensive smells. In 1932 a protest was lodged from the Independent Loyal Orange Institution regarding the wearing of civic attire (official robes) at a Eucharistic Congress in Dublin by members of the Corporation. The letter was strongly worded:

> 'We feel that the presence of the Councillors robed in their civic attire will be taken as an indication that Protestant Belfast is weakening in it's attitude to the idolatrous practices and beliefs of Rome'.

It was signed David McKnight, (Grand Secretary). There was a further meeting held in the Ulster Hall by the Ulster Protestant League and a resolution was unanimously passed seconded by Rev. Hanna in

9.   PRONI LA/7/3/A/15

which they called upon Sir Crawford and members of the Corporation to rescind permission given at a meeting on 2 May 1932[10].

In 1933 he received a threatening letter from a 'Ratepayer, Animal lover and Presbyterian' regarding the opening of Belfast Zoo. 'I do not believe in threats but I do feel that God will most assuredly hold you and the corporation responsible for cooping these poor creatures in such a place where they are inhumanly confined'. A similar letter criticising the opening of the zoo was sent by the Ulster British Israel Association who protested against the 'inhumanity and barbarity of capturing animals'.

The Ulster British Israel Association and the Macrory Memorial Presbyterian Church sent a letter strongly condemning Sunday afternoon boxing matches advertised in Ireland's Saturday Night. Sir Crawford was not opposed to entertainment being enjoyed by a depressed majority on a Sunday and openly encouraged and gave his approval to an appeal to have cinemas opened to the public on Sundays. He was a great lover of the cinema and with his secretary Major May would often attend first showings of new films that arrived in Belfast.

Letters flowed into the Lord Mayor's office every day and every one was answered personally by Sir Crawford's secretary Mr. McKinstry.

Outdoor Relief Strike

After a short post-war boom, business in Belfast became chronically depressed. The Wall Street Crash of 1929 had made a devastating impact on industrialised countries and thousands of workers found themselves without employment, shock waves surged east across the Atlantic. With the collapse of Austria's leading bank in June 1931, six million out of work in Germany in August 1931, and by January 1933 the volume of international trade was barely one third of what it had been on the eve of the Wall Street Crash.

---

10.   PRONI LA/7/3A/5 - LA/7/3A/2 Belfast Corporation Tenants Association

In Belfast grass grew on the slipways of Harland and Wolff. Queen's Island did not witness the launch of a single ship between 10 December 1931 and 1 May 1934. In 1935, Workman Clark, known in Belfast as the 'wee yard', was forced to close, with its operations taken over by Harland and Wolff. Although Harland and Wolff had built up a massive overdraft and there was talk of liquidation, the company performed creditably over the course of the 1930s. By May 1934 its work force had reached ten thousand. In 1935 its tonnage launched was a world record for the year, and by 1938 its total output was the largest for any shipyard in the United Kingdom[11].

As the economic crisis was worldwide, the Stormont Government could not continue to export the unemployed. Up to 1931 over 10,000 people a year had been emigrating in search of work. Now there were no jobs anywhere and as a result both Canada and the USA started to give 'one-way' tickets home to recent immigrants who had not become citizens. Between 1931 and 1939, 27 per cent of the insured workforce was unemployed. The lowest point was reached in July 1935 when 101,967 in the region were out of work. In Belfast's great shipbuilding and engineering industries almost half the total insured workers were idle and in the linen industry short time was general, with thirty-two percent out of work. As unemployment in Northern Ireland increased so did the need for benefits. Out of one and a quarter million people in the province over a hundred thousand had seen their jobs disappear. Of these 42,710 were getting benefit. 19,380 were on transitional benefit (which was reviewed every three months) and 13,908 got no money whatsoever. A further 24,000, mainly women and young workers were not even officially registered. Others had their benefit reduced or stopped by the operation of a 'means test'. As this 'means test' increased the number of unemployed not getting any money from the Labour Exchange, there

11. Alfred S Moore, *A Merchant Prince*

was an increase in the number applying to the Board of Guardians for 'outdoor relief'[12].

Some Boards of Guardians, notably in Newry, treated the long term employed with a fair degree of generosity. The Belfast Guardians, however, still applied the old workhouse test with rigour: applicants were carefully questioned by relieving officers; nothing would be given until savings had been exhausted; relief was in the form of groceries obtained by 'chits' from named shops; and the names of successful applicants were posted on gable walls. Patrick Shea, working for the Ministry of Labour remembered interviewing a widow whose claim for benefit he had to reject:

> I felt I had handled the situation rather well. She walked silently to the door, opened it and turning to the rows of silent men, now poring over their papers, she addressed the whole company. She spoke calmly and purposefully. "During the war my husband made bombs. He spent four years making bombs. I wish to Jaysus I had one of them now".[13']

In October 1932 the Outdoor Relief Workers went on strike and organised protest marches to demand improved assistance. This was a rare occasion when Protestants and Catholics campaigned together. On the evening of Monday 3 October a crowd of 60,000 of both religions marched from Frederick Street Labour Exchange to the traditional 'free-speech' forum at the Custom House steps where four platforms of speakers addressed the vast crowds. It was a torchlight parade, led by bands which, to avoid giving religious offence, played the neutral tune *Yes, we have no bananas*[14] over and over again. The main speakers at the meeting were Jack Beattie, MP, the two sympathetic Poor Law Guardians, Harry Diamond and James Collins, as well as Tommy Geehan and Betty Sinclair of the Belfast Trades Council. The meeting renewed its demand for increased rates of relief and added a call for rent and 'tick' (hire purchase payment) strike. This was the first time since 1919 that workers had ignored the big-

12. Paddy Devlin *Yes we have no bananas: Outdoor Relief in Belfast 1920-1939*, pp.125-6

13. Jonathan Bardon, p.524

14. Paddy Devlin *Yes we have no bananas: Outdoor Relief in Belfast 1920-1939*, pp.127-129

ots and united on class lines to fight for their own interests. The next morning 7,000 people accompanied a deputation to the Union Workhouse on the Lisburn Road where the Board of Guardians usually met and where the men lay down on the tramlines to stop the traffic. The road, one of the main routes into the city, was blocked for three hours. A delegation was received by the Guardians (after threats of what would happen if they refused) but nothing was forthcoming other than a letter to the Government asking them to provide more relief. On Wednesday October 5th the Royal Ulster Constabulary prevented another march to the workhouse by lining the route with Crossly tenders and Lancia armoured cars. Nevertheless demonstrators got past the police lines and 144 were admitted to the workhouse as inmates. Once inside they refused to obey orders and were reported singing and dancing throughout the night. Three were arrested and removed from the building. That night rioting broke out in several places. A tram was hijacked and dozens of shops and offices were looted in the main Catholic and Protestant areas. The RUC baton charged the crowds as soon as they formed. The rioting continued for the rest of the week.

On Sunday evening 9 October Sir Crawford was contacted by a number of Belfast's leading businessmen and officials from the craft unions who expressed fears concerning the implications of the rioting asking for the Lord Mayor's intervention. On Monday 10 October Sir Crawford requested an immediate conference with the Belfast Board of Guardians. The meeting, held in the Lord Mayor's Parlour in the City Hall, was attended as usual by Vice-Admiral Edward Archdale, Minister of Agriculture and Commerce, Sir Crawford and Board representatives including the Chairman of the Board of Guardians. It was announced after the meeting that a new range of relief schemes would immediately be organised which would be paid to all men of relief, and with the increased work available, give increases of payment for extra time worked. Moreover, in April Dawson Bates wrote to Sir Crawford agreeing that the grant towards the Distress Relief works should be increased from 25% to 50%. A meeting was called that afternoon in St. Mary's Hall, and as James Collins had predicted, the strikers turned down the Board's offer on the grounds that it was not adequate. They wanted full trade union rates for all work done, an increased rate on the Outdoor Relief Scheme and a general strike of all workers in the city to support them[15].

The Outdoor Relief workers planned a massive demonstration for Tuesday 1 October, which would include marches from every district to a meeting point in the centre of Belfast. It was proposed to march to the Custom House steps for a mass rally. The following morning news reached the workers that G.B Hanna M.P. secretary to the Ministry of Home Affairs, had banned all public meetings for that day and the day following under the Special Powers Act; and that he was drafting into Belfast another 700 police from outlying areas and asking for the military in Holywood to be given stand-by duties[16]. However on the day of the demonstration the unemployed attempted to resist the ban and riots spread like wildfire. They were intensive in East, West and North Belfast. Cobble stones and 'kidney-pavers' were collected, picks and shovels were retrieved from work depots and barricades were erected.

The Police moved into these areas in large numbers in an attempt to take over the main roads of Belfast. On the Falls Road, the mill workers, many of them barefoot, broke up the police cordons, reportedly to allow food supplies into the beleaguered north and west areas of the city. By late afternoon the police had opened fire and proclaimed a curfew from 11pm until 5am the following morning. Nevertheless, next day barricades were still up and hijackings were taking place frequently throughout the city. Police stopped food supplies coming in and rounded up hundreds of men in Catholic areas to dismantle the barricades. James Collins, City Councillor and sympathetic member of the Board of Guardians, was dragged out of his house with his son at gun-point and made to take down barricades close to his home in

15. Paddy Devlin *Yes we have no bananas: Outdoor Relief in Belfast 1920-1939*, p.127

16. Paddy Devlin *Yes we have no bananas: Outdoor Relief in Belfast 1920-1939*, p.128

the Short Strand. He was only partly dressed but was forced to work all night in the rain under threat of being shot[17].

John Campbell, a Guardian and secretary of the Labour Party, commenting on the rioting stated that 'Lord Craigavon's solution was to divide the workers into different religious camps and it was noteworthy that although the recent trouble was spread all over the city only in a Roman Catholic area did the police use their guns. Dawson Bates, the Minister of Home Affairs had issued instructions to the police, not merely to contain the rioting, but to use firearms in Catholic areas purportedly to prevent the IRA from overthrowing the Government, and to use batons in Protestant areas purportedly to stop looting of shops by troublemakers. When the rioting finally stopped, two people had been shot dead. Another fifteen had suffered gunshot wounds. Nineteen others suffered injuries.

At a meeting with Sir Crawford in City Hall, seventeen Belfast Councillors, including ten official Unionists signed a motion for debate in City Council calling on the Government 'promptly to take such action as may be necessary to relieve distress and starvation amongst the unemployed people of the city. At 3pm on 13 October selected representatives of the Board of Guardians were called to an urgent meeting at the workhouse to prepare them to meet Cabinet Ministers at Stormont later that afternoon. The size and power of this representation indicated that the Government was determined to stand for no further delay on the part of the Guardians and to have the matter settled before a large-scale revolution developed. The Board of Guardians' representatives, according to the Minutes, were told quite bluntly to put before their Board the following scales:-

Man and wife	20 shillings per week
With 1 or 2 children	24 shillings per week
With 3 or 4 children	28 shillings per week
With 5 or more children	32 shillings per week[18]

---

17. Paddy Devlin *Yes we have no bananas: Outdoor Relief in Belfast 1920-1939*, p.129

18. Paddy Devlin *Yes we have no bananas: Outdoor Relief in Belfast 1920-1939*, p.132

The workers went back to their jobs on 17 October. On Tuesday 18 October the Chairman of the Guardians issued a statement commentating on newspapers coverage of the strike in which he said that the increased scales were not granted because of pressure from the Outdoor Relief Strikers, but because of his Committee's efforts earlier in the year. Two of their members, Harry Diamond and James Collins told the Chairman that the increases were brought about only after blood had been shed and the city turned into a shambles by the Guardians. Eight days after the curfew was lifted the city returned to normal.

Belfast Corporation spent more than £4,000 weekly, through the Board of Guardians, on outdoor relief for able-bodied persons and in subsequent years it increased considerably. Simultaneously other expenditure was necessary to help unemployed workers over their period of penury. Thus, during the year, the City Council provided 159,546 days' work for men in various relief schemes[19].

These schemes were devised to provide work comprising the making and improving of streets, drainage plans, the construction of the Lagan Embankments, and the conversion of forty acres of land to form the Grove Playing Fields. The energy and enterprise with which Belfast City Council, under Sir Crawford's leadership, tackled the complex and grave problems arising from the inter-wars slump won unanimous recognition. Despite pessimism in many quarters, significant undertakings steadily progressed, and many buildings, now giving dignity to Belfast materialised. On 30 November 1932 Sir Crawford attended the City and Trade of Belfast at St. Andrews Dinner. In his speech regarding housing schemes and Town Planning he revealed that in the past year 1,259 dwelling houses had been erected, and in addition, 435 buildings had undergone alteration, some of these being of considerable magnitude. He went on to say that one very important step had been taken by the Belfast Corporation during

19. PRONI LA/7/1/B/10, LA/7/1//B/11, LA/7/1/B/22

the year and that was in connection with Town Planning. He stated that:-

> "The underlying principle of Town Planning was to place on a plan what is con-
> sidered to be the ideal scheme prepared in the best interests of the community
> as a whole. Bearing in mind that in any future development of the City or any
> alteration such as the result of clearance of unhealthy areas, etc., the well con-
> sidered lay-out may gradually, as circumstances permit, be effected. In preparing
> such a scheme due regard will be paid to the City's industrial and commercial
> activities as well as to its requirements as a residential area. The scheme which,
> of necessity, must be somewhat elastic, must provide in broad outline zones for
> special purposes. One zone area will be for industry, another for businesses and
> residences, with provision for roads and open spaces."

His speech contained concern for the growth of motor traffic

> "which I do not think has reached its maximum in this country, and is producing
> an entirely new set of circumstances. Not only the design of streets but the meth-
> ods of land development must be adapted to these circumstances. It is neces-
> sary not only to avoid congestion of traffic, by which improvements in mechanical
> traction are largely stultified, but also to provide for the safety and comfort both
> of pedestrians and motor transport"[20].

Crawford's speeches and addresses to public figures and dignitaries visiting Belfast throughout his mayoralty were many and varied.
Always keen to promote growth and prosperity in Ulster and to bring
innovation to the Province. In 1932 he addressed Lord Wakefield,
founder of the Castrol Oil Co., on the Development of Municipal
Airports:-

> "The Corporation of Belfast was the first Corporation in the UK to take advantage
> of the powers conferred by the Air Navigation Act of 1920 upon local Authorities
> to establish aerodromes. In 1924 the Corporation acquired 50 acres of land in
> the city for the purpose of an aerodrome and including the purchase price, spent
> £15,000 on the venture."

Crawford went on to say that according to the Air Transport
Manual there are only 16 towns in Great Britain which have license
Aerodromes.

20. PRONI LA/7/3/A/8

In 1932, a new luxury liner The Bermuda, was destroyed by fire while berthed at an out-fitting wharf in Belfast Harbour. The Corporation found it faced a £2,000,000 claim. Sir Crawford, despite his ex-of-ficio membership on the Harbour Board, argued successfully that the harbour employed its own policing force and thus was solely re-sponsible for the damages, thereby saving the Corporation this huge expense during this depressed period[21].

Sir Crawford supported the The Silent Valley Scheme. This was a project to bring water from the Mourne Mountains, fifty miles from Belfast, undertaken by the Belfast City and District Water Board. Although Belfast was in a deep economic depression and despite strong opposition from some members of the Corporation, the Water Commissioners completed their courageous project for link-ing up the available water resources from the Mountains of Mourne. The reservoir, delivering forty-two gallons of water a day per citizen, was opened on a rainy day in June 1933 by Sir Edward Carson. Afterwards he received a presentation in the Ulster Hall from Sir Crawford[22].

The Belfast Harbour Commission, of which Sir Crawford was a member, had similar faith in the future and recognised the policy 'In time of war prepare for peace; in times of peace prepare for war' had its parallel in regard to employment and idleness. Although the shipping imports and exports had decreased materially at the port, the Belfast Harbour Commissioners, entered into a very comprehen-sive programme of dock extensions during this dismal decade. Thus, in 1933, H.R.H. The Princess Alice, Countess of Athlone, formally opened the Herdman Channel and Pollock Dock. While in Belfast she also opened the 36th (Ulster) Division Bazaar in the Belfast Plaza ballroom and inspected the St. John's Ambulance Brigade after which she was the guest of Sir Crawford at City Hall.

---

21. Alfred S Moore, *A Merchant Prince*

22. Alfred S Moore, *A Merchant Prince*

In 1933 service between Belfast and Ardrossan was resumed by the Laird Lines Limited, and highlighted with pictures of Sir Crawford and visitors on the Laird's Isle at the inauguration of the run. Progress continued as the McConnell Lock and Weir were completed. The opening ceremony included a tour of the harbour with Sir Crawford navigating the barge 'Industry' with the Improvement Committee on board.

Top: Annaghdroghal House

Above: Crawford's brother Samuel McCullagh

Right: The young apprentice: A photograph of Crawford taken during his years at the Bank Buildings

Top: The Bank Buildings at the turn of the century (by kind permission of Richard Graham)

Below: Castle Junction towards Royal Avenue (by kind permission of Richard Graham)

Above: The Improvement Committee 1906

*Top: C McCullagh & Co.
Department Store c. 1905*
(by kind permission of the National
Library of Ireland)

*Far left: The Store's Art
Nouveau staircase*

Left: William Gibson

Top: The Grand Central Hotel 1906
(by kind permission of Richard Graham)

*Above and right: The Carlton Restaurant,
pictured here in the 30s, was one of
the social hubs of society life in Belfast
and was regularly used by Crawford to
meet friends and colleagues to discuss
business. Originally a private residence, it
is the oldest surviving building in Donegall
Place.*
(by kind permission of Richard Graham)

Left: Maggie Brodie's family home at 19 Greencastle Street in the townland of Ballygolan, Greencastle.

(by kind permission of James Lynne)

Below: Rust Hall, Helens Bay

Top: Lismara, Whiteabbey. It has been renamed Abbeydene and is currently run as a successful guest house by Tim and Effy Clifford (by kind permission of the National Library of Ireland)

Below: A happy family photo (minus Boysie) taken at Lismara 1919: L-R Helen, Maggie, Crawford, Daisy. (by kind permission of the National Library of Ireland)

*Above: Private Ernest McCullagh of the
Princess Patricia Light Infantry Regiment,
23rd Military Battalion.*

*Right:A young Ernest with his mother
Catherine Donaghy and step sister Evelyn*

*Left and below: Three of Crawford's
business ventures, The Metropole Hotel,
York Street* (by kind permission of Richard Graham),
*Maguire and Pattersons, Matchmakers
in Donegall Rd and The Classic Cinema,
Castle Lane* (by kind permission of Richard Graham)

*Opposite: Crawford McCullagh, High
Sheriff of Belfast 1911.*

Clockwise from top: The author's "tall, handsome and kindly looking" great grandfather; Lady Mayoress, Margaret McCullagh; Daisy McCullagh on her engagement to Victor Henderson ; Boysie McCullagh in later life displaying his love of Birds in Trafalgar Square

Top: The Floral Hall
opened in 1936
(by kind permission of John Harcourt)

Centre: Ideal Home
Exhibition 1932

Bottom: Sir Crawford's
sister Jenny Lyttle and
family in Toronto 1932
with Florrie Pat front left.

Top: Sir Crawford greets King George VI and Queen Elizabeth on the occasion of their visit to Belfast 18th July 1945

Below: L-R Sir Crawford, Randolph Churchill, Sir Thomas McConnell and Boysie McCullagh

With General Dwight D
Eisenhower unveiling a memorial
to the American Troops 24
August 1945

Top: *Field Marshall Sir Bernard Montgomery receiving the Freedom of the City 14 September 1945* (by kind permission of the Belfast Telegraph)

Below: *Sir Crawford presents Victoria Cross winner, Able Seaman James Maginnis with a cheque from the people of Belfast in recognition of his gallantry* (by kind permission of the Belfast Telegraph)

Top: Royal Visit: Sir Crawford with King George VI, Queen Elizabeth and Princess Elizabeth 1945
(by kind permission of the Belfast Telegraph)

Below: Guests including Lord Londonderry and the McCullagh family from the party for General Eisenhower hosted by Sir Crawford at Lismara (The author's father, Lionel Henderson is on the extreme right)

Top: Belfast City Hall

Below: One of the many business dinners addressed by Sir Crawford in the Grand Central Hotel

Chapter Fourteen
1932-1936

The House on the Hill

Every human society wants to be officed by a best class, who shall be
masters instructed in all the great cuts of life; shall be wise, temperate,
brave public men, adorned with dignity and accomplishments. Every
community wishes this, and each has taken its own method to secure
such service to the state. And everyone knows that in every city is always
to be found some public-spirited men who perform, unpaid, a great
amount of hard work in the public interest.

Emerson.

On 23 April 1932, Sir Crawford was appointed Deputy Lieutenant. In the same year on the 16 November the Prince of Wales (later King Edward VIII) arrived at Belfast to officially open the new Parliament Buildings. He was greeted at Donegal Quay by a twenty-one gun salute and the cheers of a vast crowd of Belfast citizens. After inspecting the Royal Marine Guard, the Prince set off in a carriage for Stormont where he was received by Viscount Craigavon and dignitaries. In his ceremonial speech he paid a glowing tribute to the 'courage, tenacity, loyalty and devotion of the Ulster people'. After the ceremony he was taken to City Hall where Sir Crawford McCullagh and over 1,500 of his guests were waiting to entertain his Royal Highness.

The Great Hall was decorated with lavish palms, tropical foliage and chrysanthemums of all colours. In bold relief to this background were brilliant splashes of crimson and blue uniforms while Sir Crawford was resplendent in his gown of gold and black. Margaret, by his side, as Lady Mayoress was dressed in a flattering gown of honey coloured silk and lace topped with her signature white mink stole. On the dais, draped in plain dark crimson cloth, stood a solitary gilded chair intended for the Prince of Wales. However he opted to stand between the Lord Mayor and the Lady Mayoress with his equerries in the rear and the Duke and Duchess of Abercorn standing close by. After a brief speech which conveyed the Prince's appreciation of Ulster's sincere welcome and his hope "that when the present wave of world depression passes the various industries of your province may once again occupy the proud place they used to do and bring back your eclipsed prosperity."[1]

During his stay of three days, he completed visits to Gallaghers' Tobacco Factory, Belfast Ropeworks, Ewart's Linen Mills and Hilden Thread Works. Finally after visiting the Royal Victoria and Mater Infirmary Hospitals, Queens University and the Belfast Harbour and Water Office, he returned to England on the Larne to Stranraer steamer.

Stormont – New Parliament Buildings

When George V came to Belfast in June 1921 to inaugurate the new Northern Ireland Parliament, the first meetings were held at City Hall before relocating in September to the Assembly College in Botanic Avenue where the Theological College of the Presbyterian Church in Ireland was based. In June the first Cabinet meeting had taken place to discuss the suitability of a site for the new Parliament Buildings. Prime Minister James Craig had proposed the site at Stormont on the outskirts of the city. This proved to be contentious and among the six objectors were the Lord Mayor Sir William Coote, and Sir Crawford McCullagh who disagreed with the proposal on the grounds that the site was too costly and too far from the city centre. A sub-committee

---

1. *Belfast Evening Telegraph* 16 November 1932

was set up and three other sites were proposed, Ormeau Park, Belfast Castle and Parkmount. After numerous meetings the original proposal for the Stormont site was agreed and the Prime Minister, Sir James Craig stated that accommodation should be provided not only for Parliament, but also for the Civil Service and the Law Courts. In December 1921 the Stormont Estate, which covered 235 acres, including Stormont Castle and seven cottages was purchased with a substantial deposit from Prime Minister Craig from his own finances. The adjacent lands were added to provide space for the processional avenue and also to prevent undesirable development.[2]

The original scheme envisaged a four-story Parliament Building, capped by a magnificent dome or cupola. Parallel to this were to be four blocks of administrative buildings at a lower level, linked to the Parliamentary tier by wings where the lower lawn terraces are today. The estimated cost of this was £1,350,000 but by the autumn of 1925 this had escalated to £1,750,000. A joint meeting of the Board of Works, Treasury, and Northern Ireland government officials was called in November 1925 and revised plans were commissioned, binding both administrative and parliamentary accommodation into a single building. The dome was unfortunately sacrificed, despite its foundations already being in place, but the costs were brought down to an acceptable level of £1,125,000 with a completion date within three-and-a-half years.

Constructed by Stewart Partners Ltd., the building is designed in the Greek classical tradition with an Ionic temple-front in the centre. The exterior is faced with Portland Stone mounted on a plinth of granite quarried from the Mourne Mountains. From the top of the building, Britannia and her guardian lions look out over Belfast, while a whole group of statuary on the pediment below depicts Ulster presenting a golden flame of loyalty to Britain and the Commonwealth. Immediately over the main entrance sits the Royal Coat of Arms.

2.   PRONI D1327/22/1

The front façade is 365 ft wide (one foot for every day of the year) and 92 ft (28m) high to the top of Britannia. [see appendix 6]

At the end of Stormont's processional Prince of Wales Avenue approaching Parliament Buildings stands a bronze statue of Edward Carson. The loyalists of Northern Ireland had commissioned the sculptor L.S. Merrifield to cast his statue in bronze. The inscription on the base read : 'By the loyalists of Ulster as an expression of their love and admiration for its subject.' On a rainy July day in 1933 he saw it unveiled by Lord Craigavon in the presence of more than 40,000 people. When the time came for Carson to speak he had to struggle with emotion. "I know of no words", he told them, "to express my gratitude to great people who all through these years never for one moment deceived or deserted me…"

Despite only one building being completed, its name has remained in the plural – Parliament Buildings. It is now affectionately known throughout Northern Ireland as 'the house on the hill'. The Foundation stone was formally laid on 19 May 1928 by the 3rd Duke of Abercorn, the Governor of Northern Ireland. Placed within this stone is a sealed casket containing a piece of The Times and several local newspapers, a volume of the Northern Ireland Hansard and collection of coinage.[3]

When the Prince of Wales arrived in Belfast to open Stormont and attend the welcoming ceremony in City Hall he had afternoon tea with his hosts in the Lord Mayor's suite of chambers. It was the first time that Crawford and Margaret had been in the Prince of Wales company without a considerable entourage and Crawford recalls in his memoirs how his wife had been quite unnerved when his Highness told her that he would be seeing her again soon. Predictably a few months later Sir Crawford and Lady McCullagh received an invitation to dinner at St. James's Palace, London.

The large white invitation card expressed that:

3.   *Stormont – The House on the Hill*

The Equerry in Waiting is directed by HIS ROYAL HIGHNESS THE PRINCE OF WALES to invite the Rt. Hon. The Lord Mayor of Belfast and the Lady Mayoress to Dinner at St. James's Palace on Friday 26 May, 1933 at 8.45 o'clock. Evening Dress: Decorations. The favour of an answer is requested to the Equerry in Waiting to H.R.H. The Prince of Wales. St. James's Palace.

The card was accompanied by two enclosures, one was a card setting forth the seating plan and the name of the guests who they would be sitting beside. The second enclosure was a smaller card bearing the engraved request to the Lord Mayor to take Lady Diana Montgomery-Massingberd into dinner. Lady Diana was one of two daughters of the Earl Temple of Stowe. She and her sister married the two sons of the Right Hon. Hugh de Fellenberg Montgomery, landowner and Ulster politician of Blessingbourne, Fivemiletown, Co. Tyrone. Her husband was General Sir Archibald Montgomery. He took her surname hyphenated to his in 1926 when she inherited family estates. He was A.D.C. to King George VI and was promoted to Field Marshall in 1936. Sir Crawford recalls the evening in his memoirs and although he found Lady Diana a most charming and interesting partner, he was fascinated by Donna Antonietta Grandi his left hand table companion and wife of the Italian Ambassador who he vividly describes in his memoirs as a striking, statuesque brunette who routinely turned the heads of all the men who were seated at the table.

Lady Margaret was accompanied into the dining room by Sir Thomas Wilford, K.C.M.G. The High Commissioner for New Zealand. Crawford relates in his memoirs how Sir Tomas immediately put Margaret at her ease by being a natural conversationalist and interested her by describing how Belfast had a town named after it in Canterbury Province, South Island. Moreover, the Province also had its Sandy Row, Donegall Street, York Street, Bedford Street and Howard Street. The evening had no ceremonial restraint in the conversation and everyone was put at their ease by His Royal Highness who as Sir Crawford reveals was in the best of spirits. There was no inclination at that time of the catastrophic turn of events that would enfold with the abdication of his regal host from the throne three years later in 1936.

When Sir Crawford was unanimously re-elected as Lord Mayor in 1933 he entertained the Corporation, civic officials, the press and friends in City Hall – again hosting the event generously from his own pocket. In addressing the guests, he called for harmony and unity. He also hoped he would not have to ask any member to retire. This was the year he introduced his 'Hore Belisha' a light that flashed red when debates got heated signalling for the over loquacious member to sit down and shut up! This was depicted in a cartoon in *The Times* in February1933. He said he looked to the future with optimism and confidence, saying unemployment was the most serious problem and there was need to provide useful work. The Nationalist representative commended him for having increased the Coal Relief Fund and for having done all possible to relieve poverty. The Labour representative said their members, while not always agreeing with him, appreciated the very fair rulings the Lord Mayor had given from the chair. Both parties supported his nomination for the coming term.

By 1934, Sir Crawford had gained control of the unruly council. In nominating him the Nationalists admired his attitude as he meted out justice to all sections, and his 'success, in holding the balance fairly between different interests was sincere and well deserved'. Upon taking the chair Sir Crawford commented on his anxiety in taking office three years previously, as there was such distrust among the members.'[4] He commended the members on how well they had responded to his appeal to support the chair. He said that the Council was now a model. Work was efficiently carried out with credit to the city. Each member was doing the best for the people they represented and they were all pulling together. They had not had to raise taxes as high as predicted by the £86,000 debt connected to the distress relief. All other committees kept spending in line for the year. A grant from the government and the fact that the trams, gas and electricity

4.   *Belfast Evening Telegraph* February 1934

had improved their position over the previous year all helped towards reducing the debt. He predicted they would turn a corner in 1934 with the shipyards getting busy again and with increased activity in the mills and factories. The city was in a good position, the highest in the Kingdom. Belfast still had the largest shipbuilding, linen and tobacco manufacturing and rope making concerns in the world and was an excellent tourist centre. In the year ahead ... he was confident they would all pull together. Every member of the Corporation would have the opportunity of expressing his views – the views he was sent to represent and those views, of whatever shade would be respected and considered.

Finishing his address to the council members Sir Crawford paid a moving tribute to Joseph Devlin who died in 1934. Entering Westminster for the first time for North Kilkenny in 1902, Devlin took West Belfast in the election of 1906 from the Unionists and became the principal spokesman for the Northern Nationalists.

Belfast Castle and Zoo

Since 1931 the Estates Committee of the Corporation had been in negotiation with the 9th Earl of Shaftesbury, Marquess of Donegall concerning his Belfast Estate. The family seat of the Donegall family since the early 19th Century had been at Ormeau Park on the outskirts of Belfast. The Marquess found the large Tudor-Revival mansion at Ormeau inconvenient and, in the late 1860s, built a sizeable Scottish-Baronial castle on 200 acres at the other side of Belfast, on the lower slopes of Cave Hill overlooking Belfast Lough. The demesne was originally part of a deer park of the old Belfast Castle and that at one time included almost the whole of Belfast.

The Shaftesbury family were philanthropists, supporting various charities and hosting garden fetes within the Castle grounds. The 9th Earl became Lord Mayor in 1907 and Chancellor of Queens University the following year. When Lord Shaftesbury took up residence in London he suggested to the Belfast Estate Committee that the Castle become a permanent residence of the Lord Mayor. When

Sir Crawford was installed as Lord Mayor following his re-election in 1934 he was further pressed by Lord Shaftesbury to make Belfast Castle his home. In his memoirs Sir Crawford writes that he had no wish to make Belfast Castle his home and sent a telegram to Lord Shaftesbury requesting an appointment. He received the following reply: 'Delighted if lunch with me Carlton Club two-after-noon tomorrow – Shaftesbury'. Within two hours Sir Crawford was on his way to London. Over lunch in the Carlton Club Sir Crawford and Lord Shaftesbury negotiated a gentleman's agreement in which Belfast Castle and two hundred acres, bordering on Hazlewood and Bellevue pleasure grounds, were to be donated to and developed for the benefit of Belfast citizens. About ten acres of this ground was regarded as suitable for building purposes. This comprised –

> 'an area fronting Antrim Road; the gate lodge adjoining, with approximate half an acre of ground; Martlett Towers; the Cavehill Post Office and gate entrance lodge; Park Lodge and grounds; buildings in the stabling yard, let jointly with grazing lands, walled in garden, with good range of greenhouses and building land, approximately ten acres'

– and was to be sold to the city for £9,750. If the Corporation did not approve the acquisition of the aforesaid lands, Sir Crawford agreed personally to pay the Earl £9,750. Sir Crawford envisioned the further development of these lands for citizens and visitors, "with which nothing could compare in the British Isles". A few years later Belfast Corporation under Sir Crawford's direction acquired 8,000 acres at Cavehill and 74 acres adjoining Hazlewood and Bellevue. With the acquisition of these lands the opening of Bellevue Zoological Gardens and Amusement Park became a reality.

On 28 March 1934 Sir Crawford formally opened the Zoo by driving a miniature railway engine in the Park with dignitaries occupying the coaches.

The *Northern Whig and Belfast Post* reported:

> 'No effort has been spared by Belfast Tramways Committee, who have spent £10,000 on the new zoo, to ensure that the enclosures for the animals shall approach as nearly as possible their natural habitat; and the dens, paddocks and

enclosures, the construction of which has kept 150 men busy for several months, are regarded by experts as the most admirable of their kind. There is even a hospital for animals which fall sick. A tour of the grounds shows large roomy dens along the bastion walls, most comfortably appointed and equipped, each with it's private sleeping compartments, dens for small mammals each fitted with it's cosy barrel, to which the animals can retire and sleep, and spacious enclosures with charming little houses tastefully arranged and finished off with wattles and logs. It is a wonderful achievement and will certainly give the city an enhanced appeal as a centre of hillside beauty and profitable instruction. To walk Leisurely through the area allocated the exhibits takes about two and one half hours Giving the necessary time for study and observation'.

The entertainments manager for the Bellevue estates strove to cater for all tastes. The traditional July holiday week when all industry shut down in Belfast was always a period of frenzied activity at Bellevue, and in 1937 was advertised 'Zoo Baby Week'. On show was a splendid collection of animals recently born at the Zoo, including baby lions, named Peter and Bunty, Swiss mountain goats, ponies, tigers, wolves, black bears, deer and coati Mundi. Year upon year new attractions were added and the July holiday period of 1938 was no exception. The Zoo was bursting at the seams with a magnificent collection of over 300 wild animals and foreign bird. New arrivals included two splendid chimpanzees, a family of sea-lions living in a specially-constructed pool, pelicans, flamingos and a further batch of baby lions.

In tandem with the excitement in the Zoo, crowds of holidaymakers were thrilled by dare-devil stuntman Sarraguna on the plateau, who slid down a wire rope hanging by his teeth, the rope was secured to the topmost pinnacle of the Mountain Dipper and his act was described as 'the great slide to death 500 ft. to earth hanging on precariously only by his molars!' By way of light relief he was also fired from a cannon and in between lifted pianos aided only by jaws and teeth! Contemporary photographs show large crowds assembled and perched at every vantage point, including bus roofs, to see the great show. Spectacular thrills were promised and delivered twice daily, at 4 o'clock in the afternoon and 8.30 in the evening.[5]

In May 1936, Sir Crawford opened The Floral Hall on the Hazlewood playgrounds at a cost of £15,000. This was an imposing, partly-glassed white-domed building nestled in a sheltered area of the Hazlewood Estate. Concerts and entertainments could now be held indoors as this was a theatre and ballroom combined. Of circular construction, the floor was eighty-five foot in diameter and was not obstructed by a single pillar. A bank of windows, facing east, offered a sweeping vista of Belfast Lough. The floor seated one thousand comfortably with a stage thirty by twenty feet and twenty-two feet high. There were accompanying dressing, storage and projection rooms. There had been criticism because of the difficulties encountered during construction, but Sir Crawford had remained optimistic and was rewarded by its eventual satisfactory completion.

The *Northern Whig and Belfast Post* reported on Tuesday 5 May:

'Sir Crawford in his opening address indicated that the Floral Hall belonged to the people. He hoped that the Corporation could make it a paying proposition, even though he was aware that a body of opinion said that they could not. However, it was his and his colleagues belief that a great city like Belfast could not count everything in pounds, shillings and pence, not let the absence of profit stand in the way of progress. He reiterated that the public should realise that the hall belonged to them and not private enterprise.

'People could come along to Bellevue and Hazlewood for the day or afternoon secure in the knowledge that the hall was there to provide entertainment, and on a wet day to offer shelter, and if so desired supply sustenance in splendid surroundings'.

'The Lord Mayor further stressed that the hall, which is on a commanding site, is the answer to a long-felt desire to complete the city's playground and to provide an entertainment hall similar in beauty and usefulness to those of the pleasure resorts across the channel'.

---

5.   Stewart McFetridge, *Bellevue - Belfast's Mountain Playground,* p.72

An insight is given into the level of entertainment that was available in Belfast at that time by Stewart McFetridge in an extract from his book *Bellevue: Belfast's Mountain Playground*:

'During the opening week of live shows at the Floral Hall, the established theatres in the city (no doubt now seen as the opposition) were presenting a varied programme. At the Grand Opera House Noel Coward's musical play Bitter Sweet, staged with a full West End cast including Betty French, Michael Cole and Renee Reel, was packing them in twice nightly.

Whist the Empire Theatre of Varieties was offering for the delectation of its patrons a revue entitled Sea Side Scandals, produced on a lavish scale and consisting of 18 scenes, skilfully combined to give a fast-moving programme. By early June a scant few weeks after the opening of the Floral Hall at Hazlewood, dancing was beginning to take over as the main attraction. Alex Monaghan and his Orchestra were in residence playing at two session daily, on Mondays, Wednesdays and Saturdays, whilst the stage show was presented on the alternate days and nights. In due course dancing was to reign almost supreme at the 'Floral'. However, there was also a varied programme of stage variety. Those companies appearing during the season included the White Blackbirds, Summer Fayre, Blue Riband, the Wows of 1939, and among other Bangor Entertainers. Whatever the round of entertainment presented, the Floral soon established itself as one of the classiest and most popular venue in which to enjoy a pleasurable night out.

Municipal Developments

Belfast Corporation organised municipal services into a number of boards, commissions and committees. Sir Crawford was active in the affairs of all these bodies, not just as an ex-officio member. While he had a keen and enlightened regard for progress he also had a prudent regard for economy. In 1933 he introduced the Wise Spending Campaign, inaugurated in Bristol, it proclaimed to 'Spend for Self-Preservation'. In the introduction to the campaign Sir Crawford said 'by spending wisely now you are putting money into circulation, which will benefit yourself and every one associated with you.[6] He promoted, encouraged and acclaimed the technical advances embodied in the fibre of Belfast. Coupling this with sound administrative

6.   PRONI LA/7/3/15

practices and good leadership much was accomplished, and despite taking office in the early stages of the industrial depression, it is evident that the city kept up with the times during his tenure. In July 1933 he spoke at an Airport Conference Dinner on the development of Municipal Airports in the United Kingdom. He said that Belfast Corporation was the first Corporation to take advantage of the powers conferred by the Air Navigation Act 1920 upon local authorities to establish aerodromes, as in 1924 when Belfast Corporation acquired some 50 acres of land in the city for the purpose of an aerodrome, and including the purchase price, expended at £15,000. Now there is a regular twice daily service between Glasgow and Belfast.

The construction of Public Housing, the Ravenhill Housing Estates, and other housing schemes continued. During the twelve months ending 31 October 1933 there were 541 dwelling houses constructed, 386 other buildings had alterations and additions and 285 motor garages were erected. In total the construction costs amounted to £577,000.[7] A new Cooperative building was built in 1932. A new Belfast Mental Hospital was opened in 1935, and an extension completed in 1936. In the same year a new fire fighting station with an ambulance section was opened. On Friday 18th December 1936 Sir Crawford officially opened the new Boyne Bridge. This replaced the old bridge of 1870 constructed over the railway tracks beside Murray's Tobacco Factory. The work was carried out by H and J Martin, the Corporation agreeing to carry out the work at their own expense. Building commenced in September 1934 at a cost of £29,270.16.2p. The Boyne Bridge was originally known as the Saltwater Bridge and is the site of the oldest bridge in Belfast mentioned in 1717 as being in need of repair. In 1936, a new branch of the National Building Society, Imperial House opened with its assets exceeding £31,000,000. These new premises became necessary because of the great need for houses and investment facilities.[8]

---

7.   PRONI LA/7/3/15

8.   PRONI LA/7/3A/45

In 1923 the Northern Ireland Education Act transferred the admin-istration and organisation of education in Belfast to the Corporation. The Education Committee was renamed as the Education Authority. The main task at the time was to replace the old, cramped, poorly lit buildings with large classrooms, and to modernise and enlarge schools transferred to the Authority. By 1931 over 20,000 children had been provided new classrooms. Much still needed to be done, and in the next eight to nine years, one or two schools a year were erected and opened. Sir Crawford and/or Lady McCullagh were involved in the stone laying or opening ceremonies of most of the public elemen-tary schools. In 1932, The 7th Marquis of Londonderry, Minister of Education for Ulster, opened Strandtown Public Elementary School on the Belmont Road. Sir Crawford presided over the ceremony and commented on the fact that although times were hard and money was scarce there was still an impressive number of new enlarged schools being built. Strandtown School was later awarded the distinction of being the best building built, in the past three years, by an architec-tural committee.[9]

In 1935 Belfast Corporation challenged the new Finance (N.I.) Act, which required local authorities to levy a rate so as to produce a pay-ment towards central expenditure on education. This legislation was determined by a policy of the British Government to distribute the burden of taxation more evenly. Sir Crawford challenged the valid-ity of the Act by a petition to the Governor, asking for a referral to the Judicial Committee of the Privy Council, on the grounds that the legislation imposed a tax substantially the same in character as income tax and, if so, was ultra vires, since only Westminster could levy income tax under the Government of Ireland Act. The Judicial Committee's response was 'the essential character' of the education levy was that it was imposed irrespective of income. The Corporation

9.   Alfred S Moore, *A Merchant Prince*

accepted their decision and proceeded to increase its ordinary education expenditure as well as to pay the levy.[10]

Civic Entertainment

In 1934 The Duke of Gloucester came to Belfast for the first time and was given a formal reception at City Hall. During the visit the Duke was accompanied by Sir Crawford to lay a wreath at the Cenotaph. He then proceeded to Wilmont House, Dunmurry, the home of Sir Thomas Dixon, H.M. Lieutenant of Belfast. The house was placed at the disposal of the Duke as the temporary official residence during the reconstruction of Government House, Hillsborough. Later that evening the Duke, his entourage, dignitaries, friends and family were guests of Sir Crawford and Lady McCullagh at a lavish ball held in City Hall. For the silver jubilee celebrations in 1935 King George V selected three cities, Belfast, Cardiff and Edinburgh. He sent his sons to each city: The Duke of Gloucester to Belfast, The Duke of Edinburgh to Edinburgh and the Prince of Wales to Cardiff. Arriving on a Saturday morning 11 May 1935, by the H.M.S. Achilles, the Duke was driven through the crowded streets of Belfast to cheers of welcome. Arriving at City Hall he was welcomed by Sir Crawford where he received the Freedom of the City. In his speech the Duke referred to the fact that, during the king's reign, Belfast had assumed greater political importance than as a mere provincial city. It was now the capital of a self-governing state within the British Empire and one result of the change had been the many architectural additions and improvements besides its advancement in prestige ... His fervent wish and prayer for both citizens of Belfast and people of Ulster was that they would continue to flourish in happiness.

Many world leaders and celebrities enjoyed 'Belfast Hospitality' courtesy of Sir Crawford, often including a visit and/or stay at Lismara. Lord Randolph Churchill had dinner at Lismara in December, 1931. The Lord Mayors of London and Dublin visited separately

10. Budge and O'Leary, *Belfast: Approach to Crisis; a study of Belfast politics 1613-1970*, p.152

in 1933 and Stanley Baldwin (British Conservative politician and statesman of the period between the two world wars) and his wife were entertained at Lismara in October 1933. Mr. Baldwin received a Doctorate from Queen's University, Belfast and his wife opened the Royal Maternity Hospital. Stanley Baldwin was the only Prime Minister to serve under three difference monarchs (George V, Edward VIII and George V1).

Much, if not most, of the expense for such lavish entertainment was met by Sir Crawford out of his own purse as was acknowledge by the Sunday Chronicle in an article published on 10 December 1932.

Until 1872 there had been a £500 mayoral salary, but since then successive sovereigns refused any emolument. It is reported that Sir Crawford McCullagh spent at least £5,000 yearly on hospitality at civic functions and receptions for city visitors. It was this generosity that endeared Sir Crawford to a host of people.

It would appear from press clippings of the time and the Lord Mayor's correspondence in the Public Record Office that Sir Crawford spent an exceptional amount of time entertaining as well as attending to other duties attached to the role of Lord Mayor. In 1936 he was invited to attend the Ulster Medical Society Dinner hosted by Dr. Robert Marshall of the Belfast Medical Institute. His speech refers to the 'onerous, numerous and varied duties of a Lord Mayor' and mentions that he is expected to receive and entertain all distinguished visitors to the city from all over the world and that in 1932 he had entertained within a fortnight 2,000 delegates to the conferences of the Education Authority of GB and NI as well as the Royal Institute of Public Health. In the same year he hosted a garden party at Lismara in honour of a number of battleships visiting Belfast. He also talks about the written and verbal requests he is expected to carry out on a daily basis, which included being called upon to trace ancestors going back 200 years, attending the birth of twins and unblocking drains.[11]

11. PRONI LA/7/3/A/8

The McCullagh's particularly enjoyed entertaining at Lismara and from 1931-1933 lavish garden parties were given in honour of visiting naval officers. (see above) The warships *Warsprite* and *Malaya* visited in 1931 and in 1932, the officers of His Majesties Ships, *Hood, Courageous, Versatile, Velox* and *Vesper* mingled with six hundred guests on the manicured lawns of the Lord Mayor's home. In October 1935 Kermit Roosevelt, son of United States President Theodore Roosevelt visited Lismara and in 1937 the Lord Mayor of Cape Town came to Belfast and was entertained at City Hall and Lismara. These events were full dress uniformed affairs when Sir Crawford and Lady McCullagh literally rolled out the carpet on the lawn to receive their honoured guests. These events were also attended by members of the family including children, spouses and grandchildren. Caterers, florists, marquee and music were all credited in the press, as was a description of each prominent ladies attire such as:-

> 'Lady McCullagh was wearing diamonds with her georgette gown of lido blue, which was decorated with an ivy leaf pattern in sequins of the same shade… Lady Spencer Portal was beautifully dressed in a gown of geranium colour…Mrs Victor Henderson (Daisy) the Lord Mayor's younger daughter, was wearing long drop ear-rings of pearl with a sumptuous gown of emerald lace….[12]

Guests were given freedom to enjoy the spacious grounds and the large aviary where Sir Crawford's son kept his collection of foreign birds housed in conditions similar to those of their natural habitat. Many improvements had been made to the gardens over the years; trees had been cut to clear a view of the Lough; a rosary planted featuring a sun dial and fountain; a greenhouse held many exotic plants; the garden merged into the woods through which ran narrow winding paths, giving shade on hot afternoons and a fruit garden had been established where trees flourished in abundance.

In 1929 Sir Crawford had written in his memoirs that his friend, Sir Edward Carson's health was not as good as it had been, and it came as no surprise when the 'father of Northern Ireland' retired on 1st November 1929. He was seventy-five years old. Lord Carson came to

12. *Northern Whig* June 1932

Belfast in 1933 for the last time to witness the unveiling of a bronze statue of himself at the opening of Parliament Buildings and Sir Crawford again noted in his diary that Sir Edward had complained to him of "having too many sleepless nights and feeling very old and very tired". At the beginning of June 1935 Sir Edward caught bronchial pneumonia, and for a while was not expected to recover. However he fought back and gradually his condition began to improve, but as summer turned to Autumn he began to weaken. The doctors diagnosed leukaemia. He died peacefully at 8.35 a.m. on 22 October 1935. In a radio broadcast from Belfast later that day Lord Craigavon announced that Lord Carson would be buried in St. Anne's Cathedral in Belfast and that he would have a state funeral provided by the Government of Northern Ireland. A warship would bring the body to Belfast.

> The funeral took place on Saturday 26th October. Shops and factories closed down and the shipyards were silent as HMS Broke steamed slowly up Belfast Lough. At eleven o'clock the coffin, covered by the Union Flag, was carried ashore by two petty officers and six seamen and placed on a gun carriage. In almost complete silence it was drawn through the streets, lined with thousands of people. With it walked the pall-bearers: Lord Craigavon; Wilfred Spender, who had devoted his life to Carson's cause; Frederick Crawford, who had brought the guns to Larne; Dawson Bates; and the Lord Mayor Sir Crawford McCullagh. Lady Carson led the family mourners. The procession stopped for a few minutes outside the Old Town Hall, which had been the headquarters of the Ulster Volunteer Force, and again at the City Hall, where he had signed the Ulster Covenant. In the Cathedral the service was conducted by his friend Primate D'Arcy. The coffin was lowered into the tomb, and from a silver bowl soil from each of the six counties was scattered on it. Buglers sounded the Last Post and Reveille, and then the congregation took up the hymn which had become the Ulster anthem: 'O God, Our Help in Ages Past'.[13]

Sir Crawford Created Baronet and 9th Term as Lord Mayor

On 1 July 1935, His Majesty King George V bestowed the honour of a baronetcy on Sir Crawford 'in recognition of his eminent public services.' Sir Crawford said the honour was a compliment to the City

13. ATQ Stewart, *Edward Carson*, p.131

of Belfast, rather than a personal tribute to him. In his memoirs he recalled the emotion he felt when entering the Council Chamber for the monthly meeting of the Corporation, his colleagues stood up en masse cheering and singing 'For he's a jolly good fellow'. After the singing they all rushed forward to individually congratulate him. In his acknowledgement, Sir Crawford said he particularly appreciated the references to his wife whose desire had been at all times to support him with her advice and assistance and to do everything in her power to promote the honour and welfare of the people and the City of Belfast which they both loved. "Honours are all very well", commented the Lord Mayor in a characteristic utterance at the succeeding luncheon, "but if one has not the goodwill and respect of the men with whom one is associated they are like sounding brass". The congratulations which every mail and telegraph messenger brought truly emphasised the universal respect the new Baronet enjoyed. The *Daily Express* created a pen portrait of Sir Crawford, describing him as:

'Bluff, cheery and of a domineering personality, he infuses the Mayoralty with a warm friendliness that enhances rather than diminishes the dignity of the office of Chief Citizen. He entertains liberally, so lavishly that Belfast is noted and admired the world over for its civic hospitality. Sir Crawford is a wise administrator, approachable and, above all, human'.

Sir Crawford McCullagh had by now been in office nearly eight years as Lord Mayor and with the Corporation thirty years. Despite being sixty-eight years old he still maintained the vigour and enthusiasm for a job that would have taxed men half his age. Although Sir Crawford said he and his wife had decided not to serve again he had been persuaded by the committee to stand again:

'He felt gratified to know that ...he had done what was right and his actions received the approval, not only of his friends but also from the general public... That morning, as he travelled back fifty years....it took him back to the days when he first came to Belfast , at that time he had no idea that he would one day occupy the position he held that day. Throughout those long years it was very uphill work and a stiff fright, but he had always endeavoured to do what he thought was right and what his conscience dictated. He was very honoured to hold this position, an honour any citizen might aspire and an honour for which he was deeply grateful'.[14]

Sir Crawford must indeed have been thinking back to those days when he first came to Belfast as a gauche fourteen year old farm boy. In March 1935, he began a radio series. His first subject was 'Small beginnings – the growth of Belfast Corporation'. The series proved immensely popular and paved the way for a further series on the history of Belfast and its surroundings. On 29 April 1936, Sir Crawford was unanimously elected as Lord Mayor for the ninth term, his sixth in succession. He was installed on 25 May 1936. Hosting his usual luncheon in City Hall, he said he did not believe there was a member of the assembly who would say one word to annoy him and noted that there was none of the rancour and nasty feeling that used to be... he thanked his son and his wife for their continued assistance and particularly welcomed his son Mr. Joseph Crawford McCullagh who was recently elected to represent Clifton Ward on 14 January 1936. His son would enter the Corporation in the spring, at twenty-nine years of age. Although Boysie is seen with his father in many press photographs and is reported to have attended almost all council sessions[15], he was subsequently only rarely seen and was never again mentioned in connection with the Corporation.

14. *Belfast Evening Telegraph* June 1936

15. In respect of Boysie's attendance and participation at Council meetings with Sir Crawford there are wide discrepancies in reports of the time – some indicate he was a regular attended while others disagree. It may well be that initial enthusiasm by Boysie soon waned so that reports of his commitment are highly dependent on their timing.

Chapter Fifteen
1936-1938

Two Kings

━━◦❦❧◦❀◦❦❧◦━━

If a man be gracious and courteous to strangers it shows that he is a citizen of the world and that his heart is no island cut off from other lands but a continent that joins them to him.

Lord Bacon

An Abdication and Coronation

The year 1936 had been a bumper year for the press. A succession of new stories of worldwide interest broke at convenient intervals – a fresh sensation almost every month. On 20 January, King George V died and was succeeded by King Edward VIII. On 7 March, Hitler's troops marched into the Rhineland. On 3 April, Bruno Hauptmann was electrocuted for the kidnap and murder of the Lindburgh baby. On 5 May, Italy completed its conquest of Abyssinia. On 18 June, Max Schmeling (boxing world heavy weight champion) defeated Joe Louis. On 16 July, the Spanish Civil War broke out. On 3 November, Franklin D. Roosevelt was re-elected President of the United States of America, and on the 30 November, the great Crystal Palace in London burnt down.

However, these news stories were pushed into the background in early December when the news broke about the King's Abdication. When Stanley Baldwin and his wife were guests of Sir Crawford and Lady McCullagh at Lismara earlier in the year, there had been some talk of the future King and his relationship with an American divorcee called Wallis Simpson. The Prince of Wales was known to have many girlfriends and it was generally assumed that she was just one of many woman who would entertain him until he found someone 'suitable' who would one day become the future Queen. Sir Crawford attended the funeral of George V in January 1936 recounting in his memoirs 'there was much talk concerning the conduct of the Prince of Wales and Wallis Simpson and the matter was being discussed with 'concern and foreboding in Buckingham Palace, Lambeth Palace, Downing Street and Whitehall'.[1] The public adored the good-looking Prince and the whole country was bitterly disappointed and saddened when the news eventually proved to be true. On the evening of 11th December 1936 families stopped whatever it was they were doing to listen to the most moving and memorable broadcast in the history of radio – transmitted around the world, wherever the English language was understood. It opened: 'At long last I am able to say a few words of my own'. He went on to praise, his brother the new King; to speak generously of the Prime Minister and the other ministers of the Crown; to express his gratitude for the kindness that the British people everywhere had shown him in his service as Prince of Wales; to absolve Mrs Simpson from all responsibility for his leaving; and to explain that he had given up the kingship because its burdens would be too heavy 'without the help and support of the woman I love'.

The whole English speaking world listened and wept as the heir to the English throne renounced his heritage and imperial splendour for love alone, the broadcast taking a mere 70 seconds to transmit. When King Edward VIII gave up the throne of England he was succeeded by his brother Albert, Duke of York. In May 1937 Sir Crawford and Lady McCullagh attended the Coronation of their Majesties King George VI and his consort, Queen Elizabeth. In his memoirs Sir Crawford gives a memorable account of that occasion:-

1.   Charles J C Murphy & J Bryan III, *The Windsor Story*

'I had gone over to London some days before with my wife and stayed at The Grosvenor House Hotel in Park Lane. Major May (his private Secretary) had travelled separately bringing with him my robes and my Deputy Lieutenant's uniform. We were woken in the morning very early as Major May was concerned about my uniform and robes. As the Deputy Lieutenant's uniform involved the wearing of a sword, he wanted to make sure it was sitting at the right angle! The scene in Westminster Abbey was very impressive and as we had seats in a special gallery, the view of the entire ceremony was perfect. There was something like 8,000 people in the Abbey, and I shall never forget the scene. The building was filled with the rustle of eight thousand souls who crowded it; men and women from the five continents, all assembled here for a moment in the amity of a great ceremonial occasion. Behind this brave new face of the Abbey, engraved upon marble, chiselled in stone, related in elegy, epitaph and superscription, was the epitome of this empire's history; the whole glittering and precarious edifice built up of service and sacrifice, violence, cunning and chicane, valour and endurance with greed and subterfuge following their footsteps, the dreams of poets and of tale-tellers, the certitudes of science, the promises of religion and scheming of statecraft. Such, too, was, in the rough, the history of every state there represented; for it was the history of restless man himself, deaf for the most part to such intimations as come now with the suspiration of this great uneasy gathering, filling the ancient church with the sound of an autumn forest, of leaves about to fall. It was all too ornate, high-wrought and over-jewelled for me to remember it in sequence.

My memory, afterwards, was of a medley of emotional and aesthetic appeals: a fanfare of trumpets sounding suddenly outside the doors, the sharp clean, classic notes piercing through the romantic jangling of bells: the surge of organ music that seemed to creep into every crack and crevice of the ancient abbey and rumble there: the slow crescendo of a procession through the standing thousands: swords and crosses, capes and tabards, gold, silver, feathers, jewels, bowed backs and pious hands of priests stiffly encrusted with vestments; orbs crowns and sceptres and all wherein do lie the dread and fear of kings; the chanting of shrill-voiced boys; the strutting of little pages, scarlet as robins, with their toy swords stuck out behind them like tails. I remember particularly how enchanting the little princesses, Elizabeth and Margaret looked. They wore long trains and were very dainty and nice. What struck me as a homely touch was the moment when the Archbishop of Canterbury twiddled the Crown round to get the proper side to the front. I remember all these things and the endless, dazing, piling-up of ritual on ritual, ceremony on ceremony, the presenting, the anointing, the crowning, then the nation's symbolic man sitting there at last in the ancient wooden chair while the priest settled the Crown with wonderful dignity. And when the crown was on, the lights increased their power, shining down strongly on the golden floor, scintillating in red and green and yellow sparks as they caught the jewels of the regal crown. From without, the boom of distant guns was heard announcing to the people that another King had been crowned in the Chair, and from within, a great shout arose - "God Save the King".

Elaborate arrangements had been made to ensure that we were picked up outside by our cars at the conclusion of the Ceremony, but something went wrong with the arrangements. All the Abbey was divided into lettered blocks, and a loud-speaker was to call the occupants of these blocks, letter by letter, telling them by which exit to leave. At the same time, telephone calls would warn the drivers in the car park which bore the same letter, and the cars would proceed to the door named, and the owners and the chauffeurs would meet. Unfortunately something went wrong with the system and the majority of the guests were left hanging around in the Abbey until 5pm. Eventually I went out to try and find my chauffeured car and walked about a mile in heavy rain without doing so. Everything was in utter confusion, Margaret was in tears, we hadn't eaten since the morning and when eventually our car turned up, the driver said he had arrived earlier but failed to pick us out in the crowd. We were both desperately tired by the time we arrived back at Grosvenor House, and although we were honoured by being present at the ceremony, the end of the day was not a happy one'.

Needless to say the incident was long forgotten when their Majesties paid a Coronation visit to Belfast. The Royal couple landed at Donegal Quay on Wednesday 28th July at 10.00 a.m. from the Royal Yacht, *Victoria and Albert*. From there they were escorted through the streets of Belfast with much cheering and flag waving to City Hall where they were received with unrestrained enthusiasm. On this occasion the Governor of Northern Ireland hosted the reception at City Hall and for a change Sir Crawford and Lady McCullagh attended as guests. The press reported that:

Everyone commented on the charm and loveliness of the Queen, and with gratification it was observed that the King looked strong and well. When his Majesty addressed the assembled company he appeared to hesitate a little, but after he had uttered a dozen words, his voice rang out clearly and he completed his speech Without the slightest symptom of hesitancy.[2]

In his address His Majesty recalled how thirteen years had intervened since they had paid their first visit to Northern Ireland. Yet, it had

2.   Belfast Evening Telegraph 29 July 1937

always remained in their memory so fragrant as to keep alive hopes that the opportunity to return would arise. It was heartfelt delight, therefore, for them to now renew their acquaintance with the loyal warm hearted Ulster people to whom they wished ever increased prosperity and happiness.

On this occasion the City Hall gardens were abloom with roses. The interior decorated with pink hydrangeas and evergreens. Sir Crawford wrote in his memoirs how the Royal couple took morning coffee in the Lord Mayor's parlour and how the Queen was so gracious when Lady Margaret presented her with a bouquet of pink Irish Hawlmark roses that she had grown in her greenhouse at Lismara. The Royal couple then reviewed the British Legion at the Garden of Remembrance. They were taken to Government House for lunch and in the afternoon reviewed the Youth Organisations at Balmoral followed by a half-hour visit to Queen's University. Then finally a garden party at Stormont where they were received by the Prime Minister and Viscount Craigavon. The visit was a resounding success and the occasion passed without incident.

Industrial Development in Northern Ireland

Northern Ireland was still in the grip of a recession. In essence it was caused by the stagnation and decline of Belfast's major traditional industries, in particular, shipbuilding and linen. These giants of the nineteenth century progressively became the dinosaurs of the twentieth. With justification, Sir Crawford observed that their contraction had been 'brought about by problems over which neither Stormont nor the municipality has any control'.[3]

With the increasing international tension in Europe during the late 1930s, industry in Northern Ireland began to revive and a small number of firms sprang up giving much needed employment to the stagnant labour force. A proportion of this growing labour force was absorbed into the engineering and building sectors which revived in

3.   Brian Barton *The Blitz: Belfast in the War Years*

the 1930s. By 1934 Harland and Wolff was beginning to recover its work load and by 1935 its tonnage launched was a world record for the year, and in 1938 its total output was the largest for any shipyard in the United Kingdom. A key to its survival was the diversification of production: it built the first diesel-electric trains in the British Isles for the Bangor and County Down Railway Company as well as more conventional locomotives for North and South America; engines for oil pipelines; and steel structures for shops and cinemas, including the Ritz which was opened in Belfast in 1936 by Gracie Fields. By late 1939 the yard was employing approximately twelve thousand – as many workers as in 1929. The aircraft factory Short and Harland began in June 1936 as a consequence of the Royal Air Force earlier that year placing so large an order for Sunderland flying boats with Short Brothers of Rochester that they could not accommodate the increased demand and were forced to expand their production capacity. In 1936 construction at Sydenham on slob land reclaimed by the Harbour Commission began and in 1937 the production of land and marine aircraft had begun. The first aircraft to be built was a Bristol Bomber L5808. Within two years, the firm was employing two thousand workers; in wartime this rose to a peak of over twenty thousand.

During the inter-war years, conditions for the vast majority of the population improved substantially. Between 70 and 80 per cent of Northern Ireland's insured workforce remained in employment throughout, and between 1932 and 1937 the number of those in work rose by 15 per cent; some being absorbed by expanding sectors of industry, while others found jobs in education, commerce and government. Overall there was a measurable improvement in health, housing, social activity, and life expectation.

In September 1924 a BBC transmitter was established locally and by 1939, roughly half of Northern Ireland had a wireless set. Among the upper and middle classes, the number of private motorcars on the roads increased ten fold between 1919 and 1937. Golf, yachting and cricket became more popular, mirroring social developments in Britain. Up to thirty thousand spectators watched rugby internationals at Ravenhill and fifty thousand gathered to see the first Newtownards Tourist Trophy race in 1928. Greyhound racing was another popular pastime and Sir Crawford officiated at the opening of the new Dunmore Stadium on the Antrim Road in the 1930s. Construction of Telephone House on the corner of May Street began in 1932. Sir Crawford opened the building and pictures in the press show him demonstrating the use of an automatic (dial) phone. During Telephone Week he is shown with a 'bank of operators' seated before and operating an early type of switchboard. The use of electricity was promoted by the Corporation's Electricity Department, which demonstrated and sold lighting and cooking appliances of all kinds as well as providing the power supply. Press coverage shows Sir Crawford opening the door to an 'all electric house' at the Ideal Home Exhibition.

On 29 November 1934 Sir Crawford deputised his son, Boysie, to switch on the new electricity supply to the Antrim side of Belfast from a new primary transmission system at the Harbour Power Station. In 1936 Sir Crawford opened the mains steam valve to set the new turbo alternator in motion at the Power Station. On 5th May 1935 he was called upon to 'turn on the floodlights' at City Hall and later each year to turn on the Christmas lights at a tree-lighting ceremony, on the lawn outside City Hall. On 22 October 1938 The Electrical Development Association of Northern Ireland called upon Sir Crawford to throw the switch on the 30,000kw. turbo alternator at the Harbour River Station. Sir Crawford, over the years, saw the successive stages of public transportation develop from the use of horses to electric street cars (trams) and hosted the inauguration of a trolley bus system in 1938. He is pictured in the press driving the last tramway car on the Falls Road on 30 April 1938.

In Ulster the pioneer of aviation was a young Belfast engineer called Harry Ferguson, he built his own aircraft and miraculously made his first flight on 31st December 1909 when he flew his aircraft at Hillsborough Park in Co. Down. Ferguson's exploits caught the public's imagination and he was soon in demand displaying his flying skills in fairs throughout Ulster. The outbreak of the First World War and the years of political upheaval which led to partition placed severe restrictions on flying, but by 1922 relative peace had returned to Ulster and a number of airline companies were establishing a pattern of regular air services between Northern Ireland and the rest of the UK In 1924 Belfast opened the first municipal aerodrome in the British Isles at Balmoral; the first flight conveyed the Lord Mayor, Sir William Turner, to Manchester.

The North of Ireland Flying Club had been formed in 1928 and was anxious to find a permanent home for its members. A solution was offered in December 1933 when the 7th Marquis of Londonderry, himself an enthusiastic aviator and Secretary of State for Air from 1931 to 1932, announced that an aerodrome would be constructed on a fifty acre portion of his estate (formerly a racecourse) adjoining the Comber Road at Newtownards. Lord Londonderry wanted his airfield to be the civil airport for Belfast and to be the main centre for private flying in Northern Ireland. The new airport was officially opened on 31st August 1934 by the Duke of Abercorn and became the main centre for private flying in Northern Ireland. The largest aircraft to land at Newtownards was a Lufthansa Junkers JU52 carrying the German Ambassador who together with his wife was to the guest of the Londonderry's at Mount Stewart. In 1947 Lord Londonderry set up Londonderry Air Charters (later renamed Ulster Aviation Ltd) using six aircraft to operate flights to the mainland. Although Lord Londonderry was keen for Newtownards to become the Province's first civil airport, Ulster's first air service officially began on 20th August 1934 to Nutts Corner, operated by Railway Air Services – the flight left from Croydon and went via Birmingham and Manchester to Belfast.[4] A year later the British Empire Service ran an airline between Belfast and England. Railways Air Services

---

4.   Ron Armstrong 2010

continued to develop and in 1938 Sir Crawford opened the Airports and Airways Exhibit in the Belfast Museum and Art Gallery.

Despite the depression Gallagher's Tobacco Factory continued to grow and increased its number of employees. By 1931 taxes paid by this firm were £3,000,000 and by 1938 £5,000,000; nearly double that paid in 1916 (Moore). In 1938 Gallagher's, Harland and Wolff, Davidson's Sirocco Works and Mulholland's York Street Flax Spinning Company were still the largest firms of their kind in the world. When chairing the many and varied committees Sir Crawford never lost the opportunity in holding their leaders up "as men imbued with ambition and love for their city".

As early as 1935, the Ulster Industrial Development was active in Northern Ireland and in 1938 the Ulster Development Council was established to expand Northern Ireland's industrial base. A lunch was hosted by Sir Crawford each year to recognise new ventures and in 1938 six new enterprises were acknowledged. One such endeavour was the Ulster Milk Bar in Lombard Street which encouraged a decrease in drunkenness. Sir Crawford and Lady McCullagh abstained from alcohol and Sir Crawford reveals in his memoirs how disappointed he was with Daisy and Boysie as their drinking had now become a problem. He said he wished that every bar that sold alcohol would be banned and milk sold instead!

Mistaken Identity

The work of the Ulster Development Council was highly successful and by 1946 Northern Ireland was exporting nine pounds of goods per head of population as compared to three pounds per head for the rest of the United Kingdom. In his capacity as Lord Mayor, Sir Crawford was asked to officiate at almost all major functions and openings. His generous hospitality was legendary and because of his long tenure as Belfast's First Citizen he was recognised the length and breadth of the United Kingdom. As he recalls in his memoirs there were a number of occasions when his status was called into question. One such incident is revealed with humour:-

'On arrival at Euston Station to cross via Heysham, I got a seat in the corner of an empty carriage. Suddenly, just as the train was about to start, there was a rush of people onto the platform, and a very beautiful and charming lady was ushered into the carriage with me. She had a lot of coats and cases with her, and someone had given her a handful of magazines. I tried to engage her in conversation, without success, till we got to Preston, when an attendant came along to look after the bookings on the steamer. He knew me and said my booking was in order. He asked the lady for her name, and after he had looked up his list, he said, "I am sorry, but there is no berth booked for you." She said, "Well, you will have to get me one!", but the attendant said that would be impossible, as every berth was booked. I then spoke, and told her not to worry, that it was a very fine steamer and that I was sure that she would be able to get a berth when she went on board. She said, "Anyhow, I have to be in Belfast tomorrow", and that ended the conversation for the time being. When we got as far as Morecombe, the train was reversed to run down to Heysham. She looked up at me, and said "What is the meaning of this?" I explained what was taking place and went on to say, "I know why the steamer is booked, there is a conference opening in Belfast tomorrow, and there are a large number of delegates coming from England." She said, "That is where I am going, and I do not want to miss it, because I hear the Corporation are giving a magnificent Ball tomorrow night". I said, "You are not quite right there. The Corporation are not giving the Ball." "Who is giving it then", she asked. "I am giving it" I replied. "You couldn't give a Ball!" she exclaimed. "Don't say that", and up went the magazine again that she was reading. No more was said until we got to Heysham, and although the lady obtained a porter to carry her luggage, I saw she was still burdened with a number of coats, so I said, "If you will allow me, I will help you", and reached out to take some of the coats off her hands. She tugged them away and snapped, "Don't bother me. I can look after myself." When I went on board the steamer I told the steward of the circumstances, and asked him to try and get a birth for her. He came along shortly afterwards and told me he had succeeded in doing this. I did not see the lady again till the following evening. Naturally, I was looking out for her at the Reception, but she was about the last to arrive. She entered, looking beautifully groomed as I would have expected. She was announced by the mace-bearer, but the moment she saw me she looked absolutely horrified and would have run back only I stepped forward and said "Come now, fellow passenger, you are perfectly all right, you need not let me frighten you now!" I took her arm and led her to her friends where she immediately started to tell the events as they unfolded the evening before, and how she had not believed that I was the Lord Mayor at all, but that I was trying to make up to her!". Then I said, "You would not walk with me last night, but come along, and you and I will have a walk now. So again I took her arm and we walked down the corridor to the ballroom listening to the music.

Sir Crawford recalls another incident, only this time it was in Belfast.

'I went into a certain establishment to buy an outside easy chair for my daughter Helen, who was in poor health, and after succeeding in getting what I wanted, I paid for the chair and told the assistant I would send the car round for it. She asked me what name and when I said the Lord Mayor she said, "Oh go on with you, none of that now!" I said, "but I am the Lord Mayor", but I'm afraid I did not succeed in convincing her, she thought I was making fun of her!'

Another time when Sir Crawford was in London he had just come out of a theatre and walking back to his hotel he encountered a group of people watching a Zeppelin pass over the Strand. He got into conversation with a gentleman who said he was delighted he had seen it because he would be able to go back to Ireland and tell his family he had seen a raid. He then asked Sir Crawford where he came from When he told the man he was Sir Crawford McCullagh, the Lord Mayor of Belfast, the man said "Och!, go on and tell that to somebody else, you can't fool me". Sir Crawford laughed and went into the hotel. A short time later in Belfast, Sir Crawford encountered the gentleman at a function who proceeded to amuse the assembled company with his story of how he had met the Lord Mayor of Belfast but didn't believe him. These occasions seemed to be rare and Sir Crawford undoubtedly found them amusing as he was photographed regularly in the press at home in Ireland, in England and on the Continent where he travelled extensively as Ambassador for Northern Ireland.

In February 1938 Sir Crawford accepted an invitation of the Ulster Association of Birmingham to be chief-guest at their annual banquet. He was to be joined in this honour by the Lord Mayor of Birmingham Councillor E.R. Canning. Lord Mayor Canning had selected a distinguished party to join Sir Crawford at luncheon in City Hall. Then during the afternoon he was taken on a tour of the city to visit the Hospital Centre, the Bournville Garden Village of the Cadbury Firm at Longbridge then to the expansive one-hundred and ten acre Austin Motor Works. Sir Crawford recalls his visit in his memoirs:

Sir Crawford felt himself very much at home at the reception and banquet. The Chairman Dr. Davison and the assemblage of 150 guests were mostly Ulster born doctors, and scientists In his speech he said Ulster Folk had every right to be proud of their Imperial Province. It had enriched both the United Kingdom and the British Empire with at least as high a proportion of leaders in all lines of civilization as England herself had. Straying beyond the British Empire, it was no empty boast to claim that Ulster's prestige was worldwide and included the United States which derived its best pioneers and goodly quota of its American Presidents from Ulster stock. Addressing the ladies present, Sir Crawford remarked:

"You have great traditions to preserve and you must never forget the fundamental Ulster advice, "Do the right thing under all circumstances. If you do you will send your sons and daughters into the great world well-equipped to keep in the forefront the name and fame of Ulster upbringing. Keep sacred that old Ulster saying that "an Ulsterman's agreement never needs any shilling stamp to make it binding".

The next day Sir Crawford was the guest of the Directors of the Dunlop Company at their great Fort Dunlop Works. Writing in his memoirs he recalls:

"We were met by the Directors, who showed us over the very extensive premises. I was particularly struck by the magnitude of the concern, and the arrangements made for the workers, as regards canteens, cloakrooms and suchlike. We were invited to luncheon, and in submitting the Toast to my health, great compliments were paid to Belfast. However, I found out that it was not generally known amongst the company present that the pneumatic tyre was invented by a Scottish born Veterinary Surgeon called John Dunlop whose veterinary yard was in May Street, Belfast. I told them that I remembered seeing Dunlop's young son Johnny riding on his tricycle around Belfast when I was an apprentice with the Bank Buildings. I said that Mr. Dunlop had first experimented with a tube made from sheet rubber and covered by a strip of linen fastened to a wooden disc the exact size of each of the tricycle's small back wheels. The idea was improved upon by Dunlop Senior and some months later the first Dunlop factory was started in Belfast for the first pneumatic tyres were made and fixed to the wheels by William Edlin at his modest Bicycle Shop in Garfield Street, behind the General Post Office. But it was not until a year later, May 18th 1889 that the invention gave the public a 'taste of its quality'. I told the assembled company that a friend of mine, William Hume, had considerable repute as captain of the Old Belfast Cruisers' Cycling club. However, meeting with a serious accident, he had intended to retire from racing, but was persuaded by William Edlin and Dunlop to show himself heroic enough to ride a safety cycle fitted with the air tyres at the Queen's University Sports Day on Easter Monday. The contraption seemed so ludicrous by conventional ideas that many of those present laughed at him and told him to take his "cart wheels" to the clown in the circus while others commented that he might dispose of his "big sausages" to some mad butcher. The mockers soon changed their tune when Hume won all four races with little or no effort.

Without the pneumatic tyre the world would never have known the development of the cycle, the motor car, the internal combustion engine, the immensely improved roads, the all-world rubber industry and the aeroplane as we know them today.'

Sir Crawford was one of Belfast's first motorists. When the production of motor-cars started in Ulster he was one of the first customers to buy from the Cuba Street Works of the Chambers Brothers in 1903. In those days the performance of cars was not always to be relied upon and frequent tyre bursts was usual. On one occasion Sir Crawford and his family were heading to the Mourne Mountains for a picnic. He recalls:

"We had progressed as far as University Street when the car suddenly stopped dead. When I got out to see what was amiss, a group of grinning urchins came breathlessly on the scene and shouted "Hey Mister, there's a big piece of her innards lying up there in the street!" We were however, able to borrow another car to reach our destination."

Sir Crawford and his son were both car enthusiasts and over the years purchased many models, among them, a Darracq V14, an Alvis, an Austin, a Bentley and eventually a Rolls Royce. Boysie famously had a Bentley engine inserted into a Rolls Royce! When the war began in 1939 and petrol was rationed, Sir Crawford owned a Vauxhall and a Rolls Royce. Even though a car was necessary for his official duties, he was refused petrol for it, and so purchased a Morris 10 which consumed less petrol.

Sir Crawford had an ability to put people at their ease. As the Belfast Telegraph reported in 1938:-

> 'he had a flair for making friends, was considered a good neighbour and a true comrade in a common cause. Said to lack ostentation, he appears modest with self-abnegation. He has a kindly disposition and uniform geniality. With such a charming personality, and never failing courtesy, he seemed to endear himself to many, in all walks of life'.

Sir Crawford and Lady McCullagh enjoyed motoring in Scotland and on one occasion he again displayed uncommon courtesy towards a fellow traveller, he wrote about the incident in his memoirs:-

> While on holiday in Turnberry in Ayrshire with my wife, we encountered an American gentleman looking for the train station. Leaving my wife to browse in an antique shop I took my bearings and led him through small streets and by-ways until we reached the station. He informed me he was crossing to Belfast by the daylight service, via Stranraer, and I told him he had no time to spare, as the train was almost due to leave. I said, "you will have to hurry." He did not seem to be too bothered and when we got inside the station, I saw the train waiting, and again urged him to hurry. He said he had to collect his suitcase first and while he was doing that I volunteered to go and see if I could do anything to prevent the train from leaving for a few minutes. I got through the barrier and saw that the Stationmaster was about to signal the train to start, so I told him there was a gentlemen from the United States who wished to catch the train. Still the man did not appear and the Stationmaster said, "I cannot wait any longer", and with that the man appeared on the overhead bridge, carrying his suitcase, and the stationmaster shouted for him to hurry up. He was shown quickly into a carriage, and he told me he was going to Belfast to enquire about his ancestors who came from Co. Monaghan. Just as the train began to move I gave him my card and told him to call with my secretary at the City Hall, and he would give him all the help he possibly could, and with that the train disappeared from sight. I forgot all about the incident, until some time afterwards, when I was giving a reception to the Pan Presbyterian Conference in Belfast to which people came from all over the world. Afterwards a gentleman came up to me and gave me the card of the man I had met in Ayreshire, who happened to be a Presbyterian Minister. He had asked him to find me and thank me for all I had done for him. He told me how on his return to the United States he had related his experience in the Church, and how he had asked for the children particularly to come along on this occasion

to preach them a special sermon. He told them of his meeting with a stranger in Turnburry, where he had become lost and how the stranger had helped him. He also said I had given him my card and how at first he did not believe I was the Lord Mayor of Belfast for at the time I was dressed in my plus-fours and a cap. However, when he called at City Hall and presented the card, he was assured that the stranger was indeed the Mayor. Then in front of the congregation he had taken my card out of his pocket and showed it to the children, saying, "Look, here is the name of that stranger - Sir Crawford McCullough", and gave a lesson to the children in showing kindness and civility to strangers.

On October 1937, Sir Crawford was again returned, unopposed, for Woodvale Ward and unanimously elected as Lord Mayor on 9 October 1937 for the period ending 23 June 1938, his tenth term.

Belfast had been elevated to the official status of 'City' in 1888 so it was fitting that the celebrations for the Jubilee Year should coincide with Sir Crawford's 70th birthday on 14th December 1938. Sir Crawford had now been Lord Mayor of Belfast for ten years and still showed no sign of slowing down. He said at his usual luncheon, "my terms of office have not affected my health or my weight," but with a laugh he added, "I won't say anything about my pocket book!". He was said to have spent between £40,000 to £50,000 on entertaining while in office.

He told the City Council General Purposes Committee that his 'life partner' as he called her had urged that he should take a rest and be relieved of the social and civic responsibilities which monopolized his leisure. Despite Lady McCullagh's resistance to his re-appointment, he was invested on 24 May 1938, for his eleventh term and said how much time, energy and immense pleasure it had given them both to serve the interests of the people in the city they both loved so much. In conclusion both agreed they could not ignore the unanimous request of the citizens' representatives. "That being so", added Sir Crawford the next day, "I place myself at the service of my colleagues, and I desire to thank them very cordially for their loyalty to me". Belfast's Jubilee Celebrations consisted of a week's festivities culminating in a Ball given by Sir Crawford at City Hall. Another celebration followed when a party was given by his colleagues in the Corporation in his honour to celebrate his three score years and ten. He was presented with a magnificent 18th Century grandfather clock. The clock was the gift of those present to mark the birthday of Belfast's First Citizen and to wish him many happy returns.

An editorial comment on Sir Crawford's remarkable record as Lord Mayor for eleven years was that it constituted an inspiring example of citizenship.

"Under the circumstances it cannot be held that the glamour of this high and honourable position can hold any novelty for him. For that reason alone the citizens are gratefully delighted he and Lady McCullagh conceded to the unanimous desire of all that, in this, the City's Jubilee Year, they should continue to hold office".[5]

5.　*Belfast Evening Telegraph* December 1938

War and Duty

━━━◆◇◆◇◆◇◆━━━

The map dissolves. Familiar town decays.
No man can ever walk these ways again,
blind to the brooding of the coming storm,
and pacing towards apocalyptic days;
and yet his boyish hope was never vain;
if it seems foolish now, it still stands firm

John Hewitt, Kites in Spring

12th Term as Lord Mayor and Outbreak of War

Throughout the summer of 1938 menacing war clouds had darkened the horizon almost continuously, the nucleus of the storm being Czechoslovakia. On 12th March 1938 the Wehrmacht crossed the Austrian Frontier and Hitler drove through Vienna soon afterwards to complete the Anschluss, the union of his homeland with the Third Reich. This first step towards the making of a Greater Germany put Czechoslovakia – the sole surviving democracy in Central Europe in mortal danger.

On 20th September the daily newspapers gave some much needed relief when it was revealed that the British Prime Minister Mr. Neville Chamberlain had flown to meet Hitler where a solemn agreement had been reached. When Chamberlain returned to London he greeted the Press from an upper window of 10 Downing Street, famously declaring that he had secured "Peace for our time".

With this declaration it seemed that the storm clouds had passed and that at last the prospect of another war had been avoided. Christmas 1938 was celebrated in Belfast with an atmosphere of 'Peace on Earth and Goodwill to All Men'. When Sir Crawford turned on the customary Christmas tree lights and the grounds of City Hall were filled with people full of festive spirit there was still no inclination of the horrors yet to come.

Sir Crawford was only too aware of the potential horror of another war and the reality was evident on 1st December 1938 when a statement was made in the House of Commons appointing Sir Crawford Chairman of the National Service Scheme. It was introduced by the Ministry of Labour for Northern Ireland as the National Voluntary Service. The House of Commons pointed out the importance of the Belfast Committee in view of the geographical position of the city and the density of the population. The shipyards and aircraft factory would be particularly vulnerable to attack and it was the duty of the committee to stimulate recruiting. National Service Guide forms were to be distributed to every household in the U.K. They included works of various kinds in connection with Civil Defence as well as the Armed Forces. Persons were required to act as air raid wardens, rescue and demolition parties, ambulance drivers, auxiliary fire services and operate report centres and communications. Women were required for first aid work, nursing and ambulance services as well as working on the land in the event of a national emergency. There would also be a requirement for the evacuation of children from dangerous areas. The first meeting of the National Service Scheme was held in the Lord Mayor's Parlour in City Hall on 3rd February 1939 with the scheme coming into effect the next day with 16,500 leaflets being distributed to households in Northern Ireland.[1]

---

1.   PRONI LA/7/3A/69, 78 and 82.

A few months later on 21st April 1939 the Belfast Telegraph head-lines announced a

> Unique civic honour for Belfast Lord Mayor – Elected Twelfth Time.
> Yielding to the unanimous appeal of the members of the General Purposes Committee of the Belfast Corporation the Lord Mayor today consented to accept again their nomination for the office of Chief Magistrate.

Once again Sir Crawford put on his chain of office and continued to serve the citizens of Belfast in every way he could at that particular time. During this time he appeared in the press as vigorous as ever. Although somewhat thinner, nevertheless he continued his role as First Citizen and one week later on the 28th April he spoke in the Ulster Hall giving a lecture on the 'Phsychological Effect of Air Raids on the Civil Population'. This was followed by an air raid film called *The Warning* which was shown at the Ritz Cinema on 5th May 1939. Meantime, Lady McCullagh had begun to lose a notable amount of weight, perhaps indicative of her failing health.

The general population however seemed reassured when the King and Queen undertook a tour to Canada and the United States during May and June of the year. On their return they had planned an afternoon Garden Party to be held on July 20th in the grounds of Buckingham Palace to which the McCullagh's had been invited. On the eve of their departure to London Sir Crawford received word that the garden party had been cancelled indefinitely due to inclement weather. Sir Crawford noted in his diary the next day 'was looking forward to seeing their Majesties, hope it is nothing more sinister than what is implied'. He did not have to wait long for an explanation.

The Belfast Telegraph issued a third edition on Sunday 3rd September 1939. The headlines read

> Britain and France at War with Germany. Formal Declaration of Hostilities.
> The following official communique was issued from 10 Downing Street: On September 1st His Majesty's Ambassador in Berlin was instructed to inform the German Government that unless they were prepared to give his Majesty's Government satisfactory assurances that the German Government would sus-

pend any aggressive action against Poland and were prepared promptly to withdraw their forces from Polish territory, his Majesty's Government would fulfil their
obligations to Poland.

At nine this morning His Majesty's Ambassador in Berlin informed the German
Government that unless not later than 11a.m. to-day, satisfactory assurances to
the above effect had been given and had reached His Majesty's Government in
London a state of War would exist between the countries from that hour.

Sir Crawford was surrounded by his family at Lismara when the news
reached the nation, listening to the wireless at 11.15 a.m. he heard
the British Prime Minister Neville Chamberlain tell the people of
Great Britain that a state of war now existed between Britain and
Germany. On Radio Éireann that same evening De Valera confirmed
that the South of Ireland would remain neutral.

"With our history, with our experience of the last war, and with part of our country
still severed from us, we felt that no other decision and no other policy was possible".

That same night the unarmed Donaldson Liner, the *Athenia*, only a
day out on her voyage from Glasgow to Canada, was torpedoed by a
Nazi U-boat off the north-west coast of Donegal and 112 of her compliment of some 1,400 passengers and crew perished. Subsequently
200 of the ill-fated liner's survivors landed at Belfast. On October
16th Sir Crawford held a remembrance dinner for the survivors at
the Grand Central Hotel in Belfast. The next day when Sir Crawford
took up his responsibilities at City Hall his concern for the people of
Belfast echoed that of Lord Craigavon who had spoken in Stormont
that morning and was affirmed in the local newspapers:

"We here today are in a state of war and are prepared with the rest of the United
Kingdom and Empire to face all the responsibilities that that imposes on the
Ulster people. There is no slacking in our loyalty. There is no failing in our determination to place the whole of our resources at the command of the Government
in Britain.[2]"

Northern Ireland would now have a key strategic role to play in the
war the province over the first seven months of 1939 received gov-

2.   Belfast Telegraph 17 October 1939

ernment contracts worth more than £6 million for equipment such as battledress, bedding, service dress, and electrical wiring. In August the 10,000-ton cruiser *HMS Belfast* left Belfast Lough ready for service, while work was well under way on the 28,000-ton aircraft carrier *HMS Formidable*. Harland and Wolff was also busy converting and arming seven passenger liners, two auxiliaries and twenty-four trawlers. By the beginning of September 1939 Short and Harland had built eleven Bristol bombers and four Hereford bombers. At the same time design work had begun on the first of the heavy bombers, the four-engine Stirling. Since the beginning of the year the region's unemployment had fallen by over thirty thousand. However, the growing importance of Belfast as a source of vital war material was certain to increase the city's vulnerability.

By the summer of 1940 German forces controlled the coasts of Europe from the Arctic to the Pyrenees and, in spite of all wishful thinking to the contrary, Belfast was well within the range of the Luftwaffe Bombers. The Germans considered Belfast to be 'a harbour and arms centre of decisive importance for the British war economy'. As early as July 1940 reconnaissance aircraft had already got a clear picture of the city, its strategic targets and its dearth of defensive installations. On Friday 18th October, they obtained clear pictures of 'the aircraft factory', Short and Harland, 'the shipyard', Harland and Wolff, Northern Ireland's chief power station, Belfast Harbour, Rank's Flour Mill, Belfast Waterworks, Victoria Barracks, Connswater Reservoir and the Gasworks on the Ormeau Road. Apart from identifying targets the photographs made clear that anti-aircraft installations, known to the army as 'ack-ack' were sparse. This confirmed to the enemy the vulnerability of their intended targets.

Sir Crawford received letters from all over requesting information about the provision of air-raid shelters in the city. Council meetings were dominated by topics regarding rationing, cross-border smuggling, and the black market. Other matters concerned the opening of cinemas and theatres. On Monday 4 September 1939 the Government issued a notice declaring that they did not consider it necessary at present to close cinemas and theatres in Northern Ireland. At the beginning of 1940 Sir Crawford received a number of letters objecting to the opening of cinemas in Belfast on a Sunday. One letter from The Congregational Union of Ireland objected on the grounds that it was 'felt to be unwise to encroach unduly upon the sanctity of the day of rest and worship, which is regarded amongst the citizens of Ulster generally as essential to the highest interest of the nation'. Another letter from the Baptist Union of Ireland wrote 'We are certain that such a step would be derogatory to the splendid traditions of the city for preserving the sanctity of the Lord's Day and would be detrimental to the moral and spiritual welfare of the men'. Sir Crawford's own thoughts on the matter would have been that cinemas not only offered warmth and entertainment to the troops but a distraction and relief from duty.

Although conscription did not apply to Northern Ireland, recruits initially had come forward at a rate of two and a half thousand per month, but rapidly this fell to less than one thousand. There was a general feeling of apathy about the war. One attitude that affected the population was the feeling that Belfast was not important enough to be bombed. A professional wartime investigator of public attitudes and behaviour who came to Belfast observed an overall 'slackness' in public attitudes that was so 'noticeable' that in his opinion, 'anyone who is keen on the war effort is liable to feel uncomfortable in Ulster'. He himself constantly experienced 'a curious feeling of guilt at being here at all. It seemed somehow as if one was getting out of the war and having too easy a life'. He noted, for example, that :

> 'people thought nothing of asking one to lunch and talking the whole afternoon. Being half an hour late for an appointment did not matter in the slightest and perhaps the most curious shock of all is seeing men lying about in the morning on the grass outside City Hall or sleeping with their feet up in the back of cars.'[3]

Sir Crawford understood the trauma of war. He was becoming increasingly worried about the attitude of the people of Ulster and their

3.   Brian Barton, *The Blitz: Belfast in the War Years*, p.58

lack of concern. He had heard Stormont ministers speak of Northern Ireland as being 'only half in the war'. So far as they were concerned an embarrassing symptom of this apathy was the disappointingly small number of volunteers for military service from the North, which it was felt 'placed the Government in a very unfavourable light'. In May, Lord Craigavon, concerned at the figures, convinced a reluctant War Office to launch a recruitment drive. Sir Basil Brooke, Minister of Agriculture was appointed to spearhead the recruitment campaign and in a letter to Sir Crawford on 12 June 1940 called on him to initiate a Belfast Recruiting Rally. In a letter dated 13 June Sir Crawford replied stating that in his opinion public meetings did not always produce good results 'the audience generally consists of men not of military age, and a certain amount of cranks who sometimes asked difficult questions. He felt better results would be produced by propaganda such as recruiting posters and using the cinema to impress men of military age that they must do their obvious duty to the country'. On 14 June Sir Crawford received a letter from The War Office and a leaflet entitled The Auxiliary Military Pioneer Corp encouraging volunteers between the ages of 35 to 50 to join two Home Defence Battalions, the 7th Battalion Royal Ulster Rifles and 5th Battalion Royal Irish Fusiliers and for overseas service men between the ages of 18 to 50 to enlist in the Royal Inniskilling Fusiliers. The rate of pay for a Sergeant was 6 shillings a day, a Corporal 4 shillings and a Private got 2 shillings a day. Recruitment began on Tuesday 16 July 1940 in the Ulster Hall.

At a rally in Bangor later in the month Lord Craigavon issued a clarion call to the youth of Ulster to enlist in the three new Ulster battalions as they had 'a high reputation to live up to'. Sir Basil Brooke spoke of the country's great history and added: "Don't live on traditions, live up to them". Sir Crawford experienced improved results when a man called Michael O'Leary who had been awarded the Victoria Cross returned home. He gave him a hero's welcome when he arrived at the Great Northern Railway station in Victoria Street and provided him with a platform in the grounds of City Hall on which to encourage volunteers to sign up.[4]

Although the rallies brought in large numbers of volunteers, they were not nearly enough and Lord Craigavon was forced to consider desperate alternatives. For a time he favoured withholding unemployment assistance from those men of military age who had failed to enlist. This potentially explosive approach was in the end rejected because of acute Unionist reaction.[5]

Sir Crawford now found himself for the second time in his adult life Lord Mayor of Belfast bound by responsibilities in a world upset by war. Daily correspondence arriving at City Hall at this time concerned requests from Ulster people living in England who wished to obtain a permit to return home. Many were from men who wished to come home to see their families at weekends. One was from a young twenty-one year old nurse working in Sheffield who wanted to visit her ill mother but her request was turned down as Permits were generally only granted for persons on business of national importance or other very strong reasons for returning to Belfast.

Boysie – Crawford McCullagh Junior

Sir Crawford had other concerns closer to home and one of his main worries at this time was the health of his only son. By April 1939 Boysie's drinking had become a major problem. He had been involved in several car accidents and on one occasion Major May interrupted Sir Crawford in a council session in City Hall with the disturbing news that his son had crashed into railings on the Antrim Road resulting in whiplash and a broken arm. At the time Boysie was attending Dr. A. P. Henderson, a well-known G.P. in Belfast who specialised in treating alcoholics. He suggested to Sir Crawford that his son should go to Knaresborough, a nursing home in England for treatment. It was felt unwise that Boysie should go on his own, so

---

4.   PRONI LA/7/3A/78

5.   Brian Barton, *The Blitz: Belfast in the War Years*

it was agreed that Major May would accompany him and stay in a nearby hotel for the seven days it was supposed to take to cure him of his addiction. Major May returned to Belfast and Boysie retreated to the South of France to stay with a friend. The cost of the treatment was £52.10s. Sir Crawford also paid £10.10s for Dr. Henderson's consultancy fee.

Boysie eventually overcame his alcohol addiction and concentrated on his vast collection of foreign birds. When his father Sir Crawford died, Boysie sold Lismara and built a smaller house in the grounds also called Lismara. He built a sanctuary to house and breed water fowl these included budgerigars, ducks, parrots and parakeets. Species from Japan, China, Africa and South America were represented in the duck and geese collection and his successful efforts to 'double cross' oriental ducks and geese with a method called 'foxing' was recognised internationally. His aviary at Lismara held his famous Parakeet collection and was the largest in Ireland. The aviary was equipped with flourescent lighting, tubular heating and ventilation and was popular with visiting aviculturists and ornithologists from all over the world and like his father before him enjoyed entertaining his fellow bird enthusiasts when they visited his collection of rare breeds at Lismara. He contributed considerably to the Northern Ireland and British Ornothological Society and was President of the Northern Ireland Budgerigar and Foreign Birds Society. He was also a member of the Belfast Zoological Society and after presenting a collection of rare parrots and parakeets to Bellevue Zoo the 'Bird House' was officially named as the McCullagh House[6].

On 7 May 1940 Sir Crawford yet again allowed his name to go forward for the position of Lord Mayor for the 13th time. The Belfast Chamber of Trade at its meeting in the Carlton Restaurant in Donegal Place produced a letter of their appreciation to Sir Crawford and on 23 May 1940 at a civic reception in City Hall, Sir Crawford appealed to the people of Belfast to pull together in the hard times ahead.

---

6.   News Letter 1 May 1963

On 18 June 1940, the Northern Whig and the Belfast Telegraph delivered a message from the Lord Mayor to the workers of Belfast. 'Don't be downhearted. Don't give in. Britain never was beaten and never will be. We have to get past these difficulties.' When asked by the BBC to give a talk on the work of NIENSA7 on 2 March 1941 (Northern Ireland Entertainments National Service Association) under the title '*Ulster Gazette*' for transmission by their overseas services to North America and the Dominions, Sir Crawford made a point of telling the listeners who had relatives in Ulster – 'Don't worry, we are quite all right, War is not a pleasant thing but if you were here you would find us in the best of spirits, going about our daily work much as usual. We are pulling our full weight, in the forces, on the farms, in the shipyards and industry generally, with the one object, and fully confident, of winning the war.'

The situation on the Western European Front was stalemate. Behind the Maginot and Siegfried Lines the contesting nations awaited an offensive which neither was ready to take. Britain's air power was being accelerated greatly, although in manpower she was much inferior both to Germany and France and by April the war had greatly extended and intensified.

Lord Craigavon now embarked on a series of strategies. Agreeing first to create a Home guard called the Local Defence Volunteers. He then established a parliamentary committee at Stormont to advise on civil defence. As a concession to the Government he created a Ministry of Public Security. It was to be responsible for public security, civil defence and the 'protection of persons and property from injury or damage in the present emergency'. John MacDermott, lawyer, King's Councillor and Unionist MP for Queens University Belfast, was duly appointed Minister of Public Security on 25th June 1940. Although he was portrayed as 'rather dull and lacked the human touch', his private secretary John Oliver described him as a 'dignified, competent,

---

7. Since 1939 NIENSA had been sending concert parties all over the six counties of Northern Ireland to provide entertainment for the British troops, the men of the Royal Navy and the crews of minesweepers. PRONI LA/7/3A/94

conscientious minister, who was hard working and in many ways the right man for the appointment. He gave a sense of stability and the public liked him'.

Some of these traits could be ascribed to Sir Crawford and its not surprising that they worked together well in their efforts to get the Corporation to accelerate the pace of war preparations. It did not take the new Minister long to appreciate the woefully inadequate defences in Belfast and his efforts were frustrated by public apathy and lack of support from his colleagues. Sir Crawford had consistently argued for the erection of air raid shelters since 1939 and was at odds with those who maintained there was little or no chance of an air raid on Belfast by the Germans. Within Northern Ireland, civil defence was widely regarded with indifference. When the war began the city had no fighter squadrons, no barrage balloons and only twenty anti-aircraft guns. Even Lady Londonderry seemed unconcerned, in a letter to her husband she wrote: 'All sorts of rot are going on here. Air raid warnings and blackouts! As if anyone cared or wished to bomb Belfast'. In a House of Commons[8] speech Sir Crawford referred to the people who said there would be no war. "They were the very people, he averred, who now tell us there were no need for shelters".

Under Sir Crawford's leadership Belfast Corporation accelerated the pace of public shelter construction. They increased the number of air raid shelters from 200 in June 1940 to 750 by the end of the year. McDermott also encouraged local authorities to advise and assist householders on ways of strengthening their own homes, using materials provided free of charge. Every man's house must be his castle was taken literally. One householder cleared his attic and lined it with asbestos, then installed steel pillars in the dining room and erected a second ceiling made of corrugated iron. In Britain most houses that had a garden or backyard space were provided with Anderson shelters, custom-made dugouts with a shell of strong cast-iron and bolstered with sandbags. They were supplied free to those whose houses had

8.   House of Commons Senate Debate. (N.I.), 22, c. 340

a Poor Law Valuation (PLV), the figure used for the calculation of Government rates. In 1940 three hundred thousand people living in houses in Northern Ireland which were eligible for free shelters had still not received them even though the Government had promised to provide them during the first week of the war under conditions which were substantially less generous than in Great Britain.

Although Belfast Corporation embarked on a major programme of public-shelter construction they were not altogether successful. In practice they were used for almost every purpose than that for which they were intended. Some were used by courting couples, children were scared of them, mostly they were used as public conveniences or waste disposal and the smell prevented most people from going near them. A belated attempt by the Government to make them more practical by installing doors and lights was a complete failure. Air raid wardens complained of the wanton destruction of electric cables and because of the filth and squalor inside the shelters, when the Blitz finally came they were woefully underused. Possibly the best-equipped air-raid shelters in Belfast were those constructed at Gallagher's tobacco factory. Roomy, well-lit and comparatively comfortable, the shelters were primarily intended for the tobacco workers. Fortunately for the local residents they were used by large numbers of people from the under protected neighbouring streets.

John MacDermott now turned his efforts to revitalising the city's fire service and again approached Sir Crawford and the Corporation to increase substantially the number of full-time firemen in Belfast. Unfortunately, additional fire engines, pumps, and steel pipe fittings had, in the meantime, become extremely difficult to obtain. Large British cities now under constant threat of attack, were seeking to augment their fire fighting provision and received priority from British Officials. This dereliction was not entirely the fault of Belfast Corporation. It was due at least in part to the apathy of the Northern Ireland Government who argued that civil defence in the region was the responsibility of Westminster. Lord Craigavon was too ill to give any leadership and his most senior colleagues John Andrews and

Dawson Bates were unsuited to dealing with the situation. The latter had become quite incoherent and could give no precise directions on policy. Wilfred Spender, the cabinet secretary, believed Bates to have been regularly drunk at his desk and his response to army communication about Belfast's vulnerability to air attack was simply a refusal to answer them. The government consistently refused to provide anything like sufficient funds to enable the Ministry of Public Security to fulfil its statutory obligations. From June 1940 they gave precedence to the provision of over twenty military airfields, scattered throughout Northern Ireland, which not only starved the shelter programme of sufficient bricks, labour and transport but much needed fire fighting equipment.[9]

At his first cabinet meeting on 1 July 1940, MacDermott won approval for the immediate voluntary evacuation of all Belfast school children, arguing that this was essential 'in the light of the present military position'. Out of a total school population in the city of seventy thousand, fewer than eighteen thousand had been officially registered for evacuation.

On the appointed day, 7 July, only seven thousand of these turned up; a further eighteen hundred arrived when a second opportunity was offered six weeks later. Failure was partly due to the fact that the attempt had been made during the school holidays, but a more fundamental reason was the all pervading assumption that Belfast would not be bombed. Sir Crawford's grandson, Lionel was evacuated from Campbell College to the Northern Counties Hotel in Portrush in September 1940.

Belfast Blitz

Belfast's first public air-raid warning, on Friday 25 October 1940, brought the war dramatically nearer home and provided its citizens with their first real test of nerve. The sirens started just after 10 p.m. Popular reactions to this unfamiliar clamour varied. Some stood on

---

9. Sean McMahon, *The Belfast Blitz: Luftwaaffe Raids in Northern Ireland 1941*

doorsteps, casually chatting. William McCready, a post office worker who was relaxing with friends in a bar, described how, at first, they had all 'rushed to the door', but soon afterwards, 'returned to the bar and had another drink'! In south Belfast Moya Woodside recorded her reaction. She had been at a poetry reading in a neighbours garden when

> Unexpectedly, unbelievably, the air raid sirens went. We looked at each other in consternation. 'It must be a practice,' someone said. Suddenly it dawned on us that this was the real thing...[A friend] went quite white, and rushed, accompanied by her husband, to put her things on...my heart was thumping and my knees positively knocked. Subconscious terror would not be suppressed.....I wonder what one does in what might be one's last moments....the slightest noise fraught with danger.

Between 25 October 1940 and the first actual raid on 7-8 April 1941, the sirens sounded almost twenty times and each was a false alarm. Moya Woodside became rather blasé in her attitude towards the sirens, she wrote of being able to go on reading, without batting an eyelid, '[bombs will] have to drop in this district before I react to a warning again'. When a friend arrived from London at Christmas 1940 she told her that the precautions were half hearted, adding, 'We feel that we are another 240 miles there and back from Liverpool and why should the Germans come all that distance when they have plenty of important targets to hand'.

The citizens of Belfast were as psychologically unprepared for the blitz and both the militarily and the civil defences were inadequately equipped to cope with its impact. Under the guidance of Sir Crawford and members of the Corporation John MacDermott started to improve the organisational structure of civil defence in Belfast by modifying the role of the city's councillors. At a meeting in City Council with Sir Crawford presiding it was agreed that the corporation's powers in relation to air raid precautions be transferred to a three-man council committee calling itself the Civil Defence Authority. This new body was to be responsible for providing the various services, with his ministry continuing to give support through grants, the supply of equipment and advice from officials. The contrast between the experience of Northern Ireland and of Great Britain in wartime was pervasive and there was severe criticism from Westminster regarding apathy for the war effort in Northern Ireland. Several ministers had resigned including Lieutenant-Colonel R.G. Gordon parliamentary secretary at the Ministry of Finance, who explained to the Commons that the Government was:

> "By nature of its personnel, its lack of drive and initiative and utter lack of what war means ... quite unfitted to sustain the people in the ordeal we have to face ... It should resign and be reconstituted immediately".

In September, Edmond Warnock, parliamentary secretary at the Ministry of Home Affairs had introduced a vote of censure, calling for a complete change in the Governments composition. He described Milne Barbour's direction at the Ministry of Commerce as 'wrong, inept and palsied', and remarked that when a person became of member of the Northern Ireland Government 'he became a tenant for life....Nothing but death, illness or promotion ever removes anybody'. Craigavon's simple response to the call to revamp his Government was: 'My answer is that I am not going to do it'.

A few months later on 24th November 1940 Lord Craigavon died peacefully in his sleep. There was widespread grief among the Unionist and Loyalist community who felt very strongly that he had been instrumental in preventing Westminster from imposing Home Rule on Ireland. The man to succeed Lord Craigavon was John Andrews but as it turned out he was barely able to cope with the burdensome demands of war. When Winston Churchill was informed of the North's negligible contribution to the war effort, he ordered an immediate investigation and called for action to ensure that fuller use was made of its resources. In December 1940 Belfast Corporation initiated the Ulster Campaign to raise five million pounds for war weapons. A barometer registered the donations. Sir Crawford, at age seventy-two and despite inclement weather, hovered over the barometer for a week until it reached the five million mark. Lady McCullagh who had been so active in raising funds in the First World War volunteered her expertise and as President of the Welfare Headquarters

Control established sixteen emergency camps, seventeen nursery centres, requisitioning schools, church halls and boy-scout centres. Large buildings not already used by the armed forces were prepared as evacuee hostels. They were equipped with sufficient food and bedding to meet the needs of ten thousand people. Sir Crawford requisitioned the Slieve Donard Hotel in Newcastle, Co. Down where he and his family had stayed on many happy occasions. He personally negotiated with the management allowing it to continue as a hotel but with severe limitations.

On Thursday 14 November 1940 there was a devastating attack on Coventry. In the course of eight hours the Germans dropped 449 bombs, 503 tons of high explosives and almost 32,000 incendiary bombs. Never before had an attack of such weight and magnitude been unleashed against a population. More than 50,000 houses were destroyed or damaged, many factories were gutted, 554 people died and 865 were seriously hurt.[10] An account of the attack was relayed to John McDermott by Rear Admiral Richard King, the Royal Navy's Flag Officer in Charge in Belfast. MacDermott's description of the account is chilling and prophetic 'this is a pen picture of what a city looked like after a raid. It made my hair stand on end because I realised that this was what Belfast would be like'[11].

In February 1941 John MacDermott voiced his concern to Sir Crawford and his colleagues, in graphic detail the probable scene in the city of Belfast in the event of an attack by the Luftwaffe; normal life brought to a standstill; extensive casualties; people shocked and dazed; multiple fires raging uncontrollably; buildings collapsing; widespread damage to private and commercial property; industry dislocated; conditions bordering on the chaotic'. The Civil Defence Authority, he suggested would be unable to cope with the circumstances unaided. He therefore advocated a strategy called The Hiram Plan. This provided for the formation of an emergency government

---

10.   Brian Barton *The Belfast Blitz: Belfast in the War Years*, p.87

11.   Brian Barton, *The Belfast Blitz: Belfast in the War Years*, p.88

which would take full charge of Belfast immediately after a raid. This would in effect help to co-ordinate the efforts of all departments, public authorities and utilities and give clear instructions to the civilian population. The cabinet at Stormont accepted this suggestion but insisted that MacDermott should himself be in control at advance headquarters.

On 18 March 1941 Sir Crawford again shouldered the responsibilities of the Lord Mayoralty, his fourteenth Year of Office, 1941-1942. He was a much loved and respected Lord Mayor, the people of Belfast felt safe in his hands and it was always his wish to fulfil the desires of the citizens. He was getting on in years, but he still had the energy to carry out his obligations to a city on the brink of .annihilation. Lady Margaret was not as robust as her husband and was now suffering bouts of ill health. She often said that "she felt, that, as Lady Mayoress, she belonged to the city and its people - that after her own family, they had first claim upon her". Despite her failing health she continued to support her husband and continued to initiate and work for many causes. Immediately, upon the outbreak of war, Lady McCullagh formed the War Hospital Supply Board and became President of the Belfast Depots and War Hospital Supply and Comfort Fund. Four depots were set up in Belfast and she was involved in organising and supporting each. She was President of the North Belfast Branch (Central Branch). In October 1939 the West Belfast Receiving Depot was opened. Margaret is pictured in the press at all these events designed to augment the funds required to obtain medical supplies and comforts for service personnel. Numerous knitting clubs were formed to supply the troops with warm garments. Lady McCullagh chaired the Ormeau knitting Club and is pictured with some forty or fifty women.

On 18 March 1941, Sir Crawford was inaugurated for the fourteenth time for the term 1941-1942. In April a brief article titled 'Thirteen Times a Lord Mayor since 1914' in the *Daily Express* reported 'his hospitality is widely known. His thirteen years as Chief Citizen of Belfast are estimated to have cost him £36,000 (probably much more); and in July 1916 he instituted a five minute silence in memory of the Ulster Division'

Sir Crawford had only been initiated as First Citizen for one month when the first wave of bombs rained down on Belfast. The first on April 7th and the fourth on the nights of May 3rd and 4th were relatively light as far as human casualties were concerned as Belfast City centre was virtually deserted at the time of the attack – the early hours of Sunday morning. In the course of these raids the Midland Hotel in York Street was burnt to the ground and a number of leading business premises were destroyed, these included Gallagher's Tobacco Factory, Dunville's Stores, the Ulster Arcade and the Bank Buldings. Bridge Street and High Street took a hit obliterating the drapery shop that Sir Crawford had leased with his first loan. The worst attack that night devastated the aircraft factory at Harland and Wolff. At about 3.30 a.m. a bomber swept in over Belfast Lough and dropped a parachute oil bomb – the last bomb of the night.

The next attacks on 15th and 16th April when from 110 to 125 planes were involved were, however, of a longer and more intense duration. An eye witness reported hearing the Luftwaffe overhead first, then the 'deafening roar of the anti-aircraft guns and only after that the anxiety-arousing notes of the 'sirens', or 'whining winnies' as they were facetiously called by Moore who describes the scene in prosaic detail:

'They had scarcely faded when the rhythmic thudding of the Nazi heavy bombers increased with their approach. Suddenly they were directly overhead in a din indescribable. Flares fell furiously from the hitherto dark sky like shot stars. Despite our blacked-out buildings and stygian streets, the revengeful enemy, "the smiler with the knife hid under his cloak" had unfalteringly outlined his objective. Rapidly everything became defined by the blazing mills, workers and buildings set on fire by his thunderbolts. For five eternity-like hours these weavers of woe wended their way to and fro, in and about, creating with their lethal shuttles a design of terror suggesting 'a lake of fire burning with brimstone'. Everywhere sounded the "whoomf" of bursting bombs, the crackling of flaming timbers, the tinkling of high pitched notes of shattering glass, the heavy leaden thumps of crashing masonry, the hail like patter of shrapnel, the pulsations of the N.F.F.

pumps, the occasional shrieks of frightened women who saw their much loved homes disappear, and the quick angry barks of our defending guns. To the ears of the nerve wracked people who suffered the long drawn agony through a period seemingly endless that "All Clear" tocsin was, in faith, divine music. In the broad daylight the next day the sun shone on a city that looked like a battlefield, a city of blasted and still smouldering buildings and homes, of great masses of rubble out of which human bodies were being dug, of fires which painted the sky a brilliant orange'.

At daybreak Sir Crawford made his way along the ruin riddled one mile York Street to do his duty at City Hall. A bomb had crashed into the large Banqueting Hall destroying the prized five-ton Donegal Carpet – but the municipal palace itself had been saved by the heroic vigilance of the fire fighting Volunteer Force. From City Hall he made his way through smoke filled and obliterated streets, passed bombed out houses and collapsing buildings, passed rescue workers and wardens until he reached the Mater Hospital. Here he witnessed some of the most horrific sights imaginable.

Ulster author Brian Moore was an air raid precautions warden attached to the Mater Hospital and he helped coffin the dead. In *The Emperor of Ice Cream* he wrote:

In the stink of human excrement, in the acrid smell of disinfectant there dead were heaped, body on body, flung arm, twisted feet, open mouth, staring eyes, old men on top of young women, a child lying on a policeman's back, a soldier's hand resting on a woman's thigh, a carter still wearing his coal-slacks on top of a pile of arms and legs, his own arm outstretched, finger pointing, as though he warned of some unseen horror. Forbidding and clumsy, the dead cluttered the morgue room from floor to ceiling.

Sir Crawford was often described as 'the human touch incarnation' and it was his decision to go out among the people of Belfast and help them individually. No efforts, physical or financial, were withheld by him, in comforting the suffering. He visited innumerable shattered homes, also the rest centres and hospitals which sheltered the maimed and homeless. Many of those he chatted to were bereft of beds to sleep upon and without roofs or walls to afford even a semblance of comfort. Lady Margaret came to the rescue on many of these occasions and found somewhere for the unfortunate homeless to have food and shelter at least until they could find somewhere more permanent.

In Belfast and its suburbs, 3,205 houses were utterly wrecked, another 3,996 seriously damaged and a further 49,684 were still erect but lacking doors, windows or floors. The public funeral of the unnamed dead took place, as arranged on 19 April, 1941. Its organisation raised some unique difficulties. The authorities first searched the unidentified bodies for personal effects, such as rosary beads and crucifixes in order to identify their religion. After separate Catholic and Protestant services were held at St. Georges Market, the dead were then taken to Milltown cemetery or to the city cemetery nearby. With regard to the organisation of the funeral, Sir Crawford stated that it would 'be difficult indeed to decide who or how many (the chief mourners) may be'[12]. Those people with relatives missing, presumed dead, followed behind the coffins. Thousands lined the streets and as the cortege passed by, both men and women wept without restraint, and civilian and military rescue squads stood with heads bowed. Controversy still surrounds the final death toll. Official statistics, first made available to the public by the Northern Ireland government in October 1944, indicated that 745 civilians were killed and over 430 seriously injured. Similarly, both the Ulster Year Book for the year 1947 and John Blakes official history of the war state that at least 700 died; Blake also states that there were some 420 serious casualties.

Although most of the direct hits from the Luftwaffe were directed at strategic points in the city the suburbs were also targeted. Sir Crawford's daughter Daisy and her husband Victor lived in Fortwilliam Park, a quiet and exclusive enclave on the Antrim Road. However in 1941 within a mile of this leafy thoroughfare a direct hit either completely destroyed or damaged beyond repair all the houses in Annadale Street.

12. Brian Barton, *The Belfast Blitz: Belfast in the War Years*, p.265

Before the war Victor had purchased a summer house in Groomsport called 'Rocklands'. It was a popular seaside spot for holidaymakers during the summer and only about 20 miles from Belfast. When the bombing over Belfast began to escalate Victor thought it would be a good idea for his wife to move out of the city so for a time Daisy and her cook Bella took up residence in Groomsport. Their son Lionel, evacuated out of Belfast with Campbell College, was now safely ensconced in Portrush while Beatrice boarded at Manor House School in Milford, Co. Armagh.

Although fishing was a sport that Victor had enjoyed with his brothers, he also was a keen golfer. He was member of Rosapenna Golf Club and he and Daisy regularly spent weekends with assorted friends and acquaintances at the Rosapenna Hotel at Downings in County Donegal. The hotel had a beautiful dining room and dance floor and even though there was a war on it didn't stop guests from enjoying themselves. Moya Woodside writing in her memoirs describes the hotel and its guests in 1941,

> Almost the last place in Europe where the lights are still alight ... Last year it was only half-full and those wearing evening dress were in a minority. This year it is crowded out mainly with Belfast's wealthier citizens and about 75 per cent are in evening wear. In fact the display of jewellery and furs is terrific. I am amused to note that a man's economic status is indicated by the number and size of the precious stones which adorn his wife's person and by the comparative length of silver fur and mink shoulder cape.[13]

The weekend's entertainment gave Daisy an excuse to show off her elaborate and expensive Paris gowns and furs as well as the fabulous jewellery that Victor liked to buy her. Sir Crawford and Lady McCullagh disapproved of their daughters extravagance especially at this time when others were suffering so terribly from the deprivations of war.

How different the circumstances of newly weds Nellie Bell and her husband Bob who joined the refugees escaping the grim reality of war torn Belfast. They ended up sharing a cottage with a family in

---

13. Jonathan Bardon, *A History of Ulster*, p.572

Donaghcloney, near Lurgan in Co. Armagh. Although they had a room to themselves, the girl of the house had a baby and to get to her room she had to go through theirs! They found their routine somewhat erratic:

> Bob was working shifts 6.00 to 2.00 and 2.00 till 10.00. Well, to get to work on early shifts, Bob and me both had to get up about 3.00 or 3.30 am. Though this is 1941, the cottage had no gas or electricity. I had to light a fire with bellows to make him a cup of tea or boil an egg for him. He walked the 4 or 5 miles to Lurgan to get a train to Belfast. After a couple of weeks he got a bicycle which helped a bit helped but after he got a puncture or two, it didn't work very well either. For the 2.00 till 10 pm it was just as bad. He had to leave Donacloney about 11.00 in the morning. [14]

Although their circumstances seemed harsh they were fortunate in having a roof over their heads and a warm bed to sleep in at night. There were many such refugees who had nowhere to go and found themselves sleeping under hedges and in barns. Looting became commonplace food was scarce and many people had fled their homes with only the clothes they stood up in. According to one official estimate, during late May and early June 1941, the number of evacuees, both voluntary and government-organised peaked at over 222,000.

In May Sir Crawford was made a member of the Northern Ireland Privy Council in the King's Birthday Honours. He took the oath upon his appointment in Buckingham Palace on 3 July 1941. This entitled him to preface his name with 'The Right Honourable'.

14. Jonathan Bardon, *A History of Ulster*, p.572

Chapter Seventeen
1941-1944

The Yanks are Coming

Sir Crawford, your record's a proud one
In wearing the Mayoral chain,
And the call is a deep and loud one
That asks you to wear it again.
There's something so genial about you,
And now skies are gloomy and drear
We feel that we can't do without you,
So wish you a Happy New Year.

Northern Whig January 1st 1941

With the outbreak of war in 1939 municipal politics in Belfast faded into the background. Elections were suspended and virtually the only municipal affairs to arouse general interest were the proposals to modify Belfast's strict Sabbatarianism. These included the opening of cinemas on Sundays to which only uniformed members of the armed forces would be allowed access and the Whiteabbey inquiry which not only involved Sir Crawford but unfortunately bore a close resemblance to the Megaw inquiry of 1926.[1]

---

1.   Budge and O'Leary, *Belfast: Approach to Crisis; a study of Belfast politics 1613-1970* p.153

The Dunlop Report

The Abbey, on the outskirts of Whiteabbey, got its name from a Cistercian Abbey on which grounds the house was built. Before it became a hospital for the treatment of Tuberculosis it was the home of the architect Sir Charles Lanyon where he lived until his death in 1889. Between the years 1889 and 1906 the number of persons dying from tuberculosis in each year was usually sustained at over 1,000. In 1894 the Royal Hospital Committee was the first in Ireland to establish a hospital for patients suffering from the disease. Another hospital for tuberculosis was opened in Fisherwick Place in October 1890 with about 6 beds. Through the generosity of Mr Foster Green (the tea merchant) new premises and grounds of about 45 acres, were obtained at Fortbreda and this became the Forster Green Hospital. In 1907 Belfast Corporation undertook to maintain 35 beds in this hospital and so was therefore responsible for half of the running costs of this institution.

In 1892 Dr Robert Hall, the Chief Medical Officer in Belfast persuaded the Board of Guardians to purchase The Abbey in order to provide an ancillary workhouse for the treatment of Tuberculosis. In 1906 the Guardians added four pavilions to the premises so that 210 patients could be accommodated. This continued under the care of Dr. Hall and the Board of Guardians until 1913. In September 1913 the Tuberculosis Committee of the Belfast City Council was founded for the prevention, detection and treatment of Tuberculosis, Dr Andrew Trimble was appointed as Chief Tuberculosis Officer.[2]

In 1914 Crawford McCullagh who was Chairman of the Improvement Committee applied to the Local Government Board for a loan of nearly £30,000 for the purchase of the Abbey Hospital. Accordingly the loan was sanctioned and Belfast Corporation renamed it 'The Belfast Sanatorium for the treatment of Pulmonary Tuberculosis.' On 1 January 1918, an open-air school was officially opened at

2. Dr. Roger Blaney, *Belfast: 100 years of Public Health*, p.34

Whiteabbey Sanatorium, it was the first official open-air school in Ireland.

In 1932 it was agreed by the T.B. Committee and Belfast Corporation that the hospital was not big enough to accommodate the rising number of patients and accordingly Belfast Corporation proposed extensions to the existing sanatorium, the first plans being selected at a competition in 1934, and the final plans being ready in 1936. However, the Tuberculosis Committee did not consider the site at Whiteabbey suitable for the proposed extensions and in 1936 the Corporation under the leadership of Sir Crawford took steps to investigate the possibility of acquiring a site for the erection of a new sanatorium.

Between 1936 and 1939 the T.B. Committee made persistent attempts to make the Corporation buy land for the purposes of a new Sanatorium at Rathmore rather than Brookhill; land which was repeatedly certified by the City Surveyor to be wholly inappropriate for the purposes of a sanatorium. Meanwhile the management and organisation of the hospital had run into severe difficulties which began with a dispute between the medical superintendent and some of his staff resulting in the Minister of Home Affairs requesting an enquiry into the entire administration of the hospital. Edward Armstrong and John Dunlop arrived at Whiteabbey Hospital in the spring of 1939 to make their inspection and according to a member of staff who was interviewed by the Belfast Telegraph said they were "always knocking about, enquiring into this and that, making ceaseless notes and holding a great many consultations. Their activity was endless and soon they became an accepted part of the institution, on the friendliest terms with everyone from the doctors to the tiny tots in the children's pavilion".

Certainly the inspectors had not been idle – The enquiry which lasted thirty-four days became known as the Dunlop Report and was published on 17 June 1941, running to over 2000 pages.

The report disclosed corruption, shocking incompetence in the running of the sanatorium and pathetic squabbling over petty issues. It disclosed serious concerns in the running of the hospital including an alleged affair between the Medical Superintendent Percy Walker and the Matron as well as the awarding of contracts for the supply of inferior and 'totally unsuitable' black out material to companies who overcharged and whose directors were members of the Corporation. On a more serious level the report asserted that the City Treasurer's Department had displayed 'complete laxity' and 'gross neglect' in the management of the sanatorium's accounts.

> 'It is perfectly clear from the forgoing that a determined effort was made by a section of the T.B Committee to force the purchase of the Rathmore site with regard to its obvious unsuitability and extravagant price, and it is therefore not surprising that evidence was forthcoming at the inquiry suggesting attempted bribery'

Towards the end of the report the Ministry's findings are listed:-

1. The T.B Committee should be dissolved.

2. Belfast Corporation should be relieved of its powers under the Tuberculosis Prevention (I) Act of 1908.

3. The Medical Superintendent, the City Treasurer, the Steward Clerk (at the hospital) and a sister (at the hospital) should all be censured.

4. The Official Stock Takers should not be re-employed.

5. The Medical Superintendent and the Matron should be "retired from their respective offices".

The end of the report supported the role played by Sir Crawford;

> 'In conclusion the Ministry desires to express its appreciation of the helpful attitude of the Right Honourable the Lord Mayor whose fearless and impartial leadership of the best elements in the Corporation, and to whom the bringing to light of certain abuses and shortcomings of the administration in Whiteabbey Sanatorium is largely due'.

Immediately after the publication of the Dunlop Report, the Corporation at a meeting on 19 June set up another 'Big Six' committee, consisting of Sir Crawford, three Unionists, one Labour and one Nationalist Councillor, to look into the entire affairs of the council. Then they traced the 'totally unsuitable' blackout material to a firm in which four Councillors were involved and asked them to resign. However at the next meeting of the council (7 August 1941) the Special Committee was dissolved, a decision which by exerting his personal influence Sir Crawford managed to get rescinded (13 August). The Big Six then proceeded to appoint a new Town Clerk and throughout the winter prepared their report.

They recommended the establishment of a special committee to control appointments; a return to direct employment instead of contract employment of semi-skilled and unskilled workers; legislation to provide more stringent definitions of 'interest' and requiring anyone tendering for a corporation contract to disclose names of Council members who might have any 'interest' at all. The Council reacted by rejecting all these recommendations at a meeting on 2 April 1942. In early June the Minister of Home Affairs introduced the Belfast County Borough Administration Act. It appointed three administrators for a three and half years period who would make all appointments, purchases, contracts and rates, and municipal taxes. In reality the three Government nominees were two leading Belfast businessmen – Messrs. William Robinson of the Bank Buildings Department Store, Charles S. Neill, President of the Belfast Chamber of Commerce – together with Mr. Charles W. Grant, an official from the Ministry of Home Affairs. On 24 July the Cabinet refused a request from a Corporation delegation to reverse its decision to appoint administrators and the Cabinet agreed to make public immediately that this would happen on 1 October and that their appointment would last for three and a half years until the 31 March 1946. The fact that the Stormont Act took 15 months to become Law after the report was published arose because of the persistent opposition of some Councillors to Sir Crawford's attempt to bring in various administrative reforms.[3]

Although Sir Crawford had tried to persuade the Government to allow a site to be selected for the purpose of building a suitable sanato-

3.   PRONI Dunlop Report

rium the Minister of Home Affairs, Sir Dawson Bates decided on the grounds of economy that the Corporation should not proceed with the scheme. However in 1942 Dr. Brice R. Clarke was appointed the new Medical Superintendent of Whiteabbey Sanatorium. Dr. Clarke had been superintendent at Forster Green Hospital for over sixteen years. He was a specialist in diseases of the respiratory organs and author of *Sanocrysin Treatment of Pulmonary Tuberculosis*. The war had raised the incidence of Tuberculosis by 20% and under Dr. Clarke's supervision Whiteabbey Hospital became a more efficient treatment centre for sufferers of this terrible disease. His recommendations included the cleanliness and sanitary condition of the surroundings, giving advice on general hygiene and on the absolute necessity of fresh air and sunlight. Windows were to be kept open both day and night, proper food was to be administered and instructions issued on how to destroy sputum so as not to spread infection. The hospital itself was updated with a new pavillion providing a ward for 25 new beds for patients, allowing in more space and light. At the same time a new kitchen annexe was added and up to date accommodation was provided to accommodate 30 nurses with four bathrooms and a drying room whereas before they had been housed in the Administration building. Dr. Clarke and his family lived on the estate of Whiteabbey Hospital for eighteen years and planted many conifers that surround the hospital today.[4]

Sir Crawford's 15th Term in Office

On 14 December 1941 Sir Crawford celebrated his 74th birthday. His daughter Helen organised a family party and they all agreed it was time for him to start slowing down. Lady Margaret's health was beginning to give some alarm and their great love for each other made it only natural for him to give her more attention and consideration. This he explained to the General Purposes Committee when

---

4. Under the Public Health (Tuberculosis) Act 1946 Whiteabbey Sanatorium was vested in the Northern Ireland Tuberculosis Authority and renamed Whiteabbey Hospital. PRONI LA/2/AB/54.

he notified them he would not accept nomination for another year of the Mayoral Office should that honour be offered to him. "With thirteen years in office, I have", he explained, "created a Municipal record. During that time I have endeavoured to uphold the best traditions of the Corporation and the honour of the City, and I think the time has come when I and my wife deserve a rest".

His decision was irrevocable and one received with much regret. The Belfast Telegraph, May 1942, reflected the sorrow:

> Both on personal and public grounds the citizens of Belfast, irrespective of their religious of political allegiance, note, with no ordinary regret, the relinquishing of the Chief Magistracy by The Right Honourable Sir Crawford McCullagh.... To have served as Lord Mayor of a great city for fourteen years, in times both of peace and war in the manner in which Sir Crawford has done is to have laid Belfast under an obligation impossible of assessment. His time and his business gifts have always been placed freely at the disposal of the public, his generosity has been unmeasured, and his bonhomie has added to his eminent fitness as holder of the office of First Citizen. The honour as been his of receiving and entertaining Royalty; at the other end of the scale he has always found happiness in extending hospitality to the least fortunate in the community... And it has always been from his personal funds.

> Throughout all his public life and service no man could have had a more helpful and sympathetic ally than he has had in Lady McCullagh. He will carry into his retirement from the chair many satisfactions, supreme amongst them must be his knowledge of the complete confidence of the public.

As his successor for the role of First Citizen, the General Purposes Committee nominated Alderman George R. Black, J.P. who was Chairman of the Finance Committee and High Sheriff in 1935. He had been a member of the City Council for sixteen years. At the Statutory Quarterly Meeting on 22 May the recommendation, when put to the vote, found support from thirty-one corporators while fourteen others – five Aldermen and nine Councillors abstained from registering their approval. Physically Alderman Black was in poor health and had to delegate many of his engagements to the Deputy Lord Mayor. After seven months in office he died in December leaving Belfast with the Deputy Lord Mayor, Alderman D. Lyle Hall performing the customary duties until a successor could be elected.[5]

The normal statutory date for the annual election of the Lord Mayor was 24 May and so it was necessary to appoint a mayor for the intervening months. At several preliminary meetings the names of suitable candidates were discussed but opinions as to their respective merits were divided. The strongest support was undeniably given to the hope that Sir Crawford could be encouraged to emerge from his retirement. Sir Crawford was not personally keen to accept the honour. His wife needed him more than ever and the rest of the family were deeply concerned about her deteriorating health. Lady Margaret's valiant efforts to rally with her husband at the beginning of the war had taken its toll and she now spent much of her time at home resting. The pictures of her in the press at the time depict her looking much thinner and rather sad. She was at her happiest when working at Sir Crawford's side and the duties she performed took her mind off the worries she had regarding her children and family. Her son Boysie still had alcohol related problems and her daughter Daisy's drinking and behaviour in public was becoming an embarrassment to all the family. Her granddaughter Beatrice left home at 16 to live with a wealthy Belfast entrepreneur old enough to be her father.

Sir Crawford finally decided to accept the nomination for his 15th year as Chief Citizen on 6 January 1943. After an absence of seven months, Sir Crawford was elected unanimously at a special meeting of the Corporation as Lord Mayor for the remaining three months of the late Alderman Black's tenure of office expiring on 23 May 1943. At his installation, Sir Crawford asked the Council to forget the past and look to the future.

"There is one thing I desire you to know and understand very thoroughly.

It is that my first interest always has been, and is today Belfast Corporation and City. Hard things have undoubtedly been said during recent months but all I will

5.   Alfred S Moore, *A Merchant Prince*

say at present is that I personally do not in the slightest degree entertain an iota of ill will towards any individual or member of the Corporation.

I have never said unkind words concerning anybody and my emphatic advice to you all is. Let us forget the past. Let us accept things as they are, and by our conduct in this assembly show the citizens and the world generally, that, despite our detractors, we of the Belfast Corporation are fit to carry on the duties assigned to us.

Our thoughts at present cannot be completely parochial. They must be concentrated and intensely on Imperial and not on civic affairs. The clouds seem to be lifting, however, and soon we may enter more placid times. Let us hope therefore, that this New Year will bring with it the success of the Allies and an early victory.

When we have attained that goal, our resolve to build up our City, of which I, and we all, are so justly proud, will be implemented. Meanwhile, our one hundred per-cent duty – I will not call it a task – is for every member of the Council to take a hold of himself and, both strenuously and conscientiously, prove to the citizens that their trust is not misplaced."

Subsequently, while entertaining the members of the Council in his traditional fashion, Sir Crawford said he had just celebrated his seventy-fourth birthday and commented on the onerous burden which the occupant of the Mayoral office now had to bear. Sir Crawford's daughter Helen stepped in as Lady Mayoress and took over many of the duties that her Mother had performed. The coming weeks and months were packed with impressive ceremonies, innumerable parades, inspections and events all designed to heighten commitment to raise funds for the war effort. Special Days were declared: Civil Defence Day, Labour Day, Flag Day, British Sailor's Day, U.S. Army Day, Army, Navy and School Children Days, when each group took the spotlight. The inauguration and closing ceremonies for these days included the military and civilian elite of the province. There were pictures of Sir Crawford in the press practically every week receiving sums as small as twenty-six pennies raised in a concert held by school children in an air raid shelter; to larger sums such as £125,000 from the Belfast Corporation's Finance Committee, £100,000 from the Co-operators Society, £50,000 from the Water Board and £25,000 from the Woolwich Equitable Building Society. The list was extensive. There were salvage drives netting over one million pounds; a student collection day; a waste paper drive by the Ulster Industrial Association. Huge military parades included: the Royal Air Force, the Women's Air Auxilliary Force, the Air Training Corps; the Women's Volunteer Service, the British Civil Defence, the Home Guard, and the Irish Home Band, the Iniskilling Fusilliers Band and others. A 'Raise the Standard' savings campaign in November, 1943, saw Sir Crawford inspecting the honour guard made up of the Ulster Home Guard after a war savings parade conducted by the War Savings Council with the Women's Voluntary Service and the Girl Guides parading. During the Wings for Victory Week in April 1943 Sir Crawford appealed to the citizens as reported in the press "to blast to smithereens Belfast's allotted target of 5,000,000 pounds". They promptly took up his challenge, before the last day of the week Sir Crawford proudly announced that their voluntary contributions totalled £5,635,646. Every effort seems to have been made to involve as many people as possible and to reward every effort, no matter how small.[6]

Northern Ireland made a vital contribution towards the food supplies in British cities. Sir Basil Brooke, Minister of Agriculture until he became Prime Minister in 1943 ordered that potatoes, carrots and cabbages be grown in lazy beds on the Stormont Estate; he got golf clubs to grow corn on their fairways; and with the help of Sir Crawford persuaded Queen's University to cultivate its lawns. The linen and tobacco industries along with the shipbuilding and munitions plants were joined by the King's Hall Airplane Construction plant in producing everything from threads to tommy-guns, from bombs to bandages and from ships to airplanes, operating day and night, Saturdays and Sundays. Sir Crawford is pictured in the press receiving donations all during the war years. Despite his advancing years he always displayed an air of youthful enthusiasm for any event that benefited the war effort. He still entertained lavishly at City

---

6.   PRONI LA/7/3/A

Hall, but infrequently at Lismara as Lady Margaret was no longer well enough to accompany her husband to many of the social events he was called upon to attend.

Sir Crawford's notable achievements in raising funds for the war effort were in themselves suggestive that his standing with the citizens, in general, had improved rather than weakened and with it the credit of the City Council since his return to the Mayoral Chair. It was therefore a foregone conclusion that the citizens of Belfast would energetically endeavour to insist on him continuing to officiate as Chief magistrate. At the statutory meeting of Belfast Corporation on 24 May Sir Crawford was once again unanimously elected Lord Mayor for the year 1943-1944, his sixteenth term in office. Reciprocating the good wishes of his colleagues, he said that he did not intend to follow the usual practice, on such occasions, of reviewing the work accomplished by the City Council and perhaps indicating something of what their aims should be for the future in civic work. No, that was outside his province at the moment. The re-building and re-planning of Belfast were decidedly important but they must be temporarily shelved. "Their thoughts", he continued, "all trended in one direction – that was the winning of the war. Happily more cheerful signs were becoming manifest and there were gleams of broadening brightness in all quarters of the compass. We must fervently hope the ensuing year, 1943-1944 would bring Peace and with it Victory for the Allies. Then they could go full steam ahead in the work of the Corporation and carry on unfettered and without deviation their plans for the betterment of Belfast in all its aspects". During the Spring of 1943 the chances of success in the War against the Germans were gradually improving. The year had opened at a very critical stage in the Battle of the Atlantic yet during the ensuing months the Allied escort forces were not only growing in strength but were turning from the mainly defensive to the offensive. Moreover, the Navy now completely dominated the Mediterranean gaining, thereby, strategic advantages of greatly shortened sea routes for men and supplies to support the fighting forces in North Africa.

Belfast had an eastern outlook that year towards the Mediterranean and the victorious leadership of their Northern Ireland hero Field Marshall Montgomery. Every school boy in 1942 knew of Mersa Matruh, Benghazi, Tripoli, Sidi Barrani and, above all, El Alamein, as familiarly as their own street names. And now during the second half of 1943 the Land War had moved from North Africa to Italy where everything was going to Montgomery's schedule; and in accordance with his battle cry of "Forward to Victory. Let us kick Italy out of the War!". At City Hall Sir Crawford enthusiastically resumed his hospitality with a stream of international and Cosmopolitan visitors who visited Belfast that year.

With his daughter Helen acting Lady Mayoress at his side he entertained guests such as Admiral Eaglin of the Russian Navy; the Rt. Hon. Stanley M. Bruce, High Commissioner of Austalia; Senator Yermaux of Montigny, Belgium, accompanied by a quartet of Belgium Members of Parliament; Mayor Earl Riley from Portland, Oregon, U.S.A. the Belgian Minister of Justice; the Czechoslavakian Minister of Foreign Affairs; and Prince Bernhardt of the Netherlands, together with the Netherland's Minister of War. This visit of the leading member of the Dutch Royal Family was particularly interesting for Sir Crawford. He writes in his memoirs how when he had talked to him of the great respect with which the memory of his illustrious ancestor, William of Orange, was still held in Northern Ireland he was amazed and even more so when Sir Crawford told him that Dutch engineers had planned Belfast's High Street and that some Dutch houses still survived in Newry and other Ulster towns.

The Arrival of American Troops in Northern Ireland

Notwithstanding Sir Crawford's role in resolving the Whiteabbey Scandal he continued to maintain his commitment to the war effort because it was realised that any German invasion in 1941 could not have been withstood. Indeed, air maps and photographs, unearthed in Germany and brought to London in 1946, proved that the Nazis had planned a large scale invasion of Northern Ireland by both sea and air. However, the focus of war eventually moved from West to East away from Great Britain and Northern Ireland towards Russia and the Western Deserts of Egypt. Nevertheless, tension did not cool off in Belfast but rather expanded. The effect of the raids on Northern Ireland in 1941 encouraged the workers to ensure that their friends fighting at the fronts would have plenty of munitions and other vital needs. This patriotic spirit was clearly apparent, when in early 1942 a Warship Week Campaign, to adopt the Belfast-built carrier *Indomitable* was launched under the leadership of Sir Crawford. The campaign proved so successful that although the target aimed at was £5,500,500, Sir Crawford was able to proudly announce that the total sum had been subscribed within less than the specified days. The same month he welcomed to City Hall General Hartle, the Commander of the United States of America's Expeditionary Force. On 26 January the first unit of American Troops disembarked at Dufferin Quay in Belfast. They were welcomed ashore by the Royal Ulster Rifles playing the 'Star-spangled Banner'. The *Belfast Telegraph* reported that the Americans had been given a 'hearty Ulster welcome' and continued:

> Over the province prowling enemy planes received a hot reception from ground defences, and for a time the thudding of distant heavy gunfire synchronised with the tramp of marching Yanks as they clattered down the gangway and on to the square-sets of the landing stage ... Many of the Americans had thought that at the beginning in camp they would have to live 'rough' and they were pleasantly surprised. The inevitable dog mascot has made its appearance, an American soldier somehow managing to bring along a mongrel known as 'jitterbug'.[7]

On arriving in Ireland the US troops were given a handbook *A pocket guide to Northern Ireland*. As well as mundane topics such as driving on the left hand side of the road, working in pounds, shilling and pence and travelling on double decker street cars called trams, there were two other very important instructions:

---

7.   Jonathan Bardon, *A History of Ulster*, p.575

'You will find the Irish very friendly. DO NOT assume you are the most wonderful guy in the world if the Irish girl smiles and talks with you. It means only Irish friendliness'.

The second instruction was even more important:

'When out socially, there are two topics of conversation about which you must not comment: POLITICS AND RELIGION.'

How well this was adhered to is open to conjecture.

The first arrivals went to the Newry-Armagh area and later contingents were based at Newcastle, Cookstown, Omagh, Lurgan and at several points in County Fermanagh. Numerous airfields, military camps and barracks were constructed, the most impressive base being built at Langford Lodge, on the shores of Lough Neagh. By May 1942 the total number of American troops in Northern Ireland reached thirty-seven thousand. Some moved in the autumn of 1942 to North Africa for the invasion of Italy with more arriving in 1943 to prepare for the Normandy landings the following year raising the total number of troops in Northern Ireland for a time to 120,000. At one stage 149 vessels were based in Derry to patrol the Western Approaches, together with some 20,000 sailors. By 1943, the official historian John W. Blake has written:-

'Derry held the key to victory in the Atlantic ... By that critical Spring when the battle for the security of our Atlantic lifelines finally turned our way, Londonderry was the most important escort base in the North-Western approaches. Everybody at Londonderry co-operated in this supreme effort'.

There was great excitement when the Americans first arrived as handsome GIs handed out Hershey bars and gum and of course nylon stockings were a great hit with the girls. However young men were less enthusiastic. A mass-observation reporter in Northern Ireland summed up the American's off-duty activities as 'pubs and pick ups'.[8]

Young women who consorted with Americans, according to Lillian Arlow were seen to have "loose morals and were subjected to vicious

8.   Jonathan Bardon, *A History of Ulster,* p.576

taunts. Many of these young girls were immature and naïve. They believed the Americans when they told them they wouldn't get pregnant if they had sex standing up!" There was racist heckling in many of the dance halls that damaged relations and caused friction between the occupying troops and the local population.

Thomas Carnduff paints an apathetic picture in his role as correspondent when he declared:-

> I don't think the authorities give a damn what Ulster people had to say about this friendly invasion. They were dumped here and that was all about it. I wish you could see their tanks, lorries and cars which crowd the Lagan Boulevards.

> They have about a mile and a half of the embankment closed off to the public with armed sentries at either end. Of course we may need them all before this war comes to an end. Two of their soldiers received ten years imprisonment last week for beating a publican to death with their tin helmets.[9]

In October 1942 a black GI was killed in a fight between local men and American troops in Antrim town. A few weeks earlier an American quartermaster had predicted 'bloodshed in the near future', observing that white soldiers were irked by the popularity of blacks. 'The girls really go for them in preference to white boys'[10].

Most people, however, were flattered by the attention Americans gave to Northern Ireland. As one woman in Newry remembers:

> Food and luxuries were in short supply, but I can tell you that Yanks did not go short. They were a great attraction to all the kids and their families. If you had a yank visiting your house, you never went short. We all learned to chew gum and smoke camel cigarettes.[11]

On 26 January 1942 Sir Crawford unveiled a memorial marking the arrival of the American Expeditionary Force to Belfast. The unveiling of the stone column was followed by a march past of US marines, sailors and nurses accompanied by the massed bands of the Royal

9. Brian Barton, *The Blitz: Belfast in the War Years*, p.45

10. Brian Barton, *The Blitz: Belfast in the War Years*, p.528

11. Jonathan Bardon, *A History of Ulster*, p.576

Ulster Rifles and the Royal Irish Fusiliers. As the Belfast Telegraph reported:

> 'Ten thousand citizens crammed the grounds and approaches of the City Hall to witness the occasion, and every vantage point, including windows, statues and the roof of the City Hall itself, was occupied'.

Those reviewing the march past included the Northern Ireland Prime Minister, J. M. Andrews, Sir Percy James Grigg, the British Secretary of State for War, Sir Crawford McCullagh, and Major General Russell P. Hartle, the commander of the American forces.

Chapter Eighteen
1944-1945

War and Peace

Here was a woman, good with pretence,
Blessed with plain reason, and with sober sense;
No conquests she, but o'er herself desired,
No arts essayed, but not to be admired,
Passion and Pride were to her soul unknown,
Convinced that virtue only is our own,
So unaffected, so composed a mind:
So firm, yet soft; so strong; yet always kind.

Pope

Death of 'My Best Pal'

To her family and intimate circle, it was known that Lady McCullagh's health had been uncertain for years. She had often complained of stomach problems and when Sir Crawford became Lord Mayor in 1914 he wrote in his diary that she did not relish the idea of having to appear in public. Despite her protestations she immediately began a round of social and philanthropic activities with evident zeal. So much so, that, when her husband was reappointed a year later, she was highly acclaimed for her accomplishments. She seemed to have benefited and even to have thrived as a result of her civic duties. Crawford loved having her at his side and she in turn supported him in his every endeavour. Her friends described her as having a 'kindly disposition and gifted with infinite tact'. Crawford's own appraisal of her when they met was that she was 'quiet, self-possessed with a simple modesty and a natural grace'. Later on in their married life he said that she had 'simplicity of character, with a cheerful disposition and was devoted to her home and garden, especially the roses and enjoyed entertaining'. The Press reported:-

> 'Her unaffected manner makes her an excellent and gracious hostess to strangers and citizens and she maintains the dignity of her position as leading lady in the City. Yet, she was solicitous for the comfort and enjoyment of guests and was seen as a friend of all grades of society'.[1]

Nothing in her background prepared her for her duties as Lady Mayoress. However, the Lord Mayor's Private Secretary (Mr Frederick Moneypenny) taught and guided her as she worked to meet the demands of her position. She must have had an inherent organisational ability in order to have met the tremendous civic and social demands, and to have done so much, with so much acclaim during both world wars. She had a pleasant voice that made her speeches agreeable. This stood her in good stead as she occupied the Chair in many organisations. She was considered a strong leader, a zealous advocate and energetic promoter of benevolent endeavours, and was noted for overcoming obstacles. Her enthusiasm, energy and devotion instilled confidence in and support of many philanthropic, civic and military causes. Again the press reported 'Even in the face of opposition and initial disinterest, she pressed her causes tirelessly and achieved her end'. She wasn't a woman to give up easily.

Sir Crawford always referred to her as 'my best pal' and when he needed sound advice and good council she would give it her utmost attention. Crawford's nephew Ernest McCullagh said she was very much in love with her husband and her indefatigable public service appear to bear this out. She was always conscious of her fluctuating weight. As a young woman she was trim and pretty, with fine features and in photographs appears to look relaxed and happy. As she got

---

1.   *Belfast Evening Telegraph* 1915

older after too many banquets and civic functions she gained considerable weight and some of the pictures in the press are less than flattering. She looks ill at ease in clothes that do not suit her and appears to look rather dour and uncomfortable. At the outset of World War II, Margaret's health was again causing problems. By 1938 she was starting to lose weight and was looking rather gaunt. At this time she started using make-up and more fashionable attire, which greatly improved her appearance, while disguising her failing health.

Her 'indifferent health' which was referred to on a number of occasions by the press was eventually diagnosed as stomach cancer to which she eventually succumbed to on Sunday 9 January 1944. She was tended to by her Doctor and her private Nurse Mary Hagan dying peacefully at Lismara surrounded by all her family. Sir Crawford and Lady McCullagh had been married for forty-seven years and most of that time had been spent working together for the benefit of Belfast and its people.

Sir Crawford was comforted in his bereavement by sincere condolences from all around the globe. Commiserations poured in from family, friends, public boards and organisations in Belfast, Ireland and Britain. The sympathy from the Duke of Abercorn, then Northern Ireland Governor, was symbolic of the general sorrow:

'Very deeply regret the passing of one whom we have always regarded as one of our oldest, dearest and truest friends and who will always leave a very great blank in the city's life'

The Belfast City Council's Special Resolution, mourning the demise of Lady McCullagh, records that:-

'She had always brought to bear upon her public duties a dignity and charm which it was the aim of many to emulate but the lot of none to surpass. Her outstanding character was emphatically her humility, a virtue manifect to all with whom she came in contact during the performance of her manifold public duties. Thus, her public persona is one of a woman "who gave herself ungrudgingly to the City of Belfast, her ideals....regarding her work were lofty'.

Her work had been formally recognised when she was elected Honorary Burgess of the City of Belfast on 23 January 1917. She was awarded the Commander of the Order of the British Empire, by Lord Lieutenant French of Vimy, on behalf of His Majesty King George V, when he visited Belfast for the peace demonstration in March 1919. Her stained glass memorial window is in the City Hall on the opposite side of the grand staircase to that of her husband on the main landing. Her likeness is depicted in the centre of the window with portrayals of her many good works featured around her. Lady Margaret had provided inspiration and support during the long years of their marriage and her loss was a devastating blow to Sir Crawford. However, it was his fundamental belief that man is granted life to make full use of it, and it was his intention to fulfil that purpose to the end. It was also what his wife would have wanted.

At a Special Meeting of the City Council, 23 May 1944, Sir Crawford was chosen to occupy the Lord Mayor's Chair. In moving the resolution, Alderman W.F. Neill MP was supported by all members of the Corporation. Sir Crawford thus registered an unprecedented record in the annals of any city in the United Kingdom by being unanimously appointed for a seventeenth term. At the same time his colleagues considered that his re-appointment was a further compliment to the late Lady Mayoress, Lady McCullagh. Sir Crawford's colleagues in City Hall, however did not know that Sir Crawford himself was unwell at this time. He had been a heavy smoker all his life and had developed a persistent cough. His Doctor told him to give up cigarettes and to reduce his work schedule. However, he ignored this advice and continued to do the job as he saw fit. Being First Citizen was his raison d'etre. He had always been first and foremost a businessman, then a politician, but now he saw it as his duty to the citizens of Belfast to see them through the troubled times of this war that had still not concluded.

The winter of 1944 was particularly harsh and Sir Crawford came down with a severe chest infection. He was admitted to Forster Green Hospital where he was diagnosed with pneumonia. Undoubtedly this had been brought about not only by the death of his wife but the multifarious duties that he performed. He had spent days standing in the cold and rain, shaking hands and congratulating schools, committees, clubs and organisations who had raised money for the war effort. He had to spend several weeks in the hospital and then time convalescing. On his return to Lismara he was taken care of by Nurse Mary Hagan who had so diligently looked after Lady McCullagh and he recovered fully by the Spring of 1945.

V.E. Day and V.J. Day

In April Sir Crawford attended preliminary meetings with the Northern Ireland Government to organise the end of war celebrations. He was anxious to control the jubilations given some minor civil disturbances, largely fuelled by drunkenness, that had erupted at the close of Armistice Day in Belfast in 1918. For the Northern Ireland Government it was important to follow arrangements in Britain as closely as possible. Therefore, in line with preparations in Britain Sir Crawford requested all churches to remain open on V.E. Day, and theatres and Dance Halls to stay open later than usual. V.E. Day and the following day were to be designated as public holidays. Church bells throughout Northern Ireland were scheduled to ring at the hour of victory, and a united Protestant service in St. Anne's Cathedral was announced for the Sunday after V.E. Day.

On Monday 7 May news spread that the Germans would surrender at midnight and preparations to celebrate the Allies' long anticipated victory in Europe were well under way. On Tuesday 8 May, as news of the surrender spread across the city, the Belfast News-Letter stated that:

> People from all parts gathered in festive mood. Along Donegall Place and Royal Avenue, long lines of revellers joined in snake-like formation, dancing in and out among rows of tramcars immobilized by the crowds. Songs were in the air everywhere. They ranged from 'Tipperary' and the favourites of 1918 to a completely new 'number' composed for the occasion which began: "Hitler thought he had us with a Ya, Ya, Ya,'[2]

2.   Jonathan Bardon, *A History of Ulster*, p.583

On the Shore Road a bugle band led a procession of youngsters carrying an effigy of the Fuehrer wearing his swastika and hanging from a gallows. At noon the Ulster United Prayer Movement held a victory thanksgiving service in the grounds of City Hall and during the day crowds gathered to hear Winston Churchill's victory broadcast at 3 p.m. and George VI's broadcast at 9pm. The crowd was estimated as larger than those that had gathered for the signing of the Covenant in 1912, the density of the crowd brought the south-bound tram traffic to a complete stop – as the Belfast Telegraph reported:

> Unforgettable scenes were witnessed in the sun-bathed City Hall grounds, gathering place for huge crowds. Flowerbeds were trampled underfoot by the deliriously happy milling mob. Soldiers, sailors, airmen, WRENS, ATS, WAAFS, American Red Cross workers and civilians made whoopee to music relayed from a battery of loud speakers.
>
> They danced Irish jigs, the Victory polka, the Lambeth Walk and played 'Kiss in the Ring' and 'Down on the Carpet'. Those who could not find room on the grass clambered to the top of the air raid shelters. There were no strangers in the crowd.
>
> All seemed intent on enjoying themselves. They did.

Following Churchill's speech Sir Crawford spoke to the happy crowd:

> "Let us remember not only those of this city who lost their lives during the air raids, but those who were injured or in any way suffered. We must not forget that we are still at war and much remains to be done before the World is at peace .... Certainly celebrate the victory and then go back to work."

At one point in the afternoon, a British Sailor climbed up a static water tank in the City Hall grounds and dived into it. He was joined by others who stripped down to their underpants for a swim before clambering out and drying themselves in the sun. With little reverence, another British sailor climbed the statue of Queen Victoria and placed a cigarette between her lips.

All this would not have passed by the gaze of the eagle eyed Lord Mayor who no doubt would have been thinking of other ceremonies and celebrations which he attended over the past 40 years. His speech may have appeared somewhat solemn amongst the cheers and jubilations but his main concern was to keep the city free from disorder and civil disturbances and a crowd caught up in revelry could easily turn the celebrations to chaos. At 10.40 p.m. the City Hall was floodlit for the first time in six years and there was a tremendous cheer as the illumination was switched on. The Belfast Telegraph reported:

> A full-throated roar greeted the switching on of the flood-lights which silhouetted the graceful lines of the municipal building against a background of gathering clouds in which glowed a dull red reflection of some of the bonfires which ringed the city. With the playing of the catchy tune 'McNamara's Band' the night's festivities started with a swing.

In other areas people such as Mary Wallace, who lived off Bloomfield Avenue, were among those who converged on the city centre. She had gone to bed and was asleep when she and her sisters were wakened by their mother. Outside, 'everyone was on the street', shouting and yelling, many of them still in their pyjamas. She pulled a coat over her night clothes, put on her shoes and joined them, following the delirious human tide along the Newtownards Road and over the Albert Bridge. It was 'as bright as day' by the time she returned home, 'freezing but so happy'. Momentously, at one minute after midnight, hostilities in Europe had officially ended.

The following Sunday 12 May Sir Crawford attended Thanksgiving Day with the state service held in St. Anne's Cathedral. It was attended by the Duke of Abercorn, the Northern Ireland Governor and members of the Corporation. Separate services were held in Belfast's Synagogue and in the Catholic St. Peter's Pro-Cathedral. Following the service in St. Anne's, a victory parade was held in the city. The parade was made up of Allied soldiers, sailors and airmen, men from the Merchant Navy, the Ulster Home Guard, the RUC Special Constabulary, St. John's Ambulance and Nursing Divisions as well as youth organisations. The parade started in May's Market passing the City Hall where the crowds cheered and the massed bands of the RUC and Ulster Regiments played *Hearts of Oak*:

> *Still Britain shall triumph, her ships plough the sea,*
> *Her standard be justice, her watchword 'Be Free',*
> *Then cheer up, my lads, with our hearts let us sing,*
> *Our soldiers, our sailors, our statesmen, and King.*

On 23 May 1945 Sir Crawford was once again nominated for the role of First Citizen. Alderman W.F. Neill, proposing his re-election as Lord Mayor for this eighteenth year of office stated that this year was undeniably a year of exceptional importance. They were celebrating the end of the Second World War and rejoicing in Sir Crawford's recovery from his severe illness. In his reply Sir Crawford thanked the Corporation and wittily confessed he was really glad to be back again in circulation. Whilst admitting he had experienced a trying illness he now believed he was fitter than ever. Except for an occasional day off for a cold, he said that it was over 40 years since he had been unable to attend to his duties due to illness. He expressed to the members of the City Council how grateful he was for the honour which they had once more conferred on him.

With the rejoicing over and Belfast's jubilant population back at work, Sir Crawford's attention now turned to the official celebrations surrounding the visit of their Majesties George VI, Queen Elizabeth and Princess Elizabeth on 18 July 1945. This was the first time a Sovereign's visit to Ulster had been by air and it was also the longest flight – two hours from Northolt, Middlesex to Long Kesh, near Lisburn – ventured by Princess Elizabeth. Although their visit to Northern Ireland only lasted two days their schedule included a varied round of engagements. They landed at Long Kesh at 4.40 p.m. on Wednesday 17 July and were welcomed by a party of Lambeg Drummers. The Royal Party then spent the remainder of the evening as the guests of the Duchess of Abercorn at Government House, Hillsborough. (Lady Moyra Campbell, daughter of the Duke and Duchess of Abercorn would later become a bridesmaid's at Princess Elizabeth's wedding). The next day they travelled to Musgrave Channel at Belfast Harbour to inspect a naval guard of honour. They were greeted by 12,000 shipyard workers, who cheered and waved their caps in the air. Wherever they went the streets were lined with tens of thousands of happy eager faces smiling and calling out their welcomes.

The Royal Party then proceeded to Parliament Buildings at Stormont, where the Sovereign addressed the Northern Ireland House of Commons and the Senate. The Belfast News Letter reported the event:

> The historic scene was full of colour. The Chamber, in its rich panelling of Empire Timber and blue upholstery under a ceiling of blue, red and gold, made an ideal setting. Every seat in the Distinguished Strangers' and Public Galleries was occupied. Women predominated, and the varied shade of their attire - red, blue, white and green, gave glamour to the picture. On the floor of the Chamber were the mere males, Senators, bewigged and begowned judges of the High Courts, Court officials, H.M.Lieutenants with British, Belgian and U.S. Officers in their respective uniforms blended pleasingly.

When the House of Commons members had been summoned by the Black Rod, the King read his historic message of thanks to the Ulster people for their notable contribution toward a hard-won victory. It included a tribute to the fighting forces and his sincere sympathy to those who mourned the sacrifice of gallant lives:

> "In every sphere of the national life men and women have shown unflinching readiness to face dangers, hardships and toil. Your homes have not escaped the ravages of war. Your ports, your shipyards, your factories have been of splendid services to the common cause. From your coast, watch and ward were kept over the waters, through which ran our vital Atlantic lifeline. On Ulster's soil the first contingent of American troops landed, and Ulster's warm welcome and hospitality have done much to strengthen our bonds of friendship with the United States".

Subsequently King George held an Investiture in the Great Hall of Stormont and presented one-hundred and twenty awards of honour. Then the Royal Party proceeded once more through the gaily bedecked streets to the festivities at City Hall. A crowd had been gathering all day to cheer their Majesties as they approached City Hall, some climbing the surrounding lampposts to get a better view of the royal family. The greeting was repeated by the robed Aldermen and Councillors and with other guests within the main entrance hall. Sir Crawford presented each Councillor individually to their majesties before guiding them to lunch up the stately marble staircase to the Banqueting Hall. On Sir Crawford's right walked the King and on his left the Queen, while the Ulster Governor conducted Princess Elizabeth and the Duchess of Abercorn.

After luncheon the King, having wished to personally thank as many war workers as possible, was taken to Botanic Gardens where their Majesties attended the greatest garden party Ulster ever convened. After the garden party a brief halt was made at Queen's University before moving on to Lisburn to inspect a Youth Parade. The memorable day continued until nightfall, with a sextet of stalwart 'Lambeggers' displaying to their Majesties a traditional demonstration of drum playing. In the evening the royals were entertained at a private dinner party held by the Duke and Duchess of Abercorn at Government House in Hillsborough.

In August 1945 the next event occurred that would remain with people for the rest of their lives. Almost daily throughout the long six years of World War II the people of Belfast had been anxiously waiting for the time when life would return to normality and the threat of conflict could be eradicated. This dream became a reality at midnight on August 14th 1945 when Prime Minister Clement Atlee in a radio broadcast announced: "Japan has to-day surrendered. The last of our enemies is now laid low".

The night sky was illuminated by a dozen bonfires as Sir Crawford stood outside City Hall and watched as the citizens of Belfast surged towards his second home. He could see that some were wearing their pyjamas under their coats but they sang and danced around the City Hall until dawn. Church bells chimed, ships' sirens and factory hooters shrieked and whined in the night air. The shops would do without customers for the next twenty-four hours and the shipyards could be left to the seagulls. The next day the cheering and shouldering of men, women and children continued.

At noon an open-air service of thanksgiving was held in the City Hall's grounds, and in the evening, as servicemen climbed lampposts and clambered over the statues in the grounds of City Hall, crowds waited to hear the King's speech and cheered when he declared:

"The war is over! These are just four simple words, yet for the Queen and myself, they have the same immeasurable significance they have for you. Our hearts are full to overflowing as are yours".

Immediately the crowd started singing *God Save the King*, and when they had finished there was more cheering when it was announced that the Lord Mayor would speak.

"Let us first of all give thanks to the Almighty God who has given us this Victory. Let us next thank those who led the nation at home and overseas. Let us thank the fighting men and women of all services. And let us never forget those who have fallen, those who have been bereaved, the wounded and the sick. Let us remember all those, not merely in our city but all who were injured, or in other ways, suffered. Our gratitude goes out likewise to our splendid Allies, particularly to the United States.

By all means let us rejoice in the Victory won. We have every right to be proud to belong to our great nation and to have played our part in the mighty struggle now past. Not a day passes over the earth, but men and women of no note do great deeds, speak great words and suffer noble sorrows. While many writers chronicle the deathless story of our armed forces in the greatest struggle between nations that the world has ever known, the complimentary story will pass "unwept, unhonoured and unsung". It is the story of the Belfast men and women behind those fighting forces; the workers who wore no uniforms, bore no arms, won few medals, yet, without whose unremitting toil the war could never have been won."

Sir Crawford's speech, in its humble sincerity was a reflection of his outlook in troubled days as in those of peace. The journalist Alfred S. Moore remarked

'He had been an example to all who would live nobly and rightly and dedicate themselves to the service of their fellow men. Every aspect of the War effort enlisted his active interest, and in the fierce light that beats upon those who occupy high positions revealed him not only maintaining but enhancing the best traditions of civic leadership. That is why there is nothing but genuine and unaffected admiration for him'.

The citizens of Belfast took their Lord Mayor's advice to their hearts. They sang and danced and cried for joy long after the milkman had completed his rounds.

Dwight D Eisenhower and Field Marshall Montgomery at Lismara

A week later on 24 August 1945 the Supreme Commander of the American Forces Dwight D. Eisenhower arrived in Belfast to person-ally thank the Lord Mayor and the citizens of Belfast on behalf of his fellow soldiers for their "surrender to them during 1942 and 1943 of their homes and hearts". His first night was spent at Lismara with Sir Crawford and his family, where a special dinner was to be held in his honour. The specially invited guests were treated to a sumptu-ous feast of local produce including wild salmon, pheasant and roast Irish lamb followed by summer fruits from the garden at Lismara. Sir Crawford recalls in his memoirs that the General had seemed like a schoolboy released for his summer holiday when he finally reached Lismara. He threw away all cares and joked with the family and seemed to enjoy the relief. He talked about his boyhood days and related humorous experiences of when he had variously been a cowboy, a boiler stoker in a creamery and semi-professional baseball player. His frank and boyish charm were infectious and it seemed im-possible to believe that this rather humble man was seriously shaping and making history. It was long after midnight when Sir Crawford withdrew to bed. The rest of the party carried on into the 'wee small hours' with Daisy, her brother Boysie and the General being the last to leave the table. The photograph taken on the steps of Lismara the following morning with General Eisenhower shows Sir Crawford surrounded by his family and those from the American Embassy in-cluding Lord Londonderry, Lord Lieutenant of County Down. At this time Sir Crawford's health was not what it was and he is looking a little crumpled and tired, whilst General Eisenhower looks remark-ably fresh considering the late hour at which he retired.

When the press had finished taking photographs General Eisenhower and his entourage made their way from Whiteabbbey to Belfast.

Along the road thousands of cheering admirers lined the route as he made his way to Queens University were he was to have his first engagement of the day. A large crowd and a military guard of honour greeted him at the University. Inside the great Hall an audience had gathered including Northern Ireland Prime Minister Sir Basil Brooke to give the general a rousing standing ovation when he was conferred the honour of Doctor of Law degree. Thousands more greeted Eisenhower at City Hall with hundred of American flags being waved and confetti and ticker tape thrown from windows as his cavalcade travelled along Donegal Square. A military band played the Star-Spangled Banner as he entered the building, where cheering members of Belfast Corporation formed a reception party. The council chamber and public galleries were packed as Sir Crawford led the procession in honour of the general's key role in the defeat of Hitler. The Town Clerk John Dunlop then read the council's resolution admitting Eisenhower as the 45th Honorary Burgess of the City. He walked slowly to the Lord Mayor's rostrum whereupon the scarlet robed Aldermen and City Councillors stood up and cheered.

Addressing the American General, Sir Crawford said they were conferring on him their highest honour in recognition of his brilliant leadership as Supreme Commander of the Allied Expeditionary Forces in Europe.

"We are honoured that your name is included in the Roll of Belfast Freemen, there to remain for all time with the names of other illustrious men and women", said the Lord Mayor. Few Ulstermen, and no one from another land, have established a stronger hold upon the admiration of the people of Northern Ireland than you. Indeed, the victories achieved by the Allied Armies in Europe are in themselves eloquent testimony of your gifts as a great Commander.

No General ever shouldered a greater responsibility, but, due to the range and vision of your plans and their brilliant execution, victory in Europe was secured much sooner than the most optimistic could have anticipated. Under your leadership the greatest alliance of fighting forces in history was built up, and this comradeship in arms could not have been achieved with your great personality."[3]

3.   *Belfast Evening Telegraph*, August 1945

Continuing, Sir Crawford said they were proud to recall that the first American soldiers to arrive in the British Isles did so within the boundaries of Belfast and that during their stay a link was forged of lasting friendship with Ulster which would not readily be forgotten.

> "Now that the tasks of war have ended we know the co-operation between your country and ours, in the fight, will continue in an effort to maintain peace in the world ... In handing you this casket containing the certificate of election, I wish you, on behalf of the citizens of this city, long life, health and happiness."

When General Eisenhower stooped and added his name to the register of the City's Honorary Burgesses the cheers were deafening. Before beginning his reply he was accorded a hearty and sustained ovation. He said:

> "In inviting me to return to Belfast to become an Honorary Burgess you have given one further proof of the ties and affection which bind the American army to the Northern Ireland people. I trust you look upon it, as I do, as a token of our common purpose to work together for a better world".

He thanked all for the hospitality shown to the American soldiers who were stationed in Ulster for so long.

> "That Ulster sojourn will remain a cherished memory in the hearts of many Americans. You received us into your community and your homes with a generosity which was evident and sincere. You put us at our ease. You gave us your friendship. For all this we are deeply appreciative. This global war has taken the American Army to many foreign fields, but it was here in Northern Ireland that we first began to concentrate for our share in the attack upon the citadel of continental Europe. From here we started the long, hard march to Allied victory which led our forced to North Africa, Sicily, the Italian mainland Normandy, and finally the dash across Germany."

Following his welcome at City Hall the general had lunch at City Hall hosted by Sir Crawford, with the Northern Ireland Prime Minister Sir Basil Brooke, Lord Londonderry and other specially invited guests. Later in the day he attended a garden party at Stormont where thousands gathered to pay him tribute, the evening ended with him being welcomed as guest of honour at the Grand Opera House.

Three weeks later on 14 September 1945 Belfast was honoured again by a visit from another great wartime leader – Field Marshall Sir

Bernard Montgomery. He told Sir Crawford he had never experienced a welcome like it: "The reception accorded me in Belfast was terrific. I have never known anything approaching it". The city centre was a mass of cheering and waving citizens. Barriers were almost broken by the pressures of the sightseers, while windows, balconies and rooftops were crowded. Each section, as the procession passed vied with each other to get a closer look at their hero. Union Jacks waved everywhere. The Field Marshall saluted smartly at the City Hall portico when he noticed nearby two very special Lambeg Drums. Both bore the Field Marshall's portrait; the Ballinderry "bugle" as it was humorously described, had been unveiled by Lady Montgomery and the other by the Earl of Caledon, brother of Field Marshall Alexander.

Cabinet Ministers and the political, legal, military and municipal leaders thronged the Council Chamber when Sir Crawford assured Field Marshall Montgomery that the City only did its duty in honouring him supremely for services immeasurable in words:

> "It is with pride the citizens followed his victorious progress from the borders of Egypt, through Northern Africa and Italy, to final victory. We Ulstermen are particularly proud that our Province has given so many leaders to the Empire, that we can claim you as one of them and especially that you, yourself, are closely connected with Ulster."

The Field Marshall, accepted the honour as symbolic of their gratitude to the British soldiers generally.

> "I am myself an Irishman. So it has been a constant source of pride to me to witness how magnificently the soldiers from this country fought during the last six years. Men of the Irish regiments have all shown that fine spirit and devotion to duty for which the British soldier is justly renowned. Among fighting men Ireland stands very high indeed for they are superb soldiers."

Sir Crawford then called on the audience to "give the three heartiest cheers we have ever given in the City Hall for a very great Irishman". His request was met with hearty enthusiasm and at the subsequent lunch at City Hall hosted by Sir Crawford in 'Monty's' honour the guests serenaded their hero with *He's a jolly good fellow* and *Land of*

Hope and Glory. Even the dishes that were served at the luncheon had names reminiscent of his victories – Alamein Crudites, Torbruck Tart, Benghazi Beef, Tunisia tuilles, Algiers and Berlin biscuits! The Chef had made a cake in the shape of a model African tank which the General autographed and sent, along with his good wishes, to the Ulster Hospital for Women and Children.

The next day the Field Marshall was the guest of Sir Crawford at Lismara. 'Monty's' character had been described by critics of the time as a harsh, narrow and silent man, a martinet much puffed with personal publicity, however in his memoirs Sir Crawford remembers:

> ... a soft-spoken sympathetic little man with steely blue eyes, free from all superlatives, a good listener and extremely tolerant to the tastes of others. The Field Marshall is of Ulster stock, although he was born in Kennington, London and spent his juvenile years in Tasmania where his father was Bishop. When he was thirteen years old the family returned to London and each succeeding summer they crossed to the family seat at Moville for six weeks holiday. During one of these vacations he came on a fortnight's visit to a Belfast family who resided on the Antrim shore; and he recalled with joy his happy days with them sailing on Belfast Lough.

Delighted with the views from Lismara, Sir Crawford recalls the Field Marshall citing lines from a poem his mother Lady Montgomery quoted when he was a boy:

> *Dominant over sea and land,*
> *Son's love built me, and I hold*
> *Mother's love in lettered gold.*
> *Would my granite girth were strong*
> *As either love, to last as long.*

He stood silent for a few moments then continued relating to Sir Crawford memories of his mother and his family at Moville. Probably Sir Crawford's thoughts at this time would have brought back fond memories of his own mother in Aghalee.

Chapter Nineteen
1945-1948

End of an Era

This I know without being told,
'Tis time to live as I grow old.
'Tis time short pleasures now to take,
O little life, the best to make,
And manage wisely the last stake

Abram Cowley

The celebrations were now over and Belfast along with other industrial cities in the United Kingdom had to face the great transition from war conditions to peace construction. The transformation was beset with more complex difficulties than those experienced in the corresponding 1919-1923 period. Among the many problems were the shortage of labour, essential building materials and construction machinery for the building of new houses.

Belfast had suffered severely as a result of the Blitz and reparations had to be met by the Government and Belfast City Council. A citizen's fund, instituted by Sir Crawford provided financial help for those who suffered from the destruction of their homes, property and personal belongings. Everything possible had been done to alleviate the loss and pain of these distressed people but much more was necessary. The City Council had repaired 51,472 houses out of a total of 56,662 damaged by enemy action, of which 3,200 were, or had to be demolished. The loss of 3,200 dwellings and the cessation of building operations during the war years had a created a serious housing shortage but all the Council members were determined to overcome all obstacles and provide the citizens with a better Belfast.

William Grant, the Minister of Health and Local Government saw that exceptional measures would have to be taken and in 1945 he set up the Northern Ireland Housing Trust. Modelled on the Scottish Special Housing Association the Trust had the power to borrow from Government to build houses and pay back the capital with interest over sixty years. Despite this state assistance, the trust was not subsidised by Government and needed to establish rents related directly to the cost of construction. The rents were fixed at 14 shillings per week and although considered high by the trust's chairman Lucius O'Brien, there were no shortage of applicants. Indeed those capable of paying the rent did much to relieve the housing shortage. More than 48,500 houses were completed by the Trust between 1945 to 1972. As well as the Trust, subsidies from Government were given to private house builders to construct new dwellings. Also the Ministry of Agriculture provided grants for replacing or reconditioning agricultural labourers' dwellings and farmhouses. These grants rebuilt or replaced 9,500 dwellings.

Reconstruction of Belfast got under way and at the same time the dramatic reforms brought in by Clement Attlee's Labour Governments at Westminster were largely applied to Northern Ireland. The outcome was a more striking increase in living standards than at any other time in the century. Never did the Unionist Governments feel more secure. Not only had Northern Ireland been promised parity but Britain agreed to pay most of the money needed to finance the new welfare legislation in Northern Ireland. Just after he resigned in 1943, John Andrews received this letter of appreciation from Winston Churchill:

> But for the loyalty of Northern Ireland and its devotion to what has now become the cause of thirty Governments or nations we should have been confronted with slavery and death and the light which now shines so brightly throughout the world would have been quenched ... During your premiership the bonds of

affection between Great Britain and the people of Northern Ireland have been tempered by fire and are now, I believe, unbreakable.

Drawing on Westminster's wartime promises and Britain's gratitude, Stormont extracted three ageements from the British Government. The first, concluded in 1946, confirmed that Northern Ireland would enjoy the same standards in social services as those prevailing in the rest of the United Kingdom, provided parity of taxation and treasury scrutiny were maintained. Then the Social Services Agreement and the amalgamation of the Unemployment Funds of Britain and Northern Ireland, both in force from July 1948, relieved the Stormont Government of most of the expense of national assistance, health provision, family allowances, pensions and national insurance, including payments during sickness, unemployment, after retirement and at death. The result was a striking advance in the material welfare of the people of Northern Ireland.[1]

James Magennis Awarded Victoria Cross

In 1946 ceremonial functions at City Hall were now less frequent than before the war. Nevertheless, there were still distinguished visitors bringing messages of goodwill to Belfast. Correspondence continued from all around the world and Sir Crawford took great pride in personally answering as many letters as possible. His secretary, Major E.H. May, D.S.O. helped him with his every day duties and his daughter Helen assisted as Lady Mayoress.

In early 1946 Sir Crawford was delighted to present Leading Seaman James Magennis with a cheque for £3,006 subscribed by the citizens of Belfast as an appreciation of his gallantry. James Magennis was born on the Falls Road in Belfast and joined the Royal Navy when he was a young boy. He served as a diver in His Majesty's Midget Submarine XE-3 commanded by Lieutenant Ian Frazer. On 31 July 1945 the submarine attacked a Japanese cruiser in the Jahore Straits, Singapore. Unfortunately XE-3 became jammed beneath the cruis-

---

1.   Jonathan Bardon, *A History of Ulster*, p.590

er such that the diver's hatch could not be fully opened. Magennis therefore had to squeeze himself out through the very narrow space that remained available. He experienced great difficulty in placing his limpets on the bottom of the cruiser due to the foul state of the keel and to the pronounced slope upon which the limpets would not hold. Before he could place a limpet Magennis had to thoroughly scrape the area clear of barnacles, and in order to secure the limpets he had to tie them in pairs by a line passing under the cruiser keel. This was very tiring work for a diver, and moreover he was handicapped by a steady leakage of oxygen. An exhausted Magennis, despite these difficulties persisted until he had placed all his limpets before returning to the submarine.

As they were withdrawing Lieutenant Fraser endeavoured to jettison his limpet carriers, but one of these would not release itself and fall clear of the submarine. Despite his exhaustion, his oxygen leak and the fact that there was every probability of being sighted by the enemy, Magennis volunteered to leave the craft and free the carrier. After seven minutes of nerve-racking work he succeeded. For displaying great courage and devotion to duty and with complete disregard to his own safety he was awarded the Victoria Cross – the highest award for bravery in the line of duty. Both James Magennis and Lieutenant Ian Fraser were invested with their Victoria Crosses by King George VI at Buckingham Palace on the 11th December, 1945.

In March 1946 Sir Crawford had the honour of again meeting H.R.H. Princess Elizabeth, this time at the launch of the giant aircraft carrier ship, *HMS Eagle* built at Queen's Island shipyard. Sir Crawford was once again delighted to be able to entertain the Princess Elizabeth and this time with his daughter Helen acting as Lady Mayoress at his side. The Princess was led to the Lord Mayor's private apartments where she met the Governor of Northern Ireland, the Earl of Granville, and the Premier Sir Basil Brooke, before being escorted by Sir Crawford into the Banqueting Hall where she was enthusiastically received by four hundred invited guests.

It is somewhat poignant to write that this was the last time that Sir Crawford entertained on a grand scale. He had other duties to perform before he retired, but his final appearance in public was a presentation on June 6th 1946 from Belfast City and its industries to the U.S. Destroyers, *Cone* and *Glennon*. It perpetuated the friendship forged between Ulster and America during war time and as Sir Crawford affirmed the bond built a mighty bridgehead: "it is the mutual wish of both peoples, east and west, that this link will ever strengthen during the years to come".

Retirement

Sir Crawford was now seventy-eight years old and until recently had enjoyed excellent health but his advancing years and his recent illness played a significant part in his desire to retire completely from public office. At the monthly City Council Meeting on 2nd September 1946 his intention not to seek re-election, as Lord Mayor, was received with heartfelt regret. He personally was unable to attend the meeting due to ill health. He had been Lord Mayor for a record period of seventeen years and was the accepted 'Father of the City Council'. Sir Crawford was the last surviving Councillor of those who had originally served at the Town Hall in Victoria Street that had been used as the Municipal Buildings forty years ago before Belfast City Hall had been built in 1906.

In Sir Crawford's absence the following resolution was adopted unanimously and with much emotion, recording the gratitude of the City for his loyal and unlimited service during his lengthy membership of Belfast Corporation:

> To him and Lady McCullagh the citizens and this Council owe a very great deal. Their kindness and generous hospitality were unlimited, and the entertainment of Royalty, distinguished members of nobility, the Government and the Services, together with the various association of professions and trade, was on a most lavish scale and added much to the good repute of Ulster. Lady McCullagh was a most gracious personality, and her loss has been greatly felt by all sections of the community..." "We regret that his health compels him to relinquish public life, and trust he may be spared for many years of retirement.

In seconding the resolution his successor, as Lord Mayor, Alderman W.F. Neill, M.P., referred to Sir Crawford as a man who set an ideal example to his fellow citizens. He had made a success of his life; and at a time when most busy men discard their business harness for rest and reflection, he had generously diverted his skill and services to the good of the citizens. All who knew and respected him – one hundred percent of Belfast's population at least – sincerely hoped his health would be restored and that he would still have many years of happiness". "A man who brought great lustre to the city, and a man who will go down in history as one of the greatest Lord Mayors Belfast ever produced", was Alderman Mercer's tribute.

These were typical of the tributes voiced by his colleagues of the City Council and that they represented the public verdict is supported by this extract from the Belfast Telegraph editorial on 3 September 1946.

> There was nothing formal about the speeches supporting this resolution of gratitude. Coming from all parties in the Corporation, they were proof of the genuine regard for Sir Crawford, not only as the First Citizen, but as Chairman in many heated debates and as friend and Councillor too". "The fact that he has occupied Belfast's highest civic office for so long, unsparing in his services and substance alike - and that he was known familiarly far and wide as "Sir Crawford" - witnesses to a unique personality. Some time must elapse before Belfast becomes accustomed to the knowledge that he is not at City Hall.

> In large measure Belfast is a self-made city owing more to the industry of its inhabitants than to anything else. Sir Crawford's career has been typical of this fundamental characteristic and he had shown those qualities which we like to think are representative of the Ulsterman - industrious, common sense, homour and generosity. That was why when he often wished to retire from the office of Lord Mayor, which he held for nineteen years, his desire was always opposed by his fellows.

> Here was a man who wore his honours well, and who could always be counted on to discharge the duties of his office with a natural sense of the fitness of things. His guests invariably found his easy congenial company. Now that health compels him to retire there is inevitably bound to be universal regret. To him and the late Lady McCullagh, who was his constant companion and helpmate in good works, the citizens owe much, and it is their sincere wish that Sir Crawford will still have many years to enjoy the fruits of his labour.

In a letter to Sir Crawford, the Northern Ireland Premier, Sir Basil Brooke, who worked closely with Sir Crawford on many issues before and after the Second World War testified:

> As head of Belfast Corporation in two World Wars and for many of the intervening years, you have been largely responsible for shaping the destinies of our capital city in most difficult times. The proud position held by Belfast to-day among the major cities of the United Kingdom testified to the skill and wisdom of its Lord Mayor. Belfast was indeed fortunate in having a man of your attainments and ability as its First Citizen for so many years. Not only, however, did you find time to devote yourself to manifold activities of the Belfast Corporation, but you freely spent your energies and talents in other important public work. Your contribution to the debates in the Senate and House of Commons has done much to enhance the prestige and dignity of our Parliament and, as leader of the Unionist Party, I should like to thank you most warmly for the influential support and help you so readily gave to the Unionist cause over a very lengthy period. Your work for numerous patriotic and benevolent objects and your intimate association with various aspects of the war effort deserve the gratitude of the whole community. My colleagues join unanimously with me in wishing you a speedy restoration to good health with which we all trust you will continue to be blessed for many years to come.

Belfast Corporation organised a committee to give the citizens of Belfast the opportunity to show their love and appreciation of the former Lord Mayor. Immediately subscriptions from all classes of the community came pouring in. A significant feature of this spontaneity showed the subscribers as being highly representative, not only of Belfast, but of Northern Ireland in general. It was agreed, and approved, by Sir Crawford that two large stained glass windows, designed by an eminent local artist, be erected in the City Hall. One as a tribute to Sir Crawford and the other to the memory of his consort, Lady McCullagh. The windows were to be placed on the principal landing on either side of the grand staircase. Unfortunately he did not live long enough to see them completed.

Sir Crawford died on Tuesday, 13 April 1948 after a lengthy battle with lung cancer. He lay in state at Lismara, where a short funeral service took place on Friday 16th. The lengthy funeral procession made its way through the streets of Belfast passing between throngs of mourners, pausing at City Hall and eventually coming to rest at Carnmoney Cemetery.

Brookeborough said of him that "A legend will hover over Belfast's City Hall for generations to come. Sir Crawford McCullagh is, indeed, one of those men whose splendid spirit and example live on long after they have gone."

To sum up the life of Sir Crawford one must understand that he reached his high level of recognition and achievement through hard work. He was a self-made man, an entrepreneur who enjoyed making money, but he was also a very altruistic public servant, advancing municipal life with his own resources. He was rewarded with a Knighthood in 1915 and although his reputation was somewhat tarnished due to the Housing Scandal in 1927 it recovered sufficiently for him to be given a Baronetcy in 1935 and to made a member of the Privy Council in June 1941. His friends included some of the most powerful and influential men and women not only in Ireland but around the world, everyone knew 'Sir Crawford'.

Sir Crawford was a man of grace and stature. With his inestimable qualities, he elevated himself to the level of statesman greatly influencing affairs of his time. He was honoured and beloved for his great public spirit, his principles of the noblest kind and his unswerving loyalty and service to Belfast through two world wars. He was a man with great presence and dignity – erect, alert, often with a smile and twinkle in his eye. He appeared to enjoy the power and theatre of his position. His long life was crowned with commercial achievement, municipal honours and social distinction.

What merit to be dropped on Fortune's Hill;
The honour is to mount it

Appendix 1 Spelling of McCullagh

Both Robert McClave McCullough and the Rev. Joseph Crawford McCullough spelt their surname in the more conventional way. Family legend has it that our branch of the family changed the spelling at the insistence of one of Sir Crawford's sisters, although which one is lost in the mists of time. Unfortunately many, if not most, of Sir Crawford's private papers were burnt by his daughter-in-law Mrs Elizabeth McCullagh, Boysie's wife. Her motivation for this act of historical vandalism is unknown. We will never know if the burnt papers could have provided an explanation for the name change.

Appendix 2 High Sheriff

The role of High Sheriff was to act as the executive arm of the Crown and in medieval times their main responsibility was the collection of revenue. By the 19th century the focus had moved to administration duties, including organising elections and appointing the grand jury. The Sheriff was usually a local landowner of some substance who in pre-Victorian times often had to pay officials out of their own pocket. During the course of the 19th century many of the Sheriff's duties were assumed by officials such as the under Sheriff but it remained an important and often controversial appointment.

Appendix 3 Ernest McCullagh

The Reverend Ernest McCullagh, Sir Crawford's nephew served with distinction in World War 1 receiving the Mons Star, the General Service Medal and the Victory Medal. After the war he returned to Canada and transferred to Knox College, University of Toronto where, in 1923, he graduated with honours Baccalaureate of Philosophy and Theology. He was inducted into the First Presbyterian Church, Pembroke, Ontario, wher he served from April 1925 to April 1930.

On 29 July 1925, Ernest (or Mac as he was affectionately called) married Annie Echo Dickson. They had seven children, Sheilagh Jean, James Crawford, Kathleen Rea, Moira Millar, Deirdre Ann, Brigid Mavourneen, and Patricia Maeve.

In 1940 he was commissioned Flight Lieutenant in the Royal Canadian Airforce and received the Canadian Volunteer Service Medal and Clasp. In 1942 he visited USA bases in Annette Islands, Anchorage and Kodiak, Alaska. He was awarded the Padre's Honorary Officer's Medal, the Queen's Coronation Medal, the Red Cross Service Medal and, in 1967) the Dunville Leading Citizen Award, Vimy Night Ceremony.

In 1946 he was inducted as minister of Knox Presbyterian Church in Dunville, Ontariao. He retired from service in 1968. Ernest 'Max' McCullagh died in 1977. His daughter Sheilagh was the inspiration for this book.

Appendix 4 The Silence.

The first recorded instance of an official moment of silence dedicated to a person's death took place in Portugal on 13 February 1912. However, in the United Kingdom the person who is credited with the idea is Sir Percy FitzPatrick, a South African born author who suggested the idea to King George V. When he heard that the 11th of November was to be recognized as Armistice Day he felt that the occasion should be marked by a 2 minute silence.

As the author has discovered, while Sir Percy FitzPatrick was the originator of the now traditional 2 minute silence on Remembrance Day, the first recorded instance of a silence as an act of remembrance in the United Kingdom was the 5 minute silence on 11 July 1916. Therefore it can be argued that Sir Crawford was the first recorded person to publicly call for a period of silence for the fallen.

Appendix 5 Joseph Devlin

Joseph Devlin, affectionately known by friends and colleagues as 'Wee Joe', began his career as a bartender and won West Belfast for the Nationalists by a margin of 16 votes in 1907, was welcomed by Redmond and Dillon as the man who could deliver the northern Catholic vote. Known as the 'pocket Demosthenes', he was a colourful figure in the Commons and for thirty years was to be the undisputed ruler of the Falls and Smithfield Wards.

Although Crawford McCullagh and Joe Devlin came from different ends of the political spectrum, Crawford's memoirs reveal a man with a sharp wit, self-depreciating humour and greatly admired by both Nationalists and Unionists. Crawford recalls how Joe was particularly fond of Crawfordsburn and remembers one occasion when he hosted a garden party in the Cinglaee Tea Gardens (Crawfordsburn Country Club) for 850 people which he paid for out of his own pocket. Devlin was well-known for bringing children from inner-city Belfast to enjoy the healthy air and beautiful beaches at Helen's Bay and Crawfordsburn.

Appendix 6 Stormont

Stormont Parliament Buildings were purpose built in the 1920s when Stormont Castle and its surrounding land was acquired by the new Northern Ireland government after the partition of 1921. The land already had an existing house, built in 1830 by John Cleland, called Storm Mount. After his death in 1859 the Cleland family demolished the house and built a large baronial style castle with 14 family bedrooms, ballroom, drawing room and other large reception rooms. The house was then renamed Stormont Castle. The house was vacated by the family in 1893 and subsequently let out to various individuals until it was acquired by the new Government of Northern Ireland. Prime Minister Sir James Craig used Stormont Castle as his official residence from 1922 until 1940.

During the Second World War the building was used by the RAF to co-ordinate the allied activity in the Atlantic Ocean, and it was from here that the attack and eventual sinking of the Bismark was planned and co-ordinated.

Appendix 7 J A Little

Dr J A Lyttle distinguished himself on Queen's University (Canada) campus with student leadership positions, scholarships and graduation magna cum laude. After graduate studies at the University of Chicago (USA) de declined a faculty appointment at Queen's in favour of pastoral ministry. In 1950 Queen's bestowed on him its highest honour, a doctorate degree. For decades he was president of Queen's Theological College Alumni Axsociation. Among many other achievements, he was president of the Toronto Conference, executive Superintendent and church planter for the United Church of Canada. He was a founding father and executive of Huntingdon University (Ontario), Dan of the Lorrain Fellowship, Board Member of the Canadian Bible Society and delegate to the World Council of Churches.

Bibliography

Books

Baguley, Margaret (2009). *World War 1 and the question of Ulster: the correspondence of Lilian and Wilfred Spender.* Belfast: Irish Manuscripts Commission.

Bardon, Jonathan (1982). *Belfast: An illustrated history.* Belfast: Blackstaff Press Ltd.

Bardon, Jonathan (1999). *Belfast: A century.* Belfast: Blackstaff Press Ltd.

Bardon, Jonathan (1992). *A history of Ulster.* Belfast: Blackstaff Press Ltd.

Barnes, William C (2015). *Thomas Andrews, a past-life memory.* Lulu.com

Barton, Brian (1989). *The Blitz: Befast in the war years.* Belfast: Blackstaff Press Ltd.

Beckett, J C et al (1982). *Belfast: the making of a city.* Belfast: Appletree Press Ltd.

Becket, J C (2014). *The Making of Modern Ireland.* London: Faber and Faber (reprint)

Beckett, J C (1967). *Belfast: The origin and growth of an industrial city.* Belfast: BBC Books.

Belfast and County Down Railway Guide. 1898.

Blake, John W (2015). *Northern Ireland in the Second World War.* Uckfield: Navy and Military Press.

Blaney, Roger (1988). *Belfast: 100 years of Public Health.* Belfast: Belfast City Council

Brett, C E B & O'Connell, Michael (1996). *Buildings of County Antrim.* Belfast: Ulster Architectural Heritage Society (1st)

Brett, C E B (1985) *Buildings of Belfast, 1700-1914.* Belfast: Friar's Bush Press.

Budge, I & O'Leary, C (1973). Belfast: *Approach to Crisis; a study of Belfast Politics 1613-1970.* London: Macmillian (1st)

Buxbaum, Gerda (2005). *Icons of Fashion: the 20th century (Prestel's Icons)* London: Prestel.

Crosby, Alfred W (2003). *America's Forgotten Pandemic: The Influenza of 1918* Cambridge: Cambridge University Press

Devlin, Paddy (1981). *Yes, we have no bananas: Outdoor relief in Belfast, 1920-39,* Belfast: Blackstaff Press Ltd.

Falls, C. (2009) *History of the 36th (Ulster) Division* Uckfield: Naval and Military Press

Fleming, N C (2005). *The Marquess of Londonderry: Aristocracy, Power and Politics in Britain and Ireland (International Library of 20th Century History)* London: I B Tauris & Co. Ltd

Gaffikin, Thomas (1894). *Belfast fifty years ago: A lecture.* Belfast: James Cleeland (3rd)

Gallagher, Jack (2008). *Stormont: the house on the hill* Holywood: Booklink

Garner, Margaret. *A History of Helen's Bay Presbyterian Church 1896-1958.*

Gray, John (1994). *Thomas Carnduff: Life and writings.* Belfast: Lagan Press

Gribbon, Sybil (1982). *Edwardian Belfast: A social profile (Explorations in Irish history).* Belfast: Appletree Press Ltd.

Haines, Keith (2009) *Fred Crawford: Carson's Gunrunner* Donaghadee: Cottage Publications.

Hennessy, Thomas (1997). *A history of Northern Ireland. Dublin*: Gill & Macmillan Ltd.

Hepburn, A C (2008). Catholic Belfast and Nationalist Ireland in the ear of Joe Devlin 1871-1934. Oxford: Oxford University Press

Hill, Myrtle & Pollock, Vivienne (1993). *Image and Experience: Photographs of Irish Women, c. 1880-1920.* Belfast: Blackstaff Press Ltd.

Howard, Ebenezer (2009). *Garden Cities of To-Morrow (Illustrated Edition).* London: Dodo Press (2nd)

Kee, Robert (2000). *The Green Flag: A history of Irish Nationalism.* London: Penguin.

Larmour, Paul *Architectural Heritage of Malone and Stranmillis* Belfast Ulster Architectural Heritage Society

Lewis, Samuel (1837). *The topographical dictionary of Ireland.* London

McDermott, Jim (2001). *Northern Divisions: The old IRA and the Belfast pogroms 1920-22.* Belfast: Beyond the Pale Publications

McIntosh, Gillian (2006). *Belfast City Hall: 100 years.* Belfast: Blackstaff Press Ltd

McMahon, Sean (2011). *Wee Joe: The life of Joseph Devlin.* Belfast: Brehon Press Ltd.

McMurray, W B, Drennan, James H, Beattie, H (1995) *Whiteabbey Presbyterian Church 1833-1933: a record of the first hundred years* – private publication

McQueen, Rod (1999). *The Eatons: The rise and fall of Canada's royal family.* Stoddart.

Maxwell, Henry (1933). *Ulster was right* London: Hutchinson

Moore, Brian (1977). *The Emperor of Ice-cream* London: Viking Childrens Books

Mulvey, K & Richards, R (1998) *Decades of Beauty: The changing image of women, 1890s to 1990s.* London: Hamlyn.

Niblock, Barry (2011) *Rembering their sacrifice in the Great War.* North Down. Self-published.

Open, Michael (1985). *Fading lights silver screen. A history of Belfast Cinemas* Antrim: Greystone Books (1st)

Potter, Matthew (2012) *A Century of Service, A History of the Association of Municipal Authorities of Ireland 1912-2012* Nenagh: Association of Municipal Authorities of Ireland, 2012.

Rankin, Kathleen (2012). *The Linen Houses of County Antrim and North County Down.* Belfast: Ulster Historical Foundation.

Stewart, A T Q (1981). *Edward Carson (Irish Lives)* Dublin: Gill & Company

Stewart, A T Q (1997). *The Ulster Crisis: Resistance to Home Rule, 1912-14.* Belfast: Blackstaff Press Ltd.

Strachan, Hew (2014). *The First World War: A new history* London: Simon & Schuster UK.

"Twixt bay and Burn" A history of Helen's Bay and Crawfordsburn. Bayburn Historical Society

Williams, John (1972). *The home fronts: Britain, France and Germany, 1914-1918.* London: Constable.

Unpublished memoirs

Shean McConnell – *private biography.*

McCullagh, Crawford. *A Memoir – An account of my early life*

McCullagh, Ernest. *Merchant Prince* – Linenhall Library

McCullagh, Ernest. *A personal account of wartime experiences.* Linenhall Library

Moore, Alfred S. (1945) *A Merchant Prince.* Linenhall Library

Lord Mayor's correspondence LA7/2EB/53 Public Record Office of Northern Ireland

Emma Duffin's Memoirs – Public Record Office of Northern Ireland

Other sources

Information on William Gibson in conversation with Martin Crozier

Itinerant Preachers, Matthew Gamble, Somme Heritage Centre.

A Veteran recalls – Billy Irvine in conversation with Mrs Jessica Getty, Journal of the Somme Association.

Report of the Enquiry into the Housing Scheme of Belfast Corporation by Mr R D Megaw. PRONI

David Cooke , *A Merchant Prince* published in Familia by the Ulster Historical Foundation

History of Nat Goorwitch and the Berwitz family supplied by Richard Graham

Dunlop Report relating to Whiteabbey Investigation PRONI

Interview with Lilian Arlow regarding American Troops in Northern Ireland

Private Newspaper cuttings regarding Whiteabbey sanatorium by kind permission of Professor Richard Clarke.

Lady Spender's Diary, PRONI D1633/2/04 1941-1943

Emma Duffin's Diaries, PRONI D2109/13

For a comprehensive and accurate account of the Belfast Blitz refer to *The Belfast Blitz* by Brian Barton 2nd Edition 2015

Newspapers

Belfast Evening Telegraph – Central Library, Belfast

Belfast NewsLetter – Central Library, Belfast

Northern Whig – Central Library, Belfast

Online articles

Famous Belfast Stores: The Bank Buildings *www.culturenorthernireland.org*

Women and the Military during World War One (Home Front) Professor Joanna Burke *http://www.bbc.co.uk/history/british/britain_wwone/women_combatants_01.shtml#four*

The Spanish flu in San Diego by Crawford Richard *http://www.sandiegoyesterday.com/?p=1051*

The Black & Tans and Auxiliaries in Ireland, 1920-1921: Their Origins, Roles and Legacy By John Ainsworth. A paper presented to the Annual Conference of the Queensland History Teachers' Association in Brisbane, Saturday, 12 May 2001 *http://eprints.qut.edu.au/9/1/Ainsworth_Black_conf.PDF*

Armstrong, Ron (2010). A History of Newtownards Airport *http://ulsterflyingclub.com/pub/ArdsAirfieldHistory.pdf*